AMELIA BLOOMER

AMELIA BLOOMER
JOURNALIST, SUFFRAGIST, ANTI-FASHION ICON

SARA CATTERALL

Belt Publishing

Printed in the United States of America
First edition 2025

1 2 3 4 5 6 7 8 9

ISBN: 978-1-9533-6889-8

Belt Publishing
6101 Penn Avenue, Suite 201
Pittsburgh, PA 15206
www.beltpublishing.com

TO SIMON

Contents

Contents

Introduction

On a scorching August day in 1889, a newspaperman caught the train across the Missouri River Bridge from Omaha, Nebraska, to Council Bluffs, Iowa, to interview Mrs. Amelia Bloomer.

The horse cab from the station dropped him at her stone steps. Above him, a rail fence guarded a two-story white frame house shaded by cottonwood trees. The gold-lettered nameplate confirmed that he was at the right address.

A white servant girl answered his knock, greeted him politely in a heavy Danish accent, and admitted him to the dim entrance hall. He removed his dusty hat by a glass case of mementoes and paused to look up at a collection of portraits. In another home, they might have been family pictures, but as his eyes adjusted to the low light, he recognized two of the largest as Susan B. Anthony and Elizabeth Cady Stanton.

The servant directed him into a spacious, low-ceilinged drawing room. Sunny windows looked out on the front terrace, and books and keepsakes crowded the polished tables and cabinets. As he waited, taking notes, he noticed a pair of portieres that veiled another doorway, and he drifted over for a glimpse of a cozy library, with an open desk in the bay window, an ornate heating stove, and two red velvet chairs, one with a sewing basket on the carpet beside it.

The door to the hallway opened, and he turned to see Mrs. Bloomer, a little old woman with earnest blue eyes, smiling a welcome. Her manner was serene and gentle, her gray hair crimped

i

and simply arranged, her gown fashionably cut and draped. Later, he wrote, inserting dramatic section breaks:

> There is nothing rugged or particularly strong
> in the delicate features of the face . . . And her
> dress?—once everyone was interested in
> **MRS BLOOMER'S DRESS.**

These paragraphed and bolded phrases read as comedy now. He was so eager to emphasize how harmless she was almost thirty years after the scandal. Her dress was no different

> from that of any other perfectly attired woman . . . No one
> would ever dream that Mrs Bloomer was, years ago, heralded—
> much against her wishes—as the great dress reformer. It was
> all an accident that her name became connected with the
> **SHORT SKIRTED COSTUMES.**

Bloomer invited him to sit with her on a horsehair couch, and she told the story again.

She first saw that costume on Mrs. Elizabeth Smith Miller, a cousin of Mrs. Elizabeth Cady Stanton. When Mrs. Miller walked past her house in it, she remembered, "she turned away from the window and laughed." It was the bold Mrs. Stanton who adopted it first in Seneca Falls. Bloomer put it on later and promoted its health benefits. But she never intended to "set the fashion." The sudden notoriety was a complete surprise to her, and

> nothing could have been more distasteful to her
> than the widespread comment which the
> **SHORT SKIRT AND TROUSERS** excited.

She continued her work as editor, writer, lecturer, and deputy postmaster without alluding to her clothes, he wrote, because she had no interest in general dress reform, only in her own comfort. The fame that it brought was "extremely unpleasant." Once lightweight hoopskirts came into fashion, she returned to conventional dress.

In her cool front parlor, Bloomer showed him her scrapbooks. She began with the volumes of her antebellum newspaper, *The Lily*, stored in black linen covers. He admired the vivacious tone of her editorials, and she pointed out an article signed "E. C. S." for Elizabeth Cady Stanton. She turned more pages, past columns on temperance and education and divorce, to an engraving of a "handsome dark-haired woman in the short skirt and full trousers. Beneath the engraving there is an autograph of the editor of the Lily—the placid gray-haired little lady who looks over the page through gold-bowed spectacles."

Later, he wrote, she moved to Iowa and retired from public life. That was not quite true either, but it suited his version of her, the suffragist wildcat grown docile with maturity. Still, he also included this anecdote: "In January, 1855, the second territorial legislature of Nebraska invited Mrs. Bloomer to deliver a lecture on woman's rights in the hall of the House of Representatives at Omaha, and she spoke with so much effect that a newspaper correspondent gave her the highest praise in his power. He said, 'A man could not have beaten it.'"

Beside him, Bloomer closed the cover of *The Lily*. She leaned on the broad volume and said, "Oh! It is all long past. I worked hard for temperance and woman suffrage and hope that I shall not always be remembered just because I wore short skirts and trousers."

Dress reform was a minor concern in the early women's movement. But it has been mistakenly labeled Bloomer's primary interest. Temperance, Bloomer's true first priority, is now a discredited cause, but it, along with abolitionism, was one of the wellsprings of the woman's rights movement. And temperance, not suffrage, was the most powerful women's political movement of the nineteenth century.

Amelia Bloomer only wore the short dress and trousers for six years of her life. But for championing a style of dress reform that did not start or end with her, for the sake of personal convenience and health, Bloomer, an influential figure in the early women's rights movement, was shamed by journalists, clergy, and the general public. The image of her that they created still persists. Despite the best attempts of her husband, Dexter, and her nieces after her death in 1894, her legacy is exactly what she feared it would be. She exists in popular culture as a dowdy fashion plate, a tale of quaint, toothless rebellion and sexless impropriety, a cautionary anecdote of a naïve woman who tried to change the world and failed. Perhaps the longer the story has been repeated, the less it has seemed that there could be anything else to say. But it is worth examining in light of her request that "future writers would seek to learn the truth concerning me and my public career, or let my memory rest in peace."[1]

Bloomer was more representative of her time in many ways than Susan B. Anthony or Elizabeth Cady Stanton, and perhaps more representative of many activists who cannot make a career of reform work. Unlike Stanton, she had little formal education, a rural upbringing, a devotion to Christianity, and no family wealth or influential connections. Unlike Anthony, she suffered chronic illness and was married, with children to raise and a husband who moved her away from the political centers of the East to a frontier town in Iowa.

Bloomer's story includes the early antebellum days of the nineteenth-century women's rights movement, when strategies were first being formed by small groups of women who had been raised to believe that they should never speak in public if men were present. Through her post office reading room, and then through her newspaper, she brought a community of like-minded women together, first in Seneca Falls and then across the nation. They supported, encouraged, debated, and educated each other and began to build a movement.

Why does it matter if we remember her? Her nerve and sarcasm and devotion are a much better story than the one we have settled for. And she offers a different perspective on the origins and ongoing struggles of the women's rights movement, and the fear and cultural resistance to change in our perceptions and definitions of gender.

Reform movements are complicated by anxiety, prejudice, discouragement, infighting, and schisms. Vital individuals drop out or work all their lives with little recognition. Studying how movements start, how they recruit people who never thought they would get involved, how they reconcile differences between factions for the sake of a common goal, and how activists carry on when nothing is getting better, is in many ways more useful than the story of a final triumph. It is also worth understanding how long many of our political debates have gone on, and gone in circles, to better perceive our most intractable problems and to understand what true progress could look like now.

CHAPTER 1
Village Girl

Not long before the last Christmas of her life in 1894, Amelia Bloomer published a short column in the *Chicago Daily Tribune*, a gentle, cranky few paragraphs of nostalgia for her central New York State childhood.

In it, Bloomer portrayed herself at five or six years old, in 1823 or '24, dancing with excitement in her nightdress while her mother hung up stockings in "a large room in which is a bed, a trundle-bed, and a fireplace large enough to admit a man going up and down the chimney." Tucked in with a kiss by her mother, who took the candle away, Amelia held "as still as a mouse" so that Santa wouldn't see her waiting for him and fell asleep watching the fire.

Adeline and Elvira, her teenage sisters, may have occupied the big bed together while Amelia shared the trundle bed with Amanda, who was two years older. Baby brother Augustus would have still been in the same room with their parents.

On Christmas morning, the children delighted in their filled stockings and wished everyone they met "Merry Christmas" in exchange for a penny. Bloomer described their presents as "simple and inexpensive." Children were "not so pampered as now," and everything was happier and less complicated, as remembered childhoods often seem to be. Her editor at the *Chicago Daily Tribune* titled this article "Bloomers Weren't Invented Then."[2]

When Amelia Jenks was born in 1818, the village of Homer, in Cortland County, New York, had less than two thousand citizens. Two generations earlier, in the spring of 1779, George Washington's army had driven out the Haudenosaunee peoples. They burned thousands of acres of crops, felled orchards, killed livestock, and destroyed at least forty towns, including Genesee Castle, the capital of the Onondagas, with over a hundred "large and elegant" houses.[3] Thousands of destitute Native refugees fled to Fort Niagara, though some remained in or near their homelands as waves of white settlers arrived from the East.

The first new settlements were along waterways: in fertile valleys threaded with trout streams; on the shores of the Finger Lakes; and near swamplands full of birds, beavers, and mosquitos. The settlers built log cabins with dirt floors, and in the early years, their cows and pigs were often killed by bears, panthers, and wolves. Where there were no established Native fields and orchards, they clear-cut the ancient forests and planted crops among the stumps.

As scattered cabins multiplied into villages, the abundant large creeks and rivers lent themselves well to mills of ever-increasing size and power. Mills sawed lumber, ground flour, and fulled wool cloth by beating it while wet to felt it and make it strong and waterproof. At this time, clothes, blankets, and household linens were mostly homespun, handwoven, and home-sewn by women. As factory-made cloth became more commonly available after 1821, the labor saved for rural women was substantial, and it gave them more time for church organizations and reading.

Homer began as a six-family settlement on the Tioga River in 1793, with a one-room school and a grist mill that also served as a church, town hall, and ballroom. Settlers farmed and produced potash for fertilizer, a profitable product they could sell along with maple sugar, pottery from the abundant clay deposits, and whiskey.

Amelia's parents were part of this post-Revolution generation of literate white Yankee settlers. Ananias Jenks, her father, was the son of a Revolutionary War corporal. Amelia's husband, Dexter Bloomer, would later tactfully describe Jenks as a man of "great force of character." He tried several lines of work but mostly settled on cloth dressing and a clothier business.[4] In 1814, he ran for state senator along with sixteen others and achieved a tie for third place with two votes. Amelia's mother, Lucy Curtiss Webb, was from Connecticut, a granddaughter of the Yale-trained minister Jeremiah Curtiss, and a descendent of Mayflower Compact signatory William Bradford. Although Lucy had relatives in Homer, including her brothers and her first cousin Adin Webb, she and Ananias married in Rhode Island in 1806.

Lucy was twenty-eight and Ananias was twenty-one when their first children, Adeline and Elvira, were born in 1807. Three years later, they had a boy, Judson. In 1816, Amanda was born in Homer. Amelia followed in 1818, and then Augustus, four years later, in 1822. They all survived to adulthood, with the possible exception of Judson, whose death date is unrecorded.

In the summer of 1815, steamboat service began on Cayuga Lake, connecting travelers with stagecoach lines.[5] More settlers and speculators arrived, and Homer grew to be the richest town in the county. That said, it was still a backwater. Most tools and dry goods were brought in from Albany via several day's journey to Schenectady, and from there by boat along a canal, a creek, Oneida Lake, and two rivers. An overland route was possible but longer and more expensive. Settlers awaited the construction of the Erie Canal, thirty-three miles from Homer, with intense anticipation.

Bloomer would write that her earliest memories were of "a pleasant home in Homer, Cortlandt County, New York." Her first were of visiting "Indians." Late in life, she would remember two who came to their house and sold a large knife to her father. Another time, she and her brother Judson mocked some Native men who knocked at the door of an empty house across the street. Judson hid with her behind the window blind and called to them, "Come in," and they laughed and danced as the men "opened the door and stepped in, then out, and looked up and around sorely puzzled at hearing a voice, but seeing no one."

She had a best friend, who walked to school and sat with her, and with whom she learned a lesson about the consequences of her actions. After school, they often explored and played together. Once they followed the little river upstream out of the village until they found an ankle-deep cove next to a millrace, a channel that carried a controlled amount of water to power mill wheels downstream. They took off their shoes and waded in. "Here with the stones which covered its bottom we built quite a city. House after house arose as if by magic." A trickle of water attracted their attention, pouring through a hole in the millrace wall. They called it "Niagara Falls," worked the stones around it loose, and pulled them out to make a satisfying cascade. They stayed until dark and went back the next day after school. To their indignation, they found all their houses knocked down and the wall repaired. They rebuilt it all but the next day found it destroyed again. "We were busily at work in water halfway to our knees, with our dresses pinned up to keep them from getting wet—talking the meanwhile with childish volubility and little heeding aught around us, when suddenly the harsh voice of a man sounded in our ears. 'Girls, did you do this?' We were startled as if by an electric shock." It was the owner of the first mill downstream. He told them that their waterfall drained the millrace, causing his mill to stop. "He gave us a good scolding, and threatened us pretty hard if we ever went there again. We were frightened at the mischief we had done, and with sorrowful hearts left the spot and never returned there more."[6]

This was far from her only moral lesson. Amelia's mother, Lucy, was her strongest early influence. She was from a Puritan New England family and was a devoted Presbyterian who trained her children in the "high sentiments of honesty, truth, duty, fidelity, and regard for the rights of others" that would motivate Amelia all her life.

Home was also where Amelia learned to hand-sew clothes and linens, knit, clean, cook, bake, preserve, do laundry, grow vegetables, and manage a budget. But her mother also valued education. Amelia would tell her niece that her early home life was a "masculine autocracy" and that what education she had was due "to the encouragement and persistence of her mother."[7] This would amount to the simplest of eighth-grade educations in village "common" schools, where she learned how to read and write, with "a little grammar and less arithmetic."

Presbyterians were the first denomination to embrace temperance as a cause rooted in concerns for public health and social stability, and Amelia's mother was probably her first teacher in this also. It is not clear whether any of the Jenks men drank.

When the Erie Canal opened in 1825, new opportunities tempted Ananias Jenks to move his young family west across Cayuga Lake. Amelia was six. The 1830 census found the family in Fayette, seven miles south of Seneca Falls. Both boys were still alive. Elvira had moved out, perhaps to teach school, perhaps already married to John Lowdon, a farmer's son.

1830 was also the year of the Indian Removal Act, which forced Native peoples west of the Mississippi. "The poor Indians," wrote an editor in the *Auburn Free Press* that June, "the original owners of the American soil, after having been persecuted for hundreds of years, are now given to understand that the same course is to be continued toward them until the last remnant of their race has been tortured from existence!"[8] But this was a minority sentiment, and the Mississippi would soon be crossed by white speculators and settlers greedy for land.

Amelia wrote little about her adolescent years, with the exception of one incident that she said laid the foundation for her later devotion to women's rights. When she was fifteen, she learned that "an old lady, a dear friend of mine, was to be turned from her home." This woman's husband had died without a will. Because they were childless, and women could not own property, the law gave her a life interest in one-third of the estate, and the rest went to a distant male cousin.[9]

At seventeen, in 1835, Amelia taught one term at a school in the village of Clyde, perhaps a "Girl's Academy."[10] She only lasted one term, though not, Dexter wrote, because she was unpopular with the children: "Her kindness of heart, united with wonderful firmness and a strict regard for truth and right, qualities which distinguished her throughout her whole life, endeared her to the children who came under her care."[11]Amelia moved in with her married sister Elvira in Waterloo, and at nineteen, in 1837, she was hired as "governess and tutor" for the three youngest girls, ages four to ten, of Oren and Mary Chamberlain. Ananias Jenks and the Chamberlain family both had mills in the hard-drinking Kingdom, halfway between Waterloo and Seneca Falls.[12] The eldest Chamberlain children, Minerva and Addis, were older than Amelia, and she seems to have fit comfortably into the household.[13]

She was strict and kind with children, and the Chamberlain girls "always manifested great affection in subsequent years for their former teacher." Her work left her with plenty of time to read and study and to expand her social circle.[14] In 1839, a friend gave her an autograph book with a stamped black and gold cover, which was quickly filled with sketches and poems by her friends and relatives. Her closest sister, Amanda, copied a poem onto one page in her open, looping script, which advised Amelia to build her life not on the deceptions of worldly wealth and love but on the reward of Christian "everlasting life."

Only three or four men signed this book. One was Dexter Chamberlain Bloomer, Oren's nephew, who was two years older than Amelia. In a careful slanting script, he wrote, "The writer of this line humbly asks that he may be numbered in the list of Amelia's favored friends—Sept 6. 1839." He wrote the word "list" twice, scratched out one, and added an elegant flourish under his signature.[15]

Dexter was a new attorney in Seneca Falls, the village clerk, a member of the volunteer fire brigade, and co-owner and coeditor of the Whig newspaper, a typical four-page weekly called the *Seneca County Courier*. Amelia's first impression, according to a thinly veiled story she wrote years later, was that he was "awkward and reserved in company." He was also a strong writer and speaker, "tall and slim, weighing about a hundred and fifty pounds," somewhat self-conscious about his long arms but with a high forehead, kind gray eyes, and thick, dark, wavy hair. Living in his uncle's house, she saw him often, and "as her acquaintance with him became more extended, she found that there was much concealed below the surface that was truly good . . . She was charmed with his talents and the virtues of his mind."[16]

He had been born in Aurora on the Fourth of July, 1816, and moved with his parents to Cortland County when he was seven, a few years after Amelia's family left. His parents were Quakers, an influential religious community with an especially progressive wing in and around Waterloo. They strove to live by the tenets of simplicity, truth, equality, and community, guided by the "inner light" of individual conscience. Dexter was strongly antislavery. He loved to read, and starting at ten, he indulged his love of books by saving his coins and walking seven miles each way to the nearest store. When he was fifteen, his mother and baby sister died within three months of each other. Dexter's father sent him and his younger brother Charles to live with the families of their Chamberlain uncles, Oren and Jacob.

Like Amelia, he had a patchy village school education, with the addition of a few years at the new Myndyrse Academy in Seneca Falls. He taught school starting at age eighteen, and after two or three years, traveled west to see Michigan by canal boats and a steamer on Lake Erie. When he returned home, with twenty dollars and a single suit of clothes to his name, he studied law, and in 1838, he passed the bar.[17] He was a promising prospective breadwinner with an active adventurous mind. The opportunities of the young United States fired his imagination, and he filled his commonplace book with economic data and notes from the lives of English kings and Roman officers.

Dexter would remember young Amelia as "much smaller" than himself, and slight, with a "well-formed head," auburn hair, bright blue eyes with dark-ringed irises, and "an exceedingly pleasant and winning smile." Though reserved with strangers, and relatively plain, she "attracted the attention and secured the confidence of her friends and associates." Their courtship was a gradual one, beginning with a friendship that "ripened as the months passed by into love."[18] They corresponded, and the "ease and grace" with which she wrote added to her attraction for Dexter. He set his eye on her as an appealing woman with demonstrated domestic and childcare skills, a strong moral character, and a compatible temperament, and also as a potential contributor to his newspaper.

Amelia married him on April 15, 1840. She was twenty-two, the average age of first marriage for women in the United States that year. They held the small ceremony in the Waterloo home of her sister Elvira. Amelia wore an ecru silk gown, and the Presbyterian minister of the village, Reverend Samuel H. Gridley, officiated. He did not use the word "obey" in the ceremony, or any wording that implied that Amelia was to hold an inferior position in her marriage, which was much appreciated by the young couple.[19] Dexter's newspaper partner, Isaac Fuller, and his wife drove over from Seneca Falls to attend.[20] No wine was served. The newlyweds spent their first night together in Waterloo, and the next day, a hired carriage drove Amelia and her groom to her new home in Seneca Falls.

CHAPTER 2
Don't Drink!

The carriage ride to Seneca Falls took about an hour from Waterloo along the south bank of the Seneca River. Amelia caught glimpses of the high flowing water through the bare gray branches of the trees. Patches of forest, ravaged clear-cut land, and plowed fields gave way to clusters of low, white frame houses until they arrived in sight of the tall, square, many-windowed mills and mercantile buildings and could hear the shouts and clatter and boom of the busy waterfront. The young couple arrived in front of their temporary home: a substantial Italianate house belonging to Dexter's good friends Isaac and Abigail Fuller. The Fullers had been married seven years but had no living children, and six boarders lived under their roof.[21] It was a good place to stay for a few months while Amelia and Dexter looked for a house of their own.

That evening, their hosts threw them a second and much less demure wedding reception. In her room, Amelia smoothed her hair back from a center part and dressed carefully in layers of petticoats over her long chemise; stays with a long steel or wooden "busk" inserted down the front; and her best dress, with a high neckline, tight dropped shoulders, tight narrow sleeves, and a long full skirt. She was not beautiful, but she was fashionably pale and delicate, and her friends and husband could have honestly said that she looked charming.

Soon Dexter's friends, including the entire volunteer fire department, packed the little lamplit rooms. The Bloomers stood together to greet the arrivals. Amelia's head was level with Dexter's shoulder, and she was still shy with strangers, but appropriate feminine modesty and reserve would have been an easy facade to hide behind while she shook hands, smiled, and tried to commit new names and faces to memory.

A band took over one corner and struck up a dance tune. Wine was poured, and with it came the first test of Dexter's commitment to his vows, perhaps a little sooner than he expected. This incident made such an impression on him that he would tell the story for the rest of his life.

Amelia watched with anxiety as her new husband drank toasts with his friends. She turned down everyone who offered to drink with her, and she sensed that this was "somewhat mortifying" to Dexter, though he did not comment.[22] At last, he collected two sparkling glasses of wine from the refreshment table and guarded them back through the festive crowd to present one to his bride for the traditional toast to each other. Amelia turned to him. He held a glass out to her. She looked at it and said, no, thank you. Several of their friends were close enough to hear their exchange.

"What," he said, according to his own report a lifetime later, "will you not drink a glass of wine with me on this joyful occasion? Surely it can do you no harm."

"No," she replied, "I cannot—I must not."

Temperance was on the rise. Like many of his class, Dexter did not drink hard liquor, but total abstinence was still odd. Temperance speakers exhorted their audiences to consider the raging epidemic of alcoholic men and their starved and abused families. Still, that all felt like someone else's problem to the moderate middle classes, who were no strangers to a drink at breakfast. Amelia's refusal to have one sip of wine with her groom would have seemed extreme.

But in the middle of that party, under the eyes of his friends, Dexter kept his promise to respect her as his equal. He did not insist. Later he would tell how "the crowd of guests standing around could but admire her great self-denial and devotion to principles."[23]

The next day, Dexter, the promising local son, may have taken Amelia for a walk through town to greet friends and family. He likely knew at least half the people on the streets—fellow students from Myndyrse Academy, mill owners, mechanics, newspapermen, lawyers, and shopkeepers. He would have pointed out the flour, paper, and cotton mills, as well as the sash factory, machine shop, hotels, taverns, grocers, printers, Union Hall, village park, and several churches, including the little wood-frame Presbyterian they would attend. In Amelia's lifetime, Seneca Falls had grown from a hamlet of about two hundred to a thriving village of over three thousand, linked to the Erie Canal and growing fast.[24] Though the depression that began in the financial panic of 1837 had set back local businesses, a fresh wave of investors was moving in. It was an exciting place to be for this idealistic young couple with little formal education and no family money.

Amelia devoted herself to domestic work and filled the rest of her time with Dexter, visits, church committees, sewing, and reading. She was shy and uncertain in these early days, still the product of her strict childhood and her years in service.

That September, the *Seneca County Courier*, with Dexter still as coeditor, reported on a woman who spoke on a political question in public. The author wrote that "a female who could thus degrade herself and her sex, for any purpose whatever, is really to be pitied; and the man who would incite her to such an act merits the scorn and contempt of all."[25] The Bloomers were not that couple. But this was a formative year for both of them. With political and business ambitions, and his new status as a married man, Dexter plunged "heart and soul" into the great Whig presidential campaign for William Henry Harrison, attending speeches, parades, and assemblies, and wearing out his printshop's supply of exclamation points and italics in editorials.[26]

Dexter wanted Amelia to join the excitement. But as a good woman, she had never taken much interest in politics, and that summer, she was not well enough to start. She came down with an "intermittent fever," which was almost certainly malaria. That disease was near its peak in North America, introduced generations before by European colonists and the West Africans they enslaved.

By the end of June, Amelia was bedridden, and Dexter was alarmed. On the Fourth of July, he was invited to give the address at a political rally, a significant honor and opportunity. But rather than linger and mingle after his speech, he maneuvered through the backslapping, hand-shaking crowd and hurried back to her bedside. When she could get up, he sent her to the health-resort town of Avon Springs, a day's journey west.[27] Thousands of invalids went there each year to bathe in and drink the spring water, gulping it down to minimize its rotten-egg smell of sulfur.

Medical science had little to offer Bloomer in the 1840s other than possibly quinine. Bloodletting, purging, and mercury treatments were standard. She was almost certainly dosed with calomel, or mercurous chloride. Large doses for long periods could loosen the teeth, hair, and nails and damage the kidneys, gastrointestinal tract, and nervous system.[28] Malaria alone can cause malnutrition, anemia, and neurological, gastrointestinal, and immune system damage.[29] This summer may have been when her chronic illnesses began.

But by August, she was well enough to return home to the arms of her relieved husband and take a wifely interest in the election. This was another new experience. Partisanship had always been considered coarse and masculine, and before 1840, women were almost entirely excluded from politics. The idea of women's suffrage was so far out on the fringe it was nearly invisible. But this year, the Whig party decided that to win, they needed to maximize turnout. To accomplish this, they recruited the respectable white women who went to religious revival meetings and ran church committees into the moral reform of politics. The Whig coalition included social reformers, evangelicals, abolitionists, opponents of the Native genocide, and now, Whig ladies. They not only sewed banners, they hosted and attended political events in numbers that astonished and angered onlookers. This campaign became a watershed in the history of women's political engagement in the United States.

This did not mean that the Whigs supported women's rights. A Virginia paper that cheered the involvement of women in the campaign also compared women's rights supporters to "Amazons" and "cackling geese."[30] Men threw eggs at one group of Whig women as they rode past a saloon in Buffalo.[31] But Bloomer was enthusiastically recruited by her husband and community. She did not write, make speeches, or run political meetings for Harrison, as a few women did, but she sewed badges and mottoes for the men, attended rallies, and visited the log cabin—the local Harrison campaign headquarters and an image used to symbolize the campaign.[32]

Another popular symbol of the campaign was hard cider, the traditional rural northeastern drink. Drunken Whig brawls in log cabins were a popular caricature, and well-founded in some places. Dexter's pro-abstinence *Courier* quoted the president of a Detroit Temperance Society who insisted that "they are generally used as READING ROOMS, and places for political conference . . . the *Friends of Temperance* will rather have reason to REJOICE AT THEIR ERECTION" because they shifted the center of political activity away from taverns and grog shops, and because the presence of Whig ladies ensured good behavior.[33]

On October 1, the Bloomers settled into a small, white frame house where Amelia could establish her first domestic domain just as the winter rain and mud set in. They had one minor conflict when Amelia refused to allow alcohol in the house. "If her friends could not visit her without being treated with alcoholic poison, they might stay away."[34] Dexter may have continued to take the odd drink with friends outside of their house, but he respected her wishes within it. He continued to ply her with books and newspapers, much to her happiness as an avid reader.[35] In the evenings, if they had no meetings to attend and no visits, they sat by the fire, each in their chair, to read, do small domestic tasks, and talk.

At last, Election Day arrived. Harrison won, and Amelia and Dexter cheered the result with their friends, though he later wrote that neither could have explained "what particular benefit it would be to either of them, except the satisfaction of being on the winning side." At the celebration dinner, he stood and raised his glass in a toast. "The Whig Ladies!" he called out to the table. "Like the Ladies of the Revolution," he continued, evoking the highest praise in the popular imagination, "their patriotism only burns the more brightly, and endears itself the more surely to the true lovers of our country, by the unceasing malignity by which it is assailed."[36] This was a fresh affirmation for Amelia that women could brave public exposure and condemnation for a good cause and be honored for their actions.[37]

The election over, everyone returned to more usual pursuits. A foot of snow fell before Christmas, and sleigh bells jingled through the village.[38] The *Courier* took up new subjects, reprinting clips from larger papers, promoting temperance, reviewing new books, and condemning "Indians" in sensational reports of "massacres" and cannibalism. It ran ads for household goods, missing cows, and—though slavery had technically ended in the state thirteen years earlier and the *Courier* was antislavery—a runaway "indentured colored boy." As was not unusual for a small-town newspaper, it also begged delinquent, cashless subscribers to pay in firewood "while the sleighing is still good."[39]

After the holidays, a new craze took hold: total abstinence. A group of "six reformed men of Baltimore" founded the Washington Temperance Reformation, and two of those founders arrived in Central New York on tour in January 1841. These "Washingtonians" were mostly from the lower classes and had no religious affiliation. They promoted mutual support to achieve and maintain sobriety, much as Alcoholics Anonymous would nearly a century later. Amelia and Dexter attended the public meeting in Ansel Bascom's Native-planted orchard, and after listening to a long and rousing speech, they stood in line with 1,300 of their friends and neighbors to sign the total abstinence pledge spread out on a table in front of the speakers.[40]

The idea of temperance had smoldered for much of Bloomer's life, and now it caught fire, the latest and one of the most influential and lasting reform movements to sweep the region.

Temperance was not motivated by sanctimonious prudery. Alcohol abuse had been the opioid epidemic of the day. Between 1800 and 1830, Americans drank more alcohol per capita than they ever had before or ever would again. Until this year, temperance mostly meant no distilled spirits. But alcohol was still ubiquitous and daily for most people. Medicines and tonics were alcohol-based. It was not unusual to give babies rum to make them sleep, or to feed toddlers sugared gin and watered wine in the belief that early introduction was the best guard against later addiction. Respectable women drank sweet wines, punches, and cocktails and pressed them on their guests, along with pickles and desserts soaked in alcohol. In 1839, Seneca Falls instituted liquor licenses and limited sales to a minimum of five gallons to discourage sales by the bottle or glass, but the village also had two distilleries, a large brewery, and thirty or more "rumshops," all for about three thousand residents. A local judge would "credit the temperance movement with reducing assaults by almost two-thirds and nearly eliminating petty offences and calls for relief."[41]

Bloomer's interest in temperance was more specific: the destructive effects of alcohol abuse on the lives of women and their families. Women were dependent on men, but all was more or less well if everyone performed their traditional roles and treated each other with respect and consideration. Drunken, violent husbands broke their side of the contract while maintaining total legal control over their wives and children. They could impoverish and terrorize their dependents with few or no consequences, protected by general respect for their authority and their privacy. If a wife ran away, her husband could sue anyone who sheltered her.

That same January, the *Courier* reprinted a column on the "Rights of Woman" by the poet Willis Gaylord Clark that sounded much like Bloomer would in a few years. It criticized men for the economic plight of women and mothers who worked outside the home. "They call themselves the defenders of women—do they protect her? They praise her virtues—does their conduct manifest real respect? . . . Men are entitled to high wages, but woman . . . must consent to be, as she has been, the drudge and slave of those who prate about *her* beauty and *their* chivalry."[42] Bloomer, comfortable beside a fire of logs delivered by her respectful and loving husband's subscribers, took note. This was a keystone of the appeal of temperance for her: the cause of women whose economic and legal dependence on men could bring financial, physical, and emotional ruin to them and their children.[43]

In the United States, the women's rights movement had emerged out of the abolitionist movement only a few years before. Feminist thought went back farther, into at least eighteenth-century Britain and the writings of Mary Astell and Mary Wollstonecraft, but there was no significant movement. Quakers Sarah and Angelina Grimké wrote and spoke on abolition and addressed mixed-gender audiences of thousands in Boston in 1838. The violent reaction against them caused them to defend their right to do so.[44] But these ideas were still beyond radical.

And Bloomer was still a quiet village wife. Her husband's paper devoted many pages to reprinting a romance from a Boston paper about a beautiful and virtuous young governess named Amelia. Mrs. Bloomer was probably amused. The *Courier* also printed articles on marriage and the duties of women, all no doubt discussed by the newly wed Bloomers. One column on "A Wife's Duties" listed childcare, cooking, cleaning, needlework, and, above all, staying home. Another advised that "on a sound education and accomplishments she should engraft a perfect and practical knowledge of domestic affairs . . . and after all romance has vanished, the sober, sedate, yet joyous and happy state of matrimony ensues . . . and such things as separation or divorce never enter into her imagination."[45] Amelia did not have much trouble adhering to such expectations. Like Dexter, she was often out at temperance and church meetings, but she was never a social butterfly. When she was well, there was no more skillful and hardworking housekeeper and needlewoman. She was still not pregnant, but she often took care of other people's children, these days without pay.

But Bloomer had also grown up in the waves of evangelical fervor that swept through Central New York in the early nineteenth century. From them, she absorbed the idea that this world could be perfected through human effort. Now the Whigs had welcomed women into politics. Temperance, which addressed a clear threat to women's lives without direct challenge to the patriarchal status quo, was a logical next step.

Bloomer embraced the movement "heart and soul." The Seneca Falls Temperance Society did not allow women, so she helped to found a ladies' temperance committee with friends from her church, a small expansion of the accepted realm of women's religious charitable work.

Amelia and Dexter organized occasional public meetings with local or visiting speakers and packed the lecture halls. Until now, temperance organizations had emphasized personal abstinence and criticized heavy drinking by the lower classes, with no program for individual support. Washingtonians shunned all alcohol and targeted respectable "moderate drinkers" for creating a culture of social alcohol consumption that tempted and pressured others to drink, with no way to tell who could tolerate it and who would succumb to addiction.

It was up to the middle class to set an example of total abstinence and offer their personal support to alcoholics. "Reformed drunkards" signed the pledge, attended weekly meetings, and shared their stories, with the longest reformed acting as mentors to new members.

By January 1842, the Seneca Falls Independent Total Abstinence Temperance Society numbered over 450 members and held meetings twice a week. Women could now attend on Wednesdays. Dexter was voted correspondence secretary and was soon a regular speaker.[46] Ansel Bascom, the first mayor of Seneca Falls, suspended his weekly newspaper to start a temperance paper for the society.[47] Bascom was an older friend of the Bloomers, an entrepreneur, a lawyer, and a Whig, and he named his new paper after the radical new alternative to alcoholic drinks at every meal, calling it the *Water Bucket*.

"Cold water" was the new cry of the temperance advocates. Until recently, water had been considered unsafe for human consumption, as in many places it was. But in Central New York, there were clear springs and creeks and plenty of rain. Bloomer was able to drink fresh water from her own well or cistern and confidently offer it to her guests.

That year, the Fourth of July was celebrated in Seneca Falls with picnics and parades. The next afternoon brought a different kind of excitement. Amelia walked out with Dexter to join a crowd at the new railway station. The completion of a railroad bridge over the canal, and a narrow single track of iron rails crosstied with red cedar and layered on locust wood, connected Seneca Falls west to Rochester by train, at a top speed of fourteen miles per hour. Townspeople and farmers gathered to stare down the tracks, and boys ran along them for the first sight of the plume of steam from the arrival of the Auburn and Seneca Railroad. Cannons roared as the locomotive clattered over the new bridge, an astonishing sight to Bloomer, who had never seen a vehicle move without horses or oxen. The crowd shouted and cheered as it pulled into the new station, the freshly painted little cars full to overflowing with passengers as exhilarated as the locals who surged forward to greet them.[48]

That night, Amelia and Dexter joined the crowd at the river park to watch the fireworks. White, yellow, silver, and red rockets, jets, and Catherine wheels burst over the broad, smoothly flowing water of the canal in a spectacle that drew gasps and cheers, terrified animals and babies, and lit up the walls and windows of the tall, square mills that crowded the banks and the central flats. It seemed as if Seneca Falls was in full recovery from the economic panic of 1837 and would soon become the prosperous competitor with Rochester and Utica that its leaders dreamed of.[49] Anyone who wanted to take the trains west in the 1840s would have to pass through Seneca Falls, and it would be much easier for city investors to discover the opportunities of this village that hoped to become a town.

The *Courier* was doing increased business as both a newspaper and a job printer. And Dexter, thinking of the letters Amelia had written to him during their courtship, wanted to make her a writer. She was doubtful. It was one thing to attend public meetings, applaud the men, and sew their banners. It was quite another to present her own thoughts to the general public. She had developed her ideas and had arguments to back them up. But though there were now a few women who left their "proper sphere" to speak in public, most people still regarded them as an immoral spectacle to be shouted down. Her church and society had always said that women must be silent in any public mixed gathering, pointing to St. Paul: "Let the women keep silence in the churches: for it is not permitted unto them to speak." On some topics, the Bible could be obscure, but this seemed fairly clear. But writing was not speaking. Plus, the Quakers had scripture-based arguments for the equality of women, and Dexter could use them to persuade her.

Still, there were almost no women journalists that she could look to as examples. They had been rare in the United States so far, and young rural wives were nowhere among them. The few working at that time were wealthy, urban, single, or all three, many of them motivated by abolitionism. The *Lowell Offering*, written by women textile workers, began publishing in 1840. Anne Royall had been publishing her muckraking paper, *The Huntress*, from her home in Washington, DC, since 1831, but she started it as a widow in her fifties and was far from respectable.[50] In January 1840, the brilliant Margaret Fuller, thirty, better educated than Bloomer, and the daughter of a congressman, became coeditor of Ralph Waldo Emerson's magazine, *The Dial*, with the promise of payment she never received.[51] The journalist Jane Grey Swisshelm had a background more like Bloomer's, but they both published their first articles in 1842, ignorant of each other's existence.[52]

But Bloomer didn't have to use her own name. Even men often hid behind initials and pseudonyms. Under Dexter's encouraging editorial eye, she began to write down her thoughts and send them to local temperance papers under pen names, including "Eugene" and "Glorvinia."

One of the first papers to publish her articles was the *Water Bucket*, the little temperance paper edited by Ansel Bascom.[53] There could be no more supportive and sanctioned place for her to start. She was not even his first woman contributor. A conventional temperance lecture written by an anonymous "lady," to be delivered by a man at a meeting, appeared in an earlier issue.

Glorvinia's first surviving piece, dated March 21, 1842, two months before Amelia's twenty-fourth birthday, was a step into public from a familiar feminine realm. In "What can the Ladies do? By a Lady," she promoted the activities of the Seneca Falls Ladies Temperance Society.[54]

Bloomer reported their full membership as an impressive 650 women. However, as is often the case with those who claim allegiance to a cause, only a handful ever showed up. "A small but faithful band" met on Fridays to make and remake clothes for "the suffering poor." Frustrated, she prodded her nonparticipant readers: "If a few can do so much, what might not be accomplished by the united aid of the whole society, if they would but come up to the work." At minimum, they could donate their old clothes.

In the following issue, she stepped out a little further and confronted the ladies in their kitchens. They might "pretend to the first respectability," she wrote, but many claimed that alcohol was indispensable in the kitchen, and some were not ashamed to say they liked a drink themselves. "Brandy on apple dumplings, forsooth!" Had they ever tried to do without it?[55]

All winter and spring, Bloomer went to meetings at Temperance Hall. She reveled in the joyful revivalist atmosphere and in Dexter's role as one of the most "thrilling and effective" speakers. The membership soon shifted their efforts from moral persuasion to legislation. That April, the central issue of the Seneca Falls election for town officers was liquor licenses. Seven hundred and fifty voters turned out—almost every eligible man—and made their village the only one in the county to deny all licenses that year. They went from twelve licensed taverns to none. The *Water Bucket* cheered. "Who then, we ask, is better entitled to the first place in the Temperance army, than Seneca Falls?"[56] Bloomer enjoyed this fresh thrill of political success. Perhaps she could dare more.

The challenge was still the moderate drinkers, the good citizens with their punches, flips, and wine. At the end of April, she wrote a column titled, "Ladies, Don't Drink!" She told women that they had the power to banish "*social* drinking." Had they served wine to gentleman visitors? And felt slighted if they declined? "Rather than offend you, they take from your hand the proffered glass—not unfrequently against their will." In turn, women should say no when offered a drink.

At this point, she took up the rhythms of a minister or lecturer, a style she had often heard. "Have you a brother just entering manhood, and would you save him from ruin and disgrace?—don't drink. Have you friends whom you love and esteem . . . —don't drink. Is there one on whom you have placed your affections . . . and does he occasionally take wine because it is the fashion?—as you value your own future happiness and prosperity . . . don't drink."

She said nothing about the men who might insist on alcohol but parroted the unexamined popular sentiments of the day, recommending that women use "influence and example . . . mildness and persuasion." If this failed, they could "find consolation in knowing, that you have not been instrumental in working your own ruin."[57]

But Bloomer soon began to question this line of reasoning. That summer, she and her friends learned that a man named Hill in Waterloo had demanded money from his family, used it to get drunk, and returned home to demand more. When his wife refused and attempted to escape him, he followed her out into the garden with a club, knocked her down, mangled her with an axe, dragged her back into her domestic realm, and forced her head into the burning kitchen stove. Their grown children and the neighbors managed to save her "from immediate death." For this crime, he was sentenced to three months in the county jail. It was hard to imagine that Mrs. Hill or her family felt consoled by the memory of her attempts to persuade her husband not to drink.

This was an extreme case, but it illuminated the social and legal structures that failed to protect women and children. After the Revolution, the law had developed a new respect for the privacy of the family. One side effect was to obscure and legitimize domestic abuse, which before had been partly a concern of the public peace.[58] And because the family was idealized as a sacred domain, with a man as master, guided by a gentle, virtuous wife, everyone put a good face on the worst realities until a woman burst out into her garden in desperate rebellion against her husband's determination to take her life.

Temperance advocates thought that those who sold Hill the alcohol shared his guilt, as did the authorities. Though they worked from simple observation, their conclusion was accurate and would be upheld by the social science of the future: society and government together had the power to prevent domestic violence fueled by alcohol.[59] Bloomer now understood that to turn this idea into reality, much more would have to be done.

CHAPTER 3

Women in the Ascendant

At church and in temperance and abolitionist meetings, many women of Seneca Falls were taking their first careful steps into public life. Many of the men welcomed their participation. But no one had been too bold just yet. They advanced more or less together, with little rushes and retreats and much private debate.

For the Fourth of July, 1842, the temperance societies of the county organized a celebration featuring their leading citizens and best speakers. Dexter served on the organizing committee and was once again appointed orator.[60]

Amelia was up early to do morning chores and dress for the parade. A light rain the night before had laid the dust and freshened the air, and by morning, the skies were clear. A cannon fired a "national salute" at sunrise, one shot for each of the twenty-six states. By nine, the Bloomers joined the crowd lining up in front of the Seneca House temperance hotel under two large United States flags that waved in the light breeze while the band played martial tunes. Participants included village officials, a rifle company in full uniform, two fire companies, with their red and yellow Red Rover engine drawn by four handsome, decorated horses, some elderly Revolutionary veterans in a carriage, clergy, Sunday schools, and the membership of all the temperance societies, led by a strong turnout of the Ladies Temperance Society, which included Amelia.

She and the ladies presented the men's temperance society with a large parade banner that they had hand-sewn for the occasion. They marched to Ansel Bascom's orchard, where there were not even enough seats for the ladies. At least a thousand people were there. Music, prayers, and readings followed. Dexter gave a literate and lectern-thumping oration that covered everything his audience expected and admired: classical references, founding fathers, "hostile savages," and the Constitution as the "most perfect form of government" ever created. But alcohol still prevented happiness. It stole free will, intelligence, and good judgment. It made voters vulnerable to demagogues. Temperance reformers were the new generation of revolutionaries, protectors of the liberty and prosperity inherited from the veterans present. "As one of that generation," Dexter ended, "I invoke your blessing."

After more prayers and music, "two or three hundred" people proceeded to the bower for a light meal provided by the Seneca House. Toasts were drunk in "clear cold water" praising the Declaration of Independence, Washingtonianism, kindness and love, and the ladies. They broke up midafternoon, delighted with the success and sobriety of the celebration. That evening, there were bonfires, rockets, and a firemen's ball. Only two men were seen to be drunk in the street, and no fights were reported.[61]

As Bloomer's temperance community united and grew, her religious one came to grips with a moral crisis. Abolitionism was also on the rise. It was more influential than temperance because it addressed, as one historian has said, both "a far more enormous evil" and was a "much more convenient challenge . . . for it did not have to do with the transgressions of friends and neighbors."[62] But it also threatened the union of states, and moderates still hoped for compromise with slaveholders. Abolition became the test of many antislavery congregations.

In the early 1840s, less than half of Seneca Falls belonged to a congregation.[63] Bloomer's devotion to her Christian faith and practice was at the center of her life, but she left the Presbyterian church less than three years after her marriage. The incident that may have provoked this is well documented by historians.[64]

Late in the summer of 1843, the radical abolitionist Abby Kelley gave a lecture series in Ansel Bascom's orchard. Kelley was an educated former Quaker from Massachusetts who opposed organized religion, promoted full civil rights for African Americans, and, simply by speaking to mixed-gender audiences, became a symbol of women's rights.[65]

Bloomer attended at least one of her lectures and came home in tears after listening to Kelley's criticism of an editorial in the *Seneca County Courier*. Dexter was unconcerned, but it was one of her first experiences with an ideological attack.[66]

Kelley also condemned the Bloomers' pastor, Horace P. Bogue, as an anti-abolitionist. The Presbyterians in Seneca Falls were a liberal congregation with progressive views that did not translate into action, and frustration among the committed abolitionists had grown.[67] Rhoda Bement was inspired by Kelley, and in the summer of 1843, she challenged Bogue for refusing to announce abolition meetings. She was put to trial by the church and condemned. Ten women of the congregation followed her to the witness stand in support.[68]

Several abolition supporters left the congregation after this incident. The Bloomers switched to the Episcopal church, the one attended by most of the village elite. Amelia involved herself in her new congregation, and her community ties continued to multiply and strengthen.

The new Wesleyan congregation of Methodists opened their meetinghouse to visiting reformist lecturers, both white and Black, which attracted touring speakers, who could now visit Seneca Falls by train.[69] Their lectures expanded Bloomer's political and intellectual world even more.

In the summer of 1846, Elizabeth Cady Stanton rumbled into town from Boston with a large check from her wealthy father. She had often visited Seneca Falls to see her adored brother-in-law and her older sister, but this time, she and her family would be moving in. Her father gave Elizabeth a neglected white frame house on the relatively isolated Locust Hill, next to the Bascoms' orchard, the Seneca Turnpike, and the flour and fulling mills on the river.[70]

Bloomer no doubt heard about them; the village was small, and Henry Stanton was a famous abolitionist and speaker. It is even possible that she attended Elizabeth's debut speech in November 1841, a temperance lecture given to about a hundred women.[71] But Bloomer would not get to know Stanton for another three years. Henry Stanton was often away, and Elizabeth was overwhelmed by the renovation and management of her new home and the care of her three small children.

Bascom became a state representative, and Bloomer and the other temperance ladies of Seneca Falls sent him a petition on the subject of liquor licenses. Petitions were an acceptable form of political participation for women, since they could be submitted by proxy. Bascom presented it to the General Assembly that spring, but as the voice of nonvoters, it achieved nothing.[72]

After six years of writing for local newspapers, Bloomer was now much more confident and skilled.[73] But the *Water Bucket* did not last long.[74] She wrote under the pen name "Ida" for the Auburn *Temperance Star*, and in February 1848 caused "quite a sensation" in Seneca Falls when she attacked local parents in the *Star* for sending their children to a dancing school held in a hotel that sold liquor illegally. [75] She was not afraid, at least under her pseudonym, to call out community members for their excuses, hypocrisy, or lack of conviction. She condemned the excise board for signing licenses and called out a Seneca Falls lawyer for speaking in defense of a rum seller after signing the pledge eight years earlier in the Presbyterian church. Many other "reformed men" had lapsed, and she thought politics and classism were involved. Successful men did not want to associate with mechanics and laborers, even though many leading citizens, including her own husband, were still active in the Temperance Society.[76]

But there was little that any woman could do about these things other than vent.[77] Even Bloomer's ability to do that was curbed this summer, when the *Temperance Star* was purchased by Samuel Chipman of Rochester, who discontinued her regular column.

But another reform, women's rights, was in the ascendant. In April of 1848, the state government passed the New York Married Woman's Property Act. Historian Judith Wellman writes that "the idea that married women could own property opened up a Pandora's box full of possibilities. If women paid taxes, what could logically keep them from voting?"[78]

That July, the *Seneca County Courier* ran a small announcement: "Women's Rights Convention: A Convention to discuss the social, civil, and religious condition and rights of Woman, will be held in the Wesleyan Chapel at Seneca Falls, NY on Wednesday and Thursday the 19th and 20th of July Current, commencing at 10 o'clock A.M. During the first day, this meeting will be exclusively for Women, which all are earnestly invited to attend. The public generally are invited to be present on the second day, when LUCRETIA MOTT, of Philadelphia and others both ladies and gentlemen, will address the Convention."[79]

Bloomer was out of town for most of this convention. She attended the evening of the second day to hear the speakers, including the admired orator and best-selling author Frederick Douglass and fifty-five-year-old Lucretia Mott, the Quaker minister, abolitionist, and cofounder of several antislavery societies with racially mixed membership.

The airy, barnlike chapel was crowded with about three hundred local reformers, almost all of whom had traveled less than a day to be there.[80] Bloomer had to find a seat in the gallery. Many familiar faces were there, including Ansel Bascom and his thirteen-year-old daughter, Mary. It may have been the first time Bloomer heard Mrs. Stanton speak, though her voice "was weak and timid, and did not clearly reach the remote parts of the house."[81]

Many of those present, including Lucretia Mott, opposed the inclusion of women's suffrage in the convention's Declaration of Sentiments. They felt it would make them look ridiculous. Bloomer thought they were right. Stanton and Douglass made strong arguments in favor, and it was left in. Sixty-eight women and thirty-two men chose to sign the final declaration. Dexter's kind and straightforward mill-owner uncle, Jacob P. Chamberlain, who was also Stanton's neighbor, was one of them. But like the majority there, Bloomer did not.

She would often follow this pattern of initial resistance when faced with new ideas. Her hesitation was a conservative impulse, but it did not prevent her curiosity from being sparked, and it was followed by private contemplation and discussion. She had strong personal principles, and any new idea that could clash with them had to go through a careful examination before she would accept it.

To others, this process was not always clear. Stanton, who lived at the opposite end of the temperamental and religious spectrums, would later tell Susan B. Anthony that at the Seneca Falls convention, Bloomer "stood aloof and laughed at us."[82]

But some of the arguments at the convention spoke to the aspect of women's rights that most interested Bloomer: the power to influence temperance legislation.[83] And she had a copy of the declaration to mull over. It was printed in the *Courier,* next to notices for agricultural prices, a lost bag, marriage and death announcements, and an advertisement to see a "Live Mammoth Crocodile!!"

On September 22, Bloomer and her friends held their own meeting at the Wesleyan chapel to resurrect the Seneca Falls Ladies Temperance Society. The first one, founded in 1841, had disbanded when the president died and members moved away. At least four of the current members had signed the Declaration of Sentiments.[84] They called themselves the "Ladies' Total Abstinence Benevolent Society of Seneca Falls," wrote a new pledge, voted for officers, and made resolutions, beginning with: "That as woman suffers most deeply from the evils of intemperance, so ought she to feel the deepest interest in removing the evils from the land." They condemned the "traffic in strong drink" and "those who are engaged in the business, as among the worst enemies to society, to virtue, and to religion," and they asserted that alcohol "kills not only the body but the soul," and that therefore its distributors were more cruel than ordinary murderers. Those who encouraged, it, legalized it, and did nothing about it were their enemies, "more guilty than the rumseller himself." No friend of temperance should trade with anyone who sold alcohol.

Finally, they resolved "that we will use our influence in all suitable ways, to discountenance the use of strong drink in the community," and not to use it themselves or give it to guests.[85]

As secretary, Bloomer sent the minutes to the *Star of Temperance* and signed them "Amelia Bloomer," perhaps for the first time in print.[86]

There were no men present to inhibit their discussions. Seated together in their voluminous skirts and starched white indoor caps, they talked over their opinions, "fired with zeal after listening to the Washingtonian lecturers and other speakers on temperance." Their resolutions gave them great satisfaction. But they had no plan to do much more.

Until, at another meeting, Bloomer made a daring suggestion. What if they published "a little temperance paper, for home distribution only?" They could share their ideas with other women, between their private homes. And Bloomer was already an experienced writer. Ideas flew, and Bloomer and Anna Mattison were named editors.[87] A committee was appointed to find out printing costs, and they adjourned, "satisfied and elated." Amelia flew home to tell Dexter.

Later, she recalled his reaction. He "threw cold water" on the whole thing. His support for her did not extend to an expensive, risky endeavor run by novices. His advice: tell the ladies "to abandon all thought" of the project. She seems to have taken this to heart. He did have years of expertise in newspaper editing and publication, and they had none. And there was no comparable women's paper that she could point to.

Sobered, at the next meeting, she reported everything that Dexter had said. But they did not listen. They issued a prospectus and began to collect subscribers for the first issue of *The Lily*, named by their president for a biblical symbol of feminine purity and worth.

Bloomer found the name insipid, but everyone else thought it was pretty.[88] They placed an order for a decorative masthead from New York City, with the name on a ribbon knotted around the stems of three botanically vague flowers.[89]

Dexter was deeply involved in the upcoming election. "National Unity" was the Whig platform, which meant they refused to embrace abolition and offend the Southern wing. Despite dissatisfaction with this stance, Seneca Falls was a Whig village in a Whig district. Some abolitionists joined Henry Stanton in the new Free Soil Party, which promised to ban slavery in new states and set Ansel Bascom against William A. Sackett of the Whigs in the congressional race. Sackett also opposed the extension of slavery, and with the support of the *Courier,* he won.[90]

In this autumn of 1848, Amelia and her family anticipated the birth of the first child of her closest sister, Amanda. The baby was born on December 11, and half an hour later, Amanda died.

Amelia already had an interest in alternative medicine, and this shock intensified it. She would later ascribe Amanda's death to the "stiff tight corsets and heavy skirts demanded by the conventions of the times."[91] From a modern perspective, she could have had anemia, which is still a common cause of severe postpartum hemorrhage.[92] In any case, like many who survive a loved one, Amelia brooded over what she or anyone could have done to keep Amanda alive.

She and her sisters Elvira and Adeline all offered to adopt the baby, but the father, Edward Frost, an educated builder and music teacher, refused. His daughter, he said, was all he had left. He named her Amanda Jane, and his widowed mother moved in to keep house and help care for the baby. The little girl beat the odds and survived. Her extended family doted on her and called her "Jennie."

Edward never remarried, and Jennie remembered how, as a little child, she followed him everywhere—to work, in their garden, ice skating—and that her "Uncle and Aunty Bloomer" often took her for a few days at a time.[93]

Bloomer was months past her third wedding anniversary and still had no biological children. Her health was unstable; she suffered from digestive and dental problems, fatigue, and chronic headaches. At least one writer has suggested, without evidence, that her symptoms were "neurotic."[94] But there is nothing to indicate that they were not real and much to show that she was determined not to be an invalid.

With so little useful medical treatment available, her suffering was not uncommon. And the nineteenth century has been called "the era of the Great American Stomachache."[95] Rich food, spices, alcohol, tobacco, and coffee were blamed by doctors, and so was lack of exercise and fresh air, and tight clothing. Bloomer attended to this advice. She tried gentle alternative treatments, modified her diet, kept active, and gave up restrictive clothes. Long, restful stays at water cures and sanatoriums made her symptoms diminish but never disappear.

Around the same time as the death of her sister, the ladies' temperance society's newspaper project suffered a setback. A traveling temperance lecturer offered to find subscribers for them, which they found a thrilling prospect. He sent them a list of names but not the money, and the man himself evaporated. In time, they realized they had fallen for a common scam, and they began to think they were in over their heads. "Very soon the society decided to give up the enterprise."[96]

Bloomer was disappointed too, but she was taken aback by this irresponsible behavior. "Our word had gone to the public and we had considerable money on subscriptions. Besides the dishonesty of the thing, people would say it was 'just like women ... what more could you expect of them?'" She went ahead with *The Lily*. Mattison was still willing to help her. And perhaps the enterprise was a useful distraction from grief. Either way, the failure or success of this "little temperance paper" would be all hers.

CHAPTER 4

A Little Temperance Paper

On New Year's Day, 1849, with many "anxious doubts and fears," Amelia Bloomer published the first issue of *The Lily*.[97] "Only two or three hundred copies" were printed on the *Courier*'s old handpress.[98] The fancy masthead had not arrived from New York City, so Bloomer resigned herself to a simple "head" of big letters. She subtitled it "A Monthly Journal, Devoted to Temperance and Literature." The next line read: "Published by a Committee of Ladies.—Terms—Fifty Cents a Year, in Advance."

Bloomer was willing to commit to a calendar year. She had a "respectable" subscriber list to start but not enough to justify more.[99] She did not expect to pay herself or her contributors, and newspapers could circulate postage-free within a thirty-mile radius, but the cost of paper and printing, and any postage outside that limit, was still substantial.[100] And she had to write much of the eight-page debut issue.

Her anxiety spilled into her first editorial. "We feel, at best, but poorly qualified for the important station that has been assigned us, and would fain shrink from public criticism; but having put our hands to the plough we cannot turn back."

Bloomer listed Mattison as her coeditor and printed the resolutions of the temperance committee with a statement of purpose. "It is WOMAN that speaks through the *LILY*. It is upon an important subject, too ... Intemperance is the great foe to her peace and happiness. It is that, above all, which has made her home desolate, and beggared her offspring . . . Surely she has a right to wield the pen for its suppression."[101]

On her first front page, she set a poem about a singing lily by a spring of fresh water that inspires a man to take a temperance pledge, and a short story on the evil of "the passion for dress." She reused two short articles in *The Lily* that she also sent to the *Temperance Star*, signed "Lily." Both were local gossip, one about a sick woman who was discovered to be "drunk, dead drunk!" and the other on the two charming sons of a local rum seller, whose doomed futures she imagined in lurid detail.[102] An editorial on the joy of reading was probably also hers. "The reading of good books is a wellspring of happiness, deep and gushing, to the human heart."

Bloomer plunged into this new endeavor "heartily and earnestly." She wrote articles, reported on meetings, sent out advertisements, selected and edited submissions, corrected proofs, wrangled with the printers, and packaged, addressed, and mailed the papers.[103] She learned new tricks to get ink out of her white linen cuffs. And she cried tears of self-doubt more than once.[104] But she got it all done, and she did it well. She did not have too much domestic work since she and Dexter were boarding again. Her head often ached, as it had for years, but her response was to keep moving. She was known for her rapid walk, her bluntness, and her smile.

To temperance and literature, she added articles on thrift, parenting, piety, grief, charity, dress, diet, and exercise, much of it clipped from her favorite publications. Clipping newspapers became one of her regular evening activities, along with sewing and reading. Her common prejudices were reflected in articles she reprinted that portrayed the degeneration of modern Italians from the classical civilization, Native people as noble savages, and the Irish as dim-witted clowns. In issue two, she shared the popular 1838 story from Cassius Clay's paper, the *True American*, that would later inspire the scene of Eliza fording an icy river with her child to escape slavery in *Uncle Tom's Cabin*.[105]

Word spread quickly of the new temperance paper. The nearby *Geneva Gazette* reported that it had "a very neat, mechanical appearance, and its editorials are very creditable. We wish the Lily much success but the work upon which it has entered, will require much labor, faith and perseverance." The *Massachusetts Cataract* called it "a neat little Monthly . . . very appropriately edited by a fine worthy pair of the teetotal Fair."[106]

Mr. Mattison, her coeditor's husband, took subscriptions for *The Lily* at his hardware store downtown and was Bloomer's sole advertiser. Bloomer made frequent visits to the post office to pick up stacks of mail for "The Editors of *The Lily*." For her March issue, she had a choice of original poetry, articles, and letters. When some Seneca Falls ladies protested her condemnation of women who served wine at New Year's parties, she retracted nothing, but wrote that she had no one particular in mind and was glad to learn that they were guiltless.

In a new section that spring, "To Correspondents," she accepted and rejected submissions, and she made an example of the unfortunate "De Forest":

> You spell badly—make use of capital letters where
> there should be none, and omit them where they
> should be used. Other errors might be pointed out, but
> these will suffice . . . It is unpleasant for us to decline
> articles sent us, and we do it with reluctance, but the
> character of our paper demands it in some cases.[107]

Before the April issue, Anna Mattison told Bloomer that she was moving away. There is no record of how Bloomer took the news, besides the fact that she hoped Mattison would still write articles, and she told her readers that "other assistance has been secured."[108] It is unclear what this "other assistance" was, but Bloomer's editorial "we" now signified only herself.

The loss of both her coeditor and sole advertiser would not have been easy to bear. Her account book was deep in the red. But she went on. She offered to pay subscription agents and appealed to her readers to sign up anyone they could. She made annual club subscriptions of five or ten copies a year available at a discount and got Isaac Fuller to replace Mr. Mattison's advertisements with one large one for his new temperance hotel.

Early that spring, Dexter bought a little white cottage. It was good to have a private home again, but repairs and resettling made more work for Amelia.[109] This move may have been due to Dexter's new job. That spring, he was sworn in as postmaster of Seneca Falls in reward for his support of the Whigs. Most government jobs turned over with every new administration as part of the "spoils system" created by Andrew Jackson, and supportive newspapermen were often rewarded this way.[110]

This job meant more money and long hours. In 1851, Dexter advertised these as "6:00 A.M. to 8:45 P.M., Monday–Saturday, and Sundays 8:00–9:00 A.M."[111]

Cheap postage and the first official postage stamps, which had been instituted two years earlier, meant a historic increase in the volume of the mail, more than one person could easily handle in a large village.[112] Dexter needed a deputy to assist him and stand in for him when he was away. This sparked Amelia's interest. Though she had enough to do without adding an office job, she was "determined to give a practical demonstration of woman's right to fill any place for which she had capacity."

Dexter was not sure about the propriety of it. He worried about what people would say. But she convinced him.[113] They were sworn in together and would serve through the four years of the Taylor and Fillmore administration.[114]

Here was a new domain, a new business to learn, and her own office next to the lobby. She and Dexter set to work on the required inventory. They learned to sort and bundle and mark and bag and lock the mail, and to serve everyone who came in to pick up and send letters and packages, since there was no home delivery. Any mail left unclaimed for long enough had to be listed in a local paper before being sent to the Dead Letter Office in Washington, DC.[115]

No doubt there was some disapproval and teasing from the customers. Post offices were social centers for men, full of newspapers and political materials; a place to meet and chat and to glean gossip and news. Now, a woman behind the desk attracted other women to pick up their own mail. Shrouded in shawls and gloves and trailing skirts, their profiles obscured by bonnets, they could greet their friend Mrs. Bloomer at the counter or step into her office where, away from the men, they might bring up a recent column in *The Lily*.

Bloomer saw an opportunity. She brought more chairs into her office, hung drapes, and made it a comfortable sitting room. On a polished wood table, she arranged newspapers and journals and invited the women of Seneca Falls to close the door on the public lobby and sit together to read and talk. Before this, the only places women could talk in private had been in their small family homes, at charitable sewing circles and committee meetings, or outdoors. And few could afford subscriptions to papers that interested them alone. Now there was a reading room and informal discussion club, out of the weather, free of charge, free of men, and open to every woman in town most days of the week. It became the center of a new form of community.

The publicly rejected "De Forest" wrote back to complain that they thought editors corrected and rewrote articles. Bloomer responded in *The Lily*. Editors did not usually do that, but if De Forest would call on her, they could sit down with a dictionary and edit the article together. Or she could publish it as is, and "then our readers could judge between us."[116] De Forest did not reply.

Miss Lydia Ann Jenkins of Waterloo became a new *Lily* contributor that spring. Jenkins was active in the temperance community and had a strong interest in women's rights. Her first article was on "Female Education." She signed her middle name only, and she stuck with that byline through the summer.[117] Bloomer asked her best contributors to write more for her and asked the many who sent poetry to try prose instead. She began to recommend books, publications, and lecturers and reprinted articles on women's intellect and the importance of "running and leaping and jumping" for growing girls. And she praised a woman in Maine who, when a rum seller ignored her pleas to stop serving her husband, walked into his shop and broke everything she could reach, for which she was fined fifty dollars.[118]

There was an uproar around a sensational new paper, the *Saturday Evening Visiter*, edited by Mrs. Jane Grey Swisshelm in Pittsburgh and founded a year before *The Lily*. It covered temperance, abolitionism, and women's rights and was supported by a Whig newspaperman.[119] Swisshelm's critics should save their breath, Bloomer wrote, "for she is more than a match for them . . . Whether our readers agree with her or not, we think it will interest them to hear a woman speak her mind." She reprinted Swisshelm's warning to liquor sellers "not to encroach on our hearth . . . if they persisted, we would *burn down* their establishments with as clear a conscience as we would build a fire to burn the June-bugs and save our plums." Women had no other recourse. "The ballot box is the creator of our dram-shops, and this *alone* can destroy them; but the use of this all-powerful weapon woman is denied . . . I tell you, you are an organized band of unscrupulous tyrants, who have united in the plentitude of your brute force to oppress the weak—to enforce taxation without representation, and I do not care one straw for your laws."[120]

Halfway through the first volume of *The Lily*, Bloomer had taken a government job, endorsed property destruction and arson, and framed women's disenfranchisement as "tyranny" and "taxation without representation." She wrote to Swisshelm, requesting an exchange—*The Lily* for the *Visiter*. Exchanges allowed editors to receive more papers than they could pay for, which meant more material to select from and a wider potential audience for their own original articles. This created a vital information network in which editors and readers debated the concerns of the day, and Bloomer especially wanted to connect with any reasonably like-minded women editors she could find.

Swisshelm sent her a note with the current issue. She was already a fan. "We should be sorry to be without *The Lily*, and rejoice to know it thinks of us." Bloomer was delighted. "We cordially take you by the hand dear sister, and whether we agree with you in all things or not, we shall have great respect for your opinions."[121]

Another key relationship began for Bloomer when, sometime in late summer, Elizabeth Cady Stanton walked into the post office and introduced herself. Stanton would remember that when Bloomer became deputy postmaster, "the improvement in the appearance and conduct of the office was generally acknowledged," and the reading room was a welcome development.[122]

Stanton was three years older than Bloomer, the mother of three boys and a few months pregnant again, elegant, plump, confident, and charming, with dark curls and sharp blue eyes. Bloomer knew her by sight and reputation as co-organizer of the previous year's women's rights convention, graduate of the elite Troy Female Seminary, wife of an admired abolitionist, daughter of a one-time congressman and current State Supreme Court justice, sister-in-law of village leader Edward Bayard, and cousin of the influential reformer Gerrit Smith, with connections to the radical hotbeds of Boston. She believed in temperance and wanted to write for *The Lily*. Bloomer welcomed her.

Alternative medicine continued to be a regular topic in *The Lily*, as Bloomer's own headaches and fragile health persisted. And that summer, cholera, a frightening new disease that could kill a healthy adult in hours, spread across the country. She recommended "cleanliness and temperance" to her readers as the best preventatives, which was reasonable, since almost nothing was understood about this waterborne illness in 1849.

The Lily was still a temperance paper, but it could not be denied that temperance fever had passed. A friend commiserated with Bloomer. "I regret the coldness and indifference or rather *inaction* of the ladies of our village . . . They seem to have laid aside much of their former interest."[123]

Bloomer was more devoted to the cause than ever. But now that she had new forums for self-education, community, and action, she gradually took up more radical ideas. In October, she sat down to compose an editorial on the controversial topic of "Woman's Rights."

She began with disarming humor. "Start not dear reader, as your eye rests upon the above words, nor think that we are going to nominate either you or ourself for the Governorship or the Presidency . . . Much, very much, must be done to elevate and improve the character and minds of our sex, before we are capable of ruling our own households as we ought, to say nothing of holding in our hands the reins of government." Many women never thought of their rights, she wrote, and were content with what they had, "but we forget how many thousand wives and mothers, worthy as ourselves, are compelled by the unjust laws of our land to drag out a weary life and submit to indignities which no man would bear."[124] She did not explicitly endorse women's suffrage but said that the "consent" of women was necessary to create just laws, and without it, civil disobedience could be appropriate.

The year was almost over, and Bloomer had to decide what to do about her paper. More success than she had expected was partnered with a workload that she still found overwhelming. She discussed the matter with Dexter and her friends and wrote an editorial in the October issue about her dilemma. "Many of our readers . . . are urging us on no account to let the paper stop, and it is our own wish that it might be continued; yet we fear unless a successor can be found to take our place, that its existence will end with the year." She had a good circulation now and could see how to increase it. She could pay the bills. But when she contemplated another year of *The Lily*, "we shrink from the undertaking, and feel impelled to retire." She would announce her decision in the next issue.

The November 1849 issue of *The Lily* marked Elizabeth Cady Stanton's first column, which contained "conversations" between a fictionalized mother and son. Her topics were "the glorious temperance cause," political vs. moral power, and her belief that grain surpluses should be sent to starving children in Ireland instead of being made into profitable whiskey.

Bloomer introduced Stanton to readers at uncharacteristic length in two spiky paragraphs titled "Sun Flower." This was Henry Stanton's pet name for Elizabeth, and her chosen pseudonym.[125] "Will some one . . .

please tell us whether the 'Sun Flower' belongs to the masculine or the feminine gender? We welcome the Sun Flower to our pages, and so long as it will act in concert with the Lily ... we shall consider it a valuable auxiliary; but should it grow proud, and in its loftiness presume too much, the Lily will ... teach it that they who hold their heads the highest are not always the best."[126] Bloomer was either joking or genuinely unsure which Stanton she was dealing with.

The reason for this prickly introduction could also have been to remind Stanton that this was Bloomer's paper. Two months earlier, Stanton had written to a clergyman friend with an idea for a sermon on nagging wives. If he wrote it, Stanton said, he should send it to her, "and I will have it published in the Lily; the reform paper we started here in Seneca Falls."[127] If the attitude behind that unearned appropriative "we" was apparent outside this private letter, it would have raised Bloomer's hackles.

Stanton responded in a long essay full of historical and literary allusions. "I humbly feel the distance there is between me and the royal Lily ... As to the gender of which you inquire, the sun-flower, like all other flowers, is both masculine and feminine ... how could you fear that one would grow proud, so wholly unnoticed and unpraised as is the Sun Flower?" Bloomer printed it and wrote: "It never occurred to us that, notwithstanding her exalted position, she might be pining from neglect, and looking with envy on her lowly neighbors. We are glad she has spoken in self-defense."

Stanton urged readers to resubscribe promptly in a second letter, signed "Sam." Seneca Falls should "strengthen and encourage the *Lily* to greater activity, for she may yet be so distinguished ... that travellers in passing through our country will visit this spot with interest, as the birth-place of the *Lily*."[128]

Bloomer also announced that she had decided to continue for another year, though she still could not afford a semimonthly. She told her readers that someone had promised to help her, but the source and nature of this promise is once again not clear. Stanton may have offered, but she was still short of time and freedom and would be for years to come.

Lydia Ann Jenkins wrote a column on "Ultraism," an argument for listening to radical new ideas, and for the first time, emboldened by her topic, she signed her full name. Bloomer shared short biographies of seventeen "Female Printers and Editors" and recommended them to "those sensitive ones who think a woman incapable of doing anything beyond the narrow sphere of her own home."[129]

Bloomer also turned in earnest to the subject of dress reform. Every spring and fall, thick, sucking mud clogged the country roads and fields. During any wet spell, the village streets became a filthy mix of wet clay soil, manure, and street debris that clotted shoes and boots, spattered trousers, and soaked skirts up to the knee. It did not help that cold wet weather made the heavy chore of washing and hanging out laundry even more arduous. "It has been a damp morning," Bloomer read in the *Edinburgh Journal.* "Our fine lady's skirts . . . are thickly dabbled for a few inches upward with mud, which they have communicated in no small quantities to her shoes and stockings . . . I am not prepared to advocate the Sclavonian [Ottoman Croatian] brevity of petticoat, with a supplement of frilled trousers . . . but I certainly recommend that the skirts of walking dresses should never come within three inches of the ground, with a supplement or not."[130] Bloomer clipped this for *The Lily.*

She also expressed her annoyance with a fashion plate in *Godey's Lady's Book.* "We do wish if the men are going to make fashions for us, they would leave us room to breathe. Now that we have laid aside our corsets and stays, we think they should encourage us in letting our forms be as nature made them, instead of asking us to pattern after such wasp like waists."[131]

For December, she continued this topic in response to the fuss in the press over an outfit worn by the touring British actor and abolitionist Fanny Kemble. "The so much talked of, 'man's clothes' which Mrs. Kemble has been guilty of putting on, is nothing more nor less than a loose flowing dress falling a little below the knees, and loose pantaletts or drawers connected to the ancle by a band or cord. This shows how very sensitive gentlemen are in regard to any infringement on what they are pleased to consider their 'rights.'

They need have no fears however on the subject, for we very much doubt whether even Mrs. Kemble could be willing to don their ugly dress." In her opinion, the "gentlemen of the press" had overreached. "We maintain that we have the right to control our own wardrobe; and when gentlemen undertake to arrange it for us they are very ill-mannered, and show that they are hard pressed for something to talk and write about."[132]

New ideas about women's health made dress reform an increasingly popular topic in the progressive journals of the day. Bloomer had never seen any of the new costumes, but she was intrigued. Her favorite *Water Cure Journal* printed a letter from a woman that brought back her own childhood freedom to explore in nature. "The free use of the arms and respiration of the lungs is certainly prohibited by the tight bodices now worn; and surely what is more inconvenient than the unwieldy shawls and flowing skirts that ladies believe they are doomed to wear? But they are not obliged to wear them." She recommended the outfit she had invented for rambles in the woods: "Stout calf-skin gaiters; white trowsers made after the Eastern style, loose, and confined at the ankle with a cord; a green kilt, reaching nearly to the knees, gathered at the neck, and turned back with a collar, confined at the waist with a scarlet sash tied upon one side, with short sleeves for summer, and long sleeves for winter, fastened at the wrist; a green turban made in the Turkish mode. With such a dress I can ride on horseback, row a boat, spring a five-rail fence, climb a tree, or find my way through a greenbrier swamp, setting aside the extra feeling of wild, daring freedom one possesses when thus equipped and alone in the woods."[133]

Before Christmas, Amelia and Dexter accepted a special invitation to take a newly completed railway line from Ithaca, at the bottom of Cayuga Lake, to New York City. At the station, Amelia picked up her skirts to step into a jewel box of a train car, "an elegant piece of workmanship, exceeding in beauty anything we have seen. It is trimmed with damask velvet and rich satin, and elaborately ornamented with carved rosewood ... every comfort and convenience of the traveler taken into consideration." This was her first trip outside the Finger Lakes region, or what was then called Western New York, and it may have been her first visit to any city.

In Manhattan, they spent a few days sightseeing, including a visit to Barnum's Museum. Amelia was interested in all she saw and happy to leave. On the return trip, she admired the fresh snow on the hills and valleys, though a snowstorm and high winds made for a hazardous ferry ride back up the lake. She was relieved to get home. "Give us the level land . . . where the eye can roam at will, rather than the rocky mountains and fearful declivities, which, though they may startle and excite admiration for a time, will in the end produce weariness."

In one year, from the security of her village home, Bloomer had built confidence, skills, and connections beyond anything she could have imagined for herself, and beyond what most of the world considered right for a respectable woman. And from charitable and temperance societies she had brought together a community of reform-minded women in her post office reading room and the public forum of *The Lily*: accessible and protected places where they could exchange ideas, educate themselves, and draw others in. She understood that they wanted guidance, and she was ready to provide it.

CHAPTER 5

The Rights We Need

In the new year of 1850, Bloomer formally dropped the pretense that *The Lily* was the work of a collective by replacing the "committee of ladies" in the masthead with her name, though she still used the traditional editorial "we."

"Oh! what a heap of good letters we are getting lately," she wrote. "We should like to publish them all, but our readers would think us so *vain* . . . We are sure we love the writers of all these letters very much, and return them many thanks for their kind regards and timely aid."[134] At least thirty people had sent her new subscribers, including "a good list" collected by an enterprising eleven-year-old girl. Bloomer ordered extra copies of the January issue, sent some to subscribers who had not yet renewed, and announced that if they did not return them by the first of February, she would consider them resubscribed. Cash in advance was now less of a concern than expansion. She ended her first year with an unexpected profit of twenty-five dollars and used it to pay herself for her year of "toil and anxiety."[135]

Labor rights were coming into focus for her now. In a column on the starvation wages paid to "the most skillful and expert seamstresses . . . driving them to crime or prostitution," she commented that women were excluded from conversations on worker protections "because they cannot vote."[136] Economic opportunities would mean the freedom for women to walk away from bad marriages, or at least to keep their families fed and clothed.

None of this was abstract for Bloomer. A dear childhood friend, "a gay, lighthearted girl," had married an alcoholic and was now trapped, exhausted with poverty and despair.[137] And that winter, Bloomer reported a conversation that inspired her to rage and tears. The impoverished wife of "a degraded sot" who abused her appealed to the poormaster of Seneca Falls for aid to feed her children, but he told her that her only option was to take them "*to the Poor House.*" The woman was horrified and begged him for any alternative, but he had nothing else to offer.[138]

Women editors were finding each other now, and Bloomer reprinted a column by Clarina Nichols that celebrated their new sense of camaraderie. "It is so like the dropping in of a friend to take tea and spend the evening, when our husband empties his capacious pockets and we find Mrs. Swisshelm, Mrs. Pierson, and Mrs. Bloomer beside us, each with heart full of stirring thoughts. We take our knitting—we always knit while we read . . . and who can say we lack anything?" Of Amelia she wrote, "*Mrs Bloomer . . .* ranges the miserable and degraded children and wife of the drunkard beside the legislation which both furnishes the rum, and consigns them to the drunken protection of its consumer, with a truthfulness and energy which, more than anything else, whispers in our heart 'to vote or not to vote,' is *that* the question?"

Bloomer replied, "We should *so like* to drop in bodily and take tea with you and meet Mrs Swisshelm and Mrs Pierson . . . how much *we* should be strengthened by an interchange of thought and sentiment . . . But then it would never do, for should some jealous gentleman editor get wind of it, he would give an alarm, and we should be arrested on a charge of treason, and a design to overturn society. So we must content ourself with spiritual communion."

She followed this with a brief column on "Woman's Rights" in which she celebrated the growing power of the movement. "Men seem to entertain fears that . . . *they* will be compelled to perform the domestic duties which belong exclusively to our sex . . . We suppose they would prefer that like the women of the harem, they should know no will but to obey their lords and masters . . . But . . . while they have women of as powerful intellect and great knowledge as Jane Swisshelm, Lucretia Mott, Lydia Jane Pierson, Clarina Nichols, and a host of others whom we might mention to contend with, they may not hope to crush or subdue the desire which has formed in woman's breast to emancipate her sex."

February brought some political news that threw gunpowder on Bloomer's smoldering sympathy for women's suffrage in an article with the arresting title: "Have Women Any Souls?" The author called it "rather the funniest thing in a Legislature we have come across." Bloomer did not laugh.

A women's property rights bill had been proposed before the Tennessee legislature. In the course of the arguments, an opponent asked for biblical proof that women had souls. Another claimed that property rights would destroy women's "delicate sensibilities" by exposing them to "the roughest scenes of life." The bill was defeated, 17–54. "Mr. Moody's doctrine, that women have no souls, and Mr. Allen's that they are too delicate and refined to hold property, is affirmed by the Tennessee Legislature!"[139]

Bloomer, outraged to her Christian core, dipped her pen and went off. "The legislature of Tennessee after gravely discussing the question, have in their wisdom decided that women have no souls, and no right to hold property!! ... Women no souls? Then of course we are not accountable beings ... We shall no longer be answerable for the violation of the laws of God or man ... We suppose the wise legislators consider the question settled beyond dispute ... it will be quite another thing to make women believe it."

She clarified her own position. "We have not designed saying much ourself on the subject of '*woman's rights*,' but we see and hear so much that is calculated to keep our sex down ... we think it high time that women should open their eyes and look where they stand."

After this, she began to address political news in more depth. Henry Stanton gave her a state legislature report on the excise question, and she wrote a column using the statistics it contained on the poverty, crime, and premature deaths caused by alcohol.

Predictable letters arrived for Bloomer in reaction to her editorial on women as accountable beings with rights. "Some of our gentlemen readers are a little troubled lest we should injure ourself and our paper by saying too much in behalf of the rights and interests of our own sex, and it has even been intimated to us that we are controlled in the matter by some person or persons ... We would here say distinctly that no one besides ourself has any control over the columns of the Lily." And "one of its objects as stated in our prospectus is, *to open a medium through which woman's thoughts and aspirations might be developed.* Gentlemen have no reason to complain if women avail themselves of this medium."[140]

When Clarina Nichols questioned why Bloomer had no time to knit, Bloomer confessed to her readers her position as post office deputy. She had hesitated to announce it because "there is a wrong impression ... that 'Uncle Sam's' Post Masters receive their letters free." But that job took up more of her time than *The Lily,* and when Dexter was away for "days and weeks" at a time, "the entire duties of the office have been entrusted to us." She published *The Lily* by herself, except the printing, and found that she could "arrange our ideas and write our editorial better while washing dishes and making puddings and pies, than we could over our knitting; so we shall lay the knitting aside until 'Jack Frost' admonishes us next fall, that we must prepare for his reception."[141]

Her favorite subscriptions and exchanges now included the health journal *Graham's Magazine, The Free School Clarion* out of Syracuse, and three publications from Fowler & Wells in New York City, including the *Water Cure Journal.* It gave better health advice, she told her readers, than "the best blistering, bleeding, calomel, pill doctor in the land."

There was a new water cure at Clifton Springs, which Bloomer promoted, and she reported on the new Female Medical College of Pennsylvania. "We are thankful that the doors to one profession at least, are now thrown freely open ... All honor to Elizabeth Blackwell who dared the frowns and ridicule of the world and thus inspired her sex with confidence to follow!" The year before, Blackwell had become the first woman to graduate from nearby Geneva Medical College, and at the top of her class.

The first New York State Convention of the Friends of Free Schools was held in Syracuse that July, and Bloomer wrote a long editorial in favor of it. Every child deserved equal access to education, and a free school system was the answer. Stanton devoted two "conversations" that summer to the subject, and Bloomer published a column on the folly of women's charitable "Education Societies" that raised funds to educate young men. Women should educate themselves first.

Stanton was now the second-most regular contributor to *The Lily* after Bloomer herself, and one of the most spirited and skilled. She wrote about the physical and mental capabilities of the sexes, and in favor of a new divorce bill in light of statistics that showed the majority of "idiots" to be the product of alcoholic parents. She recommended government regulation of marriage. Her column "Woman" explored the legal condition of the sex around the world, and she suggested that the "class of men who believe in their natural inborn inbred superiority" should read more and compare themselves with great woman leaders and scientists.

The labor and petty annoyances of editorship still made Bloomer wonder if it was worth going on. At the same time, it was all material for her columns. Her printers began to print *The Lily* on worse paper and claimed it was all they could get, though she did not believe them and argued with them in their clattering mill office to the point of tears. And then she wrote about the cheap paper. When yet another man expressed his pious concern to her that political involvement would expose women to rough crowds of men, she replied in *The Lily* using Jane Swisshelm's answer to Clarina Nichols's thoughts on the subject. Swisshelm described women at the market, "soft, white arms, with a great basket of beef and butter hanging on them . . . and the fairy feet, drooping shoulders, and taper waists . . . braced firmly to maintain their places amid coalmen and carters, hucksters and teamsters . . . Woman should be very delicate, very depending, very helpless, when men want to be loved: but she must grow very strong, very self-reliant, very efficient when he wants to be served."

But Bloomer's primary cause, temperance, still languished. The trustees of Seneca Falls said they would not enforce the village ban on alcohol sales unless they were petitioned to do so. This time, Bloomer refused to canvass for signatures. She had enough to do and "felt it to be entirely useless for women to say any thing on the subject. We have had our petitions slighted and ridiculed too often, for us to have much to do with another." Women needed the vote.

Free white women, that is to say. The only other group she considered, enslaved Black women, needed abolition first. With the Fugitive Slave Act under discussion in Congress, Bloomer devoted nearly two pages to a reprint on the "HORRORS OF THE SLAVE TRADE," from a Washington, DC, journalist on the brutal assault and abduction for sale of "a very honest and industrious colored woman" with six children who had been saving to buy her own freedom. Bloomer wrote: "Only think of it! A noble, virtuous woman, thus cruelly outraged in broad day light . . . could claim no protection from the chivalry of American men, nor from the justice of American law givers. Is it presumptuous to suppose that American women, after experimenting seventy-five years, might substitute a more wise and merciful government, for their own sex, at least, than we now endure? One that might protect the poor against the rich, the weak against the strong."

Bloomer also called out another woman editor, the New York–born Harriet Prewett of the *Yazoo Whig* in Mississippi. "So far as we know she is the only woman who has charge of a strictly political paper." Bloomer considered her a good writer but "not 'sound' on the great question of the day—that of Slavery." Her paper contained advertisements "such as . . . 'a fine lot of Virginia negroes for sale,' etc. Virginia negroes! native born Americans! for sale. Fie on you Mrs. P. thus to lend your columns to aid the inhuman traffic in the bodies and souls of your brothers and sisters!" In another issue, she again shamed Prewett for running slave auction ads. "Do not tell us on one page of your paper, of twenty women to be *sold* in front of the Court House door, in your own County, and on another, that southern women have all the rights and privileges they desire."

At the same time, Bloomer and Stanton did not regard the cause of enslaved people as more urgent than their own. And like many other white reformers, they often used the word "slavery" as a metaphor.[142] Even white abolitionists commonly used it to describe overwork, inadequate pay, addiction, love, religious experiences—anything that limited their freedom.[143] Though it was true that the law largely gave white men ownership of their families, the situation of married white women and their minor children was absolutely not equivalent to that of Black people in chattel slavery.

In one column, in support of Clarina Nichols, who had taken over the Brattleboro *Windham County Democrat* from her sick husband, Bloomer used this metaphor when she mocked the surprise of a male editor that Nichols could do the job. "You men seem to understand very well how a woman—and many times a sickly woman—can wash, iron, bake, cook your meals three times a day, mend and make clothes for half a dozen, mind the babies, keep her house in order, bring her wood and water, and sometimes cut the former; and then perhaps into the bargain take in sewing and washing to support herself and little ones and a lazy drunken brute of a husband . . . But when a woman . . . finds time '*to write leaders for a newspaper*' . . . it is more than you can understand." If "Mr. Editor" had to do half the labor done by most ordinary women, she said, "you would consider it little better than *slavery*."

Another one of Bloomer's inconsistencies on matters of race was her interest in phrenology, a popular new science that argued for a racial hierarchy and equated physical and mental power. Like many white progressives, Bloomer overlooked the racism and was intrigued by the aspects of phrenology that offered tools for self-improvement through "reading" character in the shapes of people's heads. But she balked when one editor claimed that "a man cannot be great unless he has a large and well formed brain, and a vital system powerful enough to support it." Before he judged human capacity by skull size, said Bloomer, he would have to prove that all great men such as Bonaparte and Milton "were six feet high, with the lungs of a porpoise and the head of a whale . . . small and delicate women have thought and written profoundly in the sciences, mathematics and metaphysics."

Bloomer and Stanton still had differences of opinion. And as Bloomer's circulation grew, so did the pressure from friends and others to support their preferred causes. If there is any good evidence that Stanton had no editorial control over *The Lily*, it is her lasting irritation with Bloomer for refusing to explicitly denounce the Fugitive Slave Act in its pages.

The Fugitive Slave Act became law on September 18, 1850. Anyone living in free Northern states was now required to capture and return anyone who escaped slavery. It was now a felony to aid such fugitives, many of whom traveled through Central New York on their way to Canada, or, like Frederick Douglass and Harriet Tubman, settled there. At least twenty-four Black people lived in Seneca Falls at the time, including four families who did not live with white people as servants. One was Thomas James, who refused to tell his birthplace to the census and would state his fugitive status in his will. He was a prosperous, politically active barber and a trustee of the Wesleyan church, with a family and real estate investments.[144]

In April 1852, Stanton wrote to Anthony, who was still a skeptic on women's rights, that Bloomer was an example of "the conservative element" in the temperance movement. "It was only with great effort and patience that she has been brought up to her present position. In her paper she will not speak against the fugitive slave law, nor in her work to put down intemperance will she criticize the equivocal position of the Church. She trusts to numbers to build up a cause rather than to principles."[145]

But in 1850, Stanton complained in *The Lily* that the New York State legislature spent too much time debating slavery and should focus on state concerns. Lydia Jenkins challenged her commitment to abolition. Bloomer, mediating between them, "could not repress a smile . . . Only to think that Stanton, who is an out and out abolitionist, a warm personal friend of Frederick

Douglass, Charles Lenox Remond, and many others of the colored champions of freedom . . . should be taken to task for her pro-Slavery sentiments!!" She then agreed with Stanton that horrific as slavery was, the problem of alcohol abuse was worse: "the Slave a happy man compared with the drunkard—the Slave holder innocent and respectable, when brought in comparison with the drunkard maker."[146]

Bloomer believed this, though she was antislavery and sympathized with the people she knew who aided fugitives.[147] In her October 1850 issue, she reprinted a story by Harriet Beecher Stowe about a prosperous white farmer who dreamed that he refused to help a desperate fugitive family and was condemned by the voice of God in the words of Jesus, "Depart from me ye accursed! for I hungered, and ye gave me no meat; I was thirsty, and ye gave me no drink; I was a stranger and ye took me not in." Stowe wrote, "Many in this nation . . . seem to think that there is no standard of right and wrong higher than Congress. . . . Shall any doubt if he may help the toil-worn, escaping fugitive . . . let him rather ask, shall he dare refuse him help?"

Still, this was on an inside page. Temperance was Bloomer's chosen cause, followed by women's rights. She devoted the first two pages of this issue to her manifesto on the rights of women: "ADDRESS TO THE WOMEN OF THE STATE OF NEW YORK." In it, she developed many ideas that she had presented before: Women had the same natural rights and judgment as men, and they had the right to the vote because they were taxed and on the principle of just government being derived from the consent of the governed. Boys and girls should have the same freedoms, responsibilities, and intellectual and moral training. "Instead of the selfishness found at the domestic hearth, we would have kind, conciliating companions. Our children might then have fathers as well as mothers."

Each of her readers could do something. They should not be deterred by fear of gossip, "nor allow insinuating flattery to persuade you into inactivity. Not only are your own interests involved, but the interests of posterity, the interests of the race."

Her second year of publication was coming to an end, and Amelia paused her acceptance of new subscriptions while she decided whether to quit. The temptation may have been greater now that Dexter had decided to step down from the *Courier* at the end of September. Again, her supporters protested. Her problem was not money, she told them, but health. "We have long been subject to severe attacks of headache, which unfit us for mental labor, and we feel that we cannot do justice to ourself or our readers. . . . It will be hard for us to part with our cherished bantling, and we may find when the day of trial comes, that the tie is too strong to be severed."

But she was still thinking of ending *The Lily* when a letter from Jane Swisshelm arrived. "Don't you do it, Mrs. Bloomer! If you do, you will rue it—mind! Give up 'The Lily' because you are subject to bad headaches . . . if you give up your paper you will be sure to keep the headache, and get a bad conscience into the bargain." She complimented Bloomer's "taste, thought, and ability" and cajoled her readers to subscribe if they had not already. For the headaches, she recommended "long lists of advance paying subscribers. Nothing does an editor's head and heart more good; and we will guarantee it cures her—if—if she does not drink coffee."

"There it is again!" answered Bloomer. "While we were flattering ourself that we could in a few months retire quietly from our labors, here comes this kindly remonstrance from one . . . for whom we entertain the strongest feelings of respect, and love . . . Her prescription for headache is good—for if it will not cure, it will gladden the heart, and make the pains of the head more endurable."

But she was still undecided. Readers often asked how she managed and if she had a servant. She did not. And she currently had "one little prattler under our care," one of many that she took in for weeks or years at a time. "Since April last we have done the entire work of our house, in addition to our duties as clerk and publisher. We cannot say of how much more we are capable, but think we could manage one or two more children—provided they did not want much attention. True, we have not much time to read novels, study the fashions, or gossip with idlers; yet we find time to read many things useful, to study ourself, and to visit our friends." And the interest and connection and public respect that *The Lily* brought her would not be easy to give up.

For now, she praised "the sewing girls of Adrian, Mich." for striking for better wages and expressed her gratitude to Henry Stanton for a beautiful copy of the *Catalogue of the Cabinet of Natural History of the State of New York*. She accepted columns from Jenkins on self-reliance, and Stanton on housekeeping advice and temperance. She clipped a quote on the evils of smoking in public places. At least there were signs forbidding it. She wished they would also forbid spitting. "A woman can hardly take a seat in the cars, or any other public place, without having her dress drabbled in tobacco juice, the stains of which cannot be erased ... if a smoker stop too long near us, we can ask him to leave, or refrain ... But setting down in a puddle of tobacco juice, or having our floor and stove besmeared with it, is too much for our patience."

A two-day women's rights convention in Worcester had been a great success. Bloomer read the report of it in the *New York Tribune*. It was the first national one, organized by members of the Anti-Slavery Society, including Abby Kelley (now Abby Kelley Foster), Lucy Stone, and Paulina Wright Davis, who had helped lobby for the Married Woman's Property Act of 1848. Attendees and speakers included Frederick Douglass, William Lloyd Garrison, Sojourner Truth, the young Oberlin graduate Antoinette Brown, Lucretia Mott, and the Polish Jewish suffragist Ernestine Rose, who had also worked for the property act.

Bloomer gave an equal amount of space to a more local "Festival" by the Daughters of Temperance in Oswego. In late November 1850, Bloomer received a long, friendly letter from Mary C. Vaughan, a temperance activist who had read a poem at the Oswego event and who had received two issues of *The Lily* from a friend. She agreed with some of what she read but disagreed that women should be involved in politics or the ministry. Bloomer replied in *The Lily*, "You talk confidently of the good woman may do in the *temperance* cause ... Have you no wish to do more than you can now do?—Does your heart never yearn for *power*... would your sense of *delicacy* and *refinement* prevent your expressing your hatred of the liquor traffic thro' the ballot-box, had you the privilege of doing so?"

After much internal debate and another scuffle with the printers, who made her November issue late because they were focused on the election, Bloomer finally resolved that this year was her last as an editor and publisher. She could still read, write, and attend meetings when she felt well and be free to do none of those things when she was sick. She wrote an "announcement of discontinuance" for her December issue and sent it to the typesetter.

But she could not rest in this decision. There were other papers for women now, but none so successful or so dedicated to temperance and women's rights. *The Lily* had opened up the world to her and given her an unmediated outlet for her thoughts, and she knew it was vital to many women who had felt themselves alone before. They told her so in letters every week. If she shut down *The Lily*, this network would go dead, for them and for herself. "Some unseen power seemed to direct otherwise—some voice to whisper 'Do it not!'" She tried to put it aside, but the still small voice kept whispering in the back of her mind as she sorted mail, walked home, and washed the dishes.

At last, she wrote another editorial, carried it down to the printing office, and swapped it for the announcement.[148] "We cannot bear the thought of separation, yet would fain shrink from the duties and responsibilities connected with it . . . Our little sheet has found a welcome in many circles where no other temperance paper would be tolerated, and thus aroused the attention of many who were indifferent . . . And while our opinions, and those of our correspondents on the so called question of 'woman's rights' may have been distasteful to some, we know that they have waked an echo in many hearts."

She had more subscribers in other states now and had even authorized a London agent. But she knew that most of her audience did not have much pocket money, so she kept the annual rate at fifty cents.

"Those who have borne us company so far, know about what to expect of us in future," she wrote. "We should be glad to enlarge, and otherwise improve our paper, but cannot afford it; so it must e'en be content to wear its old dress another year. . . . It has already, through its friends, importuned us for a change of name; but we dislike calling an old friend by a new name . . . We hope, however, it may yet earn for itself, both a new name, and a new dress."

CHAPTER 6

The Trousers

As she would remind people for the rest of her life, Amelia Bloomer did not invent "bloomers." No one individual did. Origins that have been suggested for them—that they were inspired by men's trousers, or the women's dress of the Haudenosaunee peoples of New York State—are often oversimplified or wrong. Anxiety about European women "wearing the trousers" is as old as gender-specific clothing, and at times they did put on "men's clothing" for various reasons. Haudenosaunee women who dressed traditionally wore versions of a loose dress, shawl, and half leggings tied above the knee. But gartered half leggings are not trousers. After the Civil War, several white nineteenth-century woman's rights advocates would credit the intellectual influence of Haudenosaunee women's rights, but none of the dress reformers said they used Native dress as a model, despite the obvious external resemblance. No contemporary report refers to the short dress and trousers as "Indian," or by the name of any tribe. Some described it as children's dress or exercise wear. But Bloomer, other promoters of dress reform, and their critics often called these trousers, and the entire outfit, "Turkish," and in some cases, accessorized accordingly.

Traditional Turkish aesthetics and garments had migrated into European dress through trade, diplomacy, and illustrated books since the fourteenth century, and Turkish women and men have worn trousers for three thousand years.[149] Turkish dress started to be worn in European reform and artistic circles not long after Lady

Mary Wortley Montagu brought it back to London from a visit to Constantinople between 1716 and 1718. She admired the rights of Turkish women as well as their clothes, writing, "'Tis very easy to see, they have in reality more liberty than we have." They kept control of their property through marriage, and when they divorced, they took it with them, plus an addition from their husbands.[150] British married women would not enjoy comparable property or divorce rights until the Married Women's Property Act of 1882. Lady Mary wrote essays on marriage and women's education and sometimes wore and posed for portraits in her Turkish clothes. After her death in 1762, her letters were published, and her descriptions helped inspire a craze for Turkish-inspired fashions and themes. Turkish dress was popular for fancy dress costume but was also worn as leisure wear—for portraits, by elite women with ties to the region or to revolutionary politics; or by those with unconventional lives.[151] And perhaps most relevant to Bloomer's circles, this outfit had long become familiar as exercise and health wear at sanatoriums, water cures, and elsewhere, unconnected with the politics of women's rights. In 1838, when Bloomer was a twenty-year-old governess, Henriette d'Angeville became the first woman to climb Mont Blanc unaided. To do so, she wore a long button-front wool dress with a short skirt and matching wide-leg trousers tucked into gaiters.[152]

More British women published Eastern travel memoirs in the nineteenth century. Some glossed over the constraints faced by Ottoman Turkish women, but the relative legal, marital, and social freedoms they admired were real. In 1837, Julia Pardoe wrote, "It is the fashion in Europe to pity the women of the East; but it is ignorance of their real position alone which can engender so misplaced an exhibition of sentiment."[153] It was the fashion in the United States, too, this image of pitiable or desirable submissive femininity, a useful scapegoat for a culture eager to imagine itself at the peak of civilization. Their full trousers, gathered at the ankles, were distinct from the straight-legged trousers of Western men, and because of this, to some early reformers, Turkish trousers seemed like an attractive yet modest alternative to long skirts. And now, white women in the US were slowly gaining property rights, state by state. Increased political and economic power led to other experiments with personal freedom.

Dress reform was needed in 1851. Fashionable dress had become a burden. The ideal silhouette was a tiny waist, full bosom, fuller hips, and trailing hemlines. To achieve this shape, women wore stays or corsets or structured bodices augmented by padding. To give volume to their skirts, they wore layers of heavy petticoats that tangled their legs, collected dirt and debris, and soaked up moisture from the ground. Sleeves were long and tight, shoulders dropped and tight, daytime necklines were high, and shoes were paper-thin and flat. Voluminous shawls, gloves, and profile-obscuring bonnets, sometimes with the addition of veils to protect against sun and dust, made them almost as modest in public as Turkish women, though more likely to trip.

Corsets and bodices were often laced tight for fashion's sake, though most women with any work to do wore them just snug enough for support and a respectable, neat appearance. As with any restrictive fashions, most stylish people accepted whatever made them feel put together and attractive until illness made them uncomfortable. Whether clothing caused illness was an ongoing debate. Right or not, medical professionals railed against "tight lacing" in both mainstream and alternative medical journals, and some patients, like Bloomer, had already taken their advice to abandon all tight clothes for the sake of their health.

But trousers were another matter. Western women did not even wear two-legged underwear until the eighteenth century's pantalettes and drawers. And those garments were open-crotched, attached only at the waist.[154] Children often wore pantalettes with a closed crotch under a shorter skirt but only until puberty, when girls changed into long skirts and boys changed into trousers.[155]

There are various stories of how the short dress and trousers spread in the United States. Children's dress for adults in utopian communities that promoted relative gender equality was an early influence. Robert Owen's New Harmony society, founded in Indiana in 1825, made both men and women wear loose pantaloons.[156] Because Owen advocated equality in marriage, they were accused of "free love" and dissolved in 1827.

In the summer of 1848, the Oneida Community, led by John Humphrey Noyes, moved in about ten miles from the home of the wealthy and influential reformer Gerrit Smith, whose daughter Elizabeth is often credited with inventing the short dress and trousers in 1851. Noyes felt that conventional women's dress was immodest because it overemphasized gender, and that children's dress was in better taste. He described how some of the women changed to "short gowns or frocks, with pantaloons ... The women say they are far more free and comfortable in this dress than in long gowns; the men think that it improves their looks." Many of them also cut their hair to shoulder length.[157]

But in January of 1851, Bloomer was preoccupied by the charter election results in Seneca Falls. Many temperance men she trusted had voted along party lines for rum sellers. Her remaining hope rested on the two or three village trustees who were "good Temperance men and true," though she knew they were now outnumbered.[158]

More letters than she could answer stacked her desk. Lydia Ann Jenkins sent one on the damage done by "Tight Dressing." Elizabeth Cady Stanton wrote on daily cold baths in reaction to a medical journal that claimed more than one a week was "injurious." And Bloomer clipped some compliments from other editors to reprint. The *Concord Free Press* in Massachusetts called her "a pleasing, energetic writer, and the *Lily* is one of the best temperance advocates we know of . . . it is positively a shame for anyone to be without it."

Bloomer promoted two petitions to the state legislature, one on suffrage and property rights and one on tax exemption for poor women, though again, she felt they were probably futile. "Men are willing to pay deference to us in little things . . . when we complain of real wrongs, then we are out of our spheres." In another article, she commented, "One thing is certain, we are not to be frightened by these *dictators*, and so long as we are proprietor of the Lily . . . we shall say just what we please. . . . It is an independent, woman's paper, and will remain such so long as our name stands at the editorial head. We are happy to state that in our own village, out of about a hundred subscribers, three only have ordered their papers stopped—two of these say they love *temperance* very much, but they 'will not *countenance* this subject of woman's rights'. Glad *we* are not *their wife!*"

But she did find time amid her other preoccupations to consider the short dress and trousers. To her surprise and amusement, in a late January issue of the *Seneca County Courier*, an anonymous author wrote about "Female Attire." "Who has not been pained to witness the inconvenience attending the act of entering a carriage or alighting? Ten to one but the dress is soiled, if not utterly ruined. This can scarcely be avoided, to say nothing of the indelicate exposure ... Then how painful to the sensitive female must it be to strive to walk, her dress flapping in the breeze and assuming all the gyrations of a ship's sails in a storm." He suggested a "pair of Turkish pantaloons, wide, and nearly meeting the shoe, of such material and texture as the season demanded ... and a garment neatly fitting the person, buttoned, or permanently closed on all sides, extending just below the knee."

She suspected the author might be Isaac Fuller, who had sparred with her on "the woman's rights question" more than once. This was a good chance "to score him one on having gone so far ahead of us."[159]

"Really," she wrote:

Had we broached this subject the cry would have been
raised on all sides, "She wants to wear the pantaloons," and
a pretty hornet's nest we should have got into. But now
that our cautious editor of the *Courier* recommends it, we
suppose there will be no harm in our doing so. And what is
this dress, which we are to don at the bidding of our self-
constituted lords and guardians? As near as we can get at
it, it is simply a sack-coat and pantaloons, and a cap or hat
similar to those worn by men. One thing we object to on the
start, and that is having the coat entirely closed. Men like

to display a handsome vest, and nicely plaited shirt-bosom, and why may we not have the same privilege? Nothing is said about our hair, whether we shall have it cut short—or about our boots ... The latter, we think, ought not to have been omitted. We go for high thick boots that are impervious to cold or wet ... Really, ladies, will it not be nice? ... Yet the convenience of the thing is nothing when compared to the health and comfort. Small waists and whalebones can be dispensed with, and we shall be allowed breathing room; and our forms will be what nature made them."

She reminded readers of the fuss made over Fanny Kemble's ensemble the year before, which was essentially the same. "This only shows that women should not dare to make a change in their costume till they have the consent of men."[160]

Her March issue took up the subject more thoroughly. She clipped articles on dress from the *Water Cure Journal*.[161] One asked, "Why are short dresses, which all agree are decidedly becoming for a young miss, so improper, indelicate and immodest, as soon as she has passed into her teens?"

That February, a surprising figure appeared on the streets of Seneca Falls: the first woman ever to walk them in a knee-length dress and trousers.

Bloomer was soon introduced to her by Stanton, and, like several other Seneca Falls women, she was fascinated by this intelligent and congenial woman, tall and healthy and beautiful, with glossy black hair and deep brown eyes, standing before them in the clothes that, until now, Bloomer had only read about.

The woman was Elizabeth Cady Stanton's cousin, Elizabeth Smith Miller, who had appeared in Stanton's columns as "Sobriny Jane." They had spent summers together as teenagers and called each other "Johnson" and "Julius" after characters in a Christy's Minstrels blackface comedy routine.[162]

Like Stanton, Miller was married with young children. Her family was devoted to reform, and she had never worn a corset.

Their home was a stop on the Underground Railroad and welcomed what Stanton's husband, Henry, would later call a "miscellaneous" assortment of urban sophisticates, religious and political radicals, and a few Oneida tribal members who mostly stopped by for supplies and left. They must have known about the white Oneida Community nearby and their innovation in women's dress. That would be the origin story asserted by the dress reformer Mary Tillotson in 1885. But Miller would remember her creation as inspired by the frustration of a long gardening session.

"Mr. Courier" mock-accused Bloomer of too much "levity" in her reply to his article on female dress. Not at all, she replied, "we made ourself a little merry over it, at the editor's expense; but we were really very serious in all we said in favor of the proposed change. The *Courier* now attempts to make a fling at us about the boots; but let us tell you, Mr. Courier, that whether we take 'a seat in the Legislative Hall, drive a team on the tow path' or follow the more proper and delicate business of cook and dishwasher, we need the boots all the same; for . . . there are times when the most refined and gentle find it necessary to brave both mud and snow." She continued: "We have reason to know that several women in our village are ready to assume the Turkish dress as soon as a sufficient number will join them, or they can muster courage to be independent; and we hope and believe that ere long it will be generally adopted. More absurd changes than this have been made in the fashion of woman's dress within our recollection."

She brought the subject back to her primary concern. "The *Courier* says that the fashion of woman's dress has been a great cause of intemperance. Men have found the burden of supporting sickly wives so great, that it has driven them to drunkenness. We don't know but this is so; but women certainly have been the greatest sufferers from their own folly, and if anybody was privileged to get drunk on account of it, we think they have the best right."[163]

Stanton wrote her own response to "Mr. Courier" in the form of another "Sobriny Jane" column for the March issue. She told how Miller had shortened all her skirts in December "in the presence of her liege lord and all her sons ... She then slipped her neatly turned foot and ankle into a masculine boot, leaped into a pair of Turkish trowsers, and walked forth ... to the home of her childhood. There having received the paternal nod of approval, she shrinks not, now, from encountering the vacant gaze, the vulgar laugh, and idle jeers, of ill-bred men, women and children ... Is it not better, voluntarily to imitate the Turkish nobility, than meekly bow to the dictation of a vulgar French milliner? ... If Mrs. Bloomer will persist in talking lightly of ten or twenty pounds of petticoats, console yourself with the reflection that she feels their weight as grievous as the least of us. Entre nous, I have every reason to think she is already perpetrating some mutilations on her own wardrobe. She had several interviews with Sobriny, and has an exact pattern of the costume."[164]

Amelia consulted with Dexter. Though she considered her clothing her own business, she was also aware that, as with the post office position, he might be concerned about gossip. But he had no objection. She got out her shears. Whether she chose to cut the skirt of a dress she had and use the remnant to construct a pair of matching trousers, or whether she bought new fabric and started from scratch, it was a significant investment.

Within the week, Stanton left her house in a new black satin outfit, her skirt cut a little above the knees of her matching trousers.[165] A few days after that, Bloomer debuted a more modest ensemble with a longer skirt. Soon afterward, the *Courier* writer said he was glad to see that "several of the most respectable ladies of our village" had put on the new style. "It is now quite common to see the short dress and pantalettes in our streets, and it is admitted by nearly all that they are a decided improvement." The editor of the *Cayuga Chief* from Weedsport, north of Auburn, said he was "pleased to learn that some of the ladies of Seneca Falls have commenced a reform in the style of female attire. We ... suppose it to be that of the short dress and Turkish trowsers—the most beautiful and graceful female dress in the world."

The Lily continued to report on other fronts as well. Earlier in the year, another woman writer came to her attention, the gifted and prolific Frances Gage of Ohio, who was twenty years older than Bloomer and used the pen name "Aunt Fanny."[166] She became a regular contributor.

Henry Stanton dropped off copies of the legislature's reports on state license laws. Bloomer wrote an editorial on them and called out the lukewarm "temperance men" of Seneca Falls who voted on party lines. And a flattering request arrived: "Only think, the Secretary of State has requested two copies of our Lily; he wishes 'to send one copy to the Grand Industrial Fair to be held in London, to be afterwards deposited in the Royal Museum, and to place another copy in the New York State Library!'"[167]

She was reading more history and ran a series of short biographies of women leaders in *The Lily*, more than a modern reader might expect. "That there have been, comparatively, a greater number of good queens, than of good kings, is a fact stated by several historians." Among these she listed the ancient Syrian queen Zenobia; Isabella of Spain; Maria Theresa of Austria; Catherine of Russia; Elizabeth I of England; and "the brave, intelligent, proud hearted Zinga, the negro Queen of Angola." From these rulers, she turned to the American Revolutionary writer Hannah More, "one of the great minds of her day."

Combining the topics of tobacco spit and short dresses, Stanton wrote in the April issue, "The women of Seneca County have found out how to keep their dresses out of this extract of the Virginia weed—and that is by cutting them off to the knee." She bemoaned the new distillery on the river in front of her house, with pens for hogs to consume the rich mash created by the brewing process. "I would not willingly exchange the perfume of linden and locust trees . . . for the heavy odors of fermenting grains and filthy hogs . . . Is there nothing, dear Lily, we can do to make distillers 'dreadful uncomfortable.'"

Bloomer commented that the distillery posed more danger to Stanton's family than bad smells. "But what of it? Two or three men will get rich and live luxuriously, (or, what is more probable, in the end become poor) and they stop not to enquire how many poor souls they will grind in the dust." As to what Stanton could do about it, "We should think she had learned, ere this, the extent of woman's power . . . but as we are appealed to . . . We advise that the distillery be complained of as a nuisance . . . and if our friend has more money to bribe drunken lawyers and judges, than have the distillers, she will gain her case, otherwise it is hopeless."[168]

"Our Costume" was Stanton's third topic, and Bloomer placed it on the next-to-last page. "Some say the Turkish costume is not graceful. Grant it . . . but nowhere is the ideal female form to be found in a huge whaleboned bodice and bedraggled skirt," and in them, "one might as well work with a ball and chain." As to mockery, "that is a strong reason in its favor. It is good to be laughed at; the more ridicule you encounter the better. It strengthens and develops the character to stand alone."

On the page before this, Bloomer set her own column, titled "Our Dress": "Behold us now in short dress and trowsers, and then, if you please, give free vent to your feelings on the subject . . . We did not think, when we expressed our approval of the proposed change, that we should so soon be drawn into it ourself; but . . . we feel it incumbent upon us to practice what we preach." Most men, she said, were in favor of it, though some laughed or glared at her. "The women are many of them decidedly opposed to the change; others laugh, and say 'you look so queer,' others still, come out in our favor, and many have already adopted the dress." Some of her friends were distressed by her change, "but we are such an unfortunate mortal that we cannot turn without stepping on some one's toes . . . So we must e'en go our own way, and our friends must make allowance for our ignorance and awkwardness."

At least one of those friends had lectured Dexter on his duty to order Amelia back into long skirts. Dexter was polite but dismissed her and told Amelia. She addressed this woman without naming her:

> It is our pleasure in all things important to consult the wishes
> of our husband, and to do nothing without his consent and
> approval . . . we are happy to say that in this matter of dress,

he is on our side. If she would have him, at any time, exert an influence for good over us, she must find some other way for him to do it than by the exercise of 'authority' ... A silken cord is sometimes stronger than an iron chain, and a respectful entreaty has more power than the tyrant's command ... Those who think we look 'queer,' would do well to look back a few years, to the time when they wore ten or fifteen pounds of petticoat and bustle around the body and balloons on their arms ... If men think they would be comfortable in long, heavy skirts, let them put them on—we have no objection ... We do not say we shall wear this dress and no other, but we shall wear it for a common dress; and we hope it may become so fashionable that we may wear it at all times, and in all places, without being thought singular. We have already become so attached to it that we dislike changing to a long one.[169]

Many in this close-knit community of progressive Seneca Falls women and men thought that this new dress for women was a practical, attractive, and modest alternative to the restrictive fashions of the day. The strength of the greater public reaction would take them by surprise.

CHAPTER 7

Infamy and the Art of Disagreement

S pring sunlight glittered on the waters of Lake Ontario below the mill town and fort of Oswego as travelers boarded a steamboat to travel west. There was a stir of excitement on the landing as four people made their way through the crowd: two gentlemen with two ladies in skirts that ended just below their knees, exposing loose trousers to the tops of their shoes. They "were evidently people of cultivation," wrote the *Oswego Journal*. "In point of beauty, no costume is equal to that of the Turkish. Its convenience is superior to all others."

In Syracuse, a downpour turned the unpaved streets to mud and running water. A journalist "saw several splendid silks with about four inches of mud plastered around the bottom ... Several of our city ladies however, have had the good sense to adopt the new fashion, without waiting until it loses its oddity by becoming universal, and tripped over the damp pavements without any more inconvenience than if they were walking in a parlor."[170]

A woman in St. Louis reported four young women traveling to California with their father and brother, all dressed in stylish "male attire," with their hair cut short. The other passengers found them "very genteel," and the eldest daughter told her that "the day will yet come when all women will wear male attire."[171]

Bloomer and Stanton's April announcements of their new clothes, and the *Water Journal* column on "Woman's Dress," traveled across the nation within weeks. They elicited both praise and protest, but to begin with, mostly praise. Only one *Lily* subscriber canceled. Bloomer experienced some rude stares and remarks in public, but curiosity was the main reaction. People dropped by the post office and her home to see how she looked. Dexter thought that because she had a slight figure, "they became her very well . . . fortunately or otherwise."[172]

She continued to tinker with the design. For now, it was similar to current fashion, "except that our skirts have been robbed of about a foot of their former length, and a pair of loose trowsers of the same material as the dress, substituted. These latter extend from the waist to the ankle, and may be gathered into a band and buttoned round the ankle, or, what we think prettier, gathered or plaited up about two inches in depth, and left sufficiently wide for the foot to pass through, and allow of their falling over the top of the gaiter." She tried an elastic cuff, and at last, let them hang straight like the trousers of men. Bodices she made with loose "sack fronts," with a light belt or sash at the natural waist. Corsets she had given up before. Shawls she replaced with sack coats, a boxy unisex style that hung straight down from the shoulders. For her, as for many, the "new costume" was now an amalgam of ideas, altered to suit her own needs and personal aesthetic.

Word spread of the new dress. The New York City *Home Journal* wrote that there was "a town somewhere in the interior of the State, where the common gymnasium dress, of trousers and frock, had been adopted . . . where the sex is not subjected to wet heels and bedraggled petticoats in wet weather, and that town is 'Seneca Falls.'"[173]

In May 1851, the American Anti-Slavery Society held a convention in Syracuse. The entrance of Gertrude Burleigh and her grown daughters was widely reported. All three wore the "new costume," and as everyone stared at them, they strolled up the center aisle and took their seats on the platform. A Virginia paper reported it as "The Progress of Turkish Fashion" and worried that this "good work" of dress reform had "fallen into bad hands . . . at the incendiary abolition convention."[174]

After that convention, the main speakers, William Lloyd Garrison and George Thompson, toured smaller towns in the region. On May 13, they gave an afternoon lecture in Seneca Falls.[175] Bloomer was there with her overnight guest, Susan B. Anthony, who had followed them down from Syracuse.

Anthony was a Quaker, thirty, unmarried, and handsome, with smooth dark hair and calm, direct blue eyes. Bloomer seems to have befriended her at temperance meetings, and Anthony recruited subscribers for *The Lily* in Rochester.[176] She had developed confidence and a manner of authority as a teacher and headmistress, and she gave her first public speech at a temperance dinner in 1849. She met the famous Frederick Douglass at her father's antislavery meetings, and he recruited her as a lecturer for the Anti-Slavery Society. By 1850, Anthony was devoted to full-time reform work, though she was not yet converted to woman's rights. But she admired Stanton's writings and was eager to meet her.

When the meeting adjourned, Bloomer and Anthony lingered on the street corner to look for Stanton, who was hosting the speakers. Bloomer wore a short dress and trousers, bonnet, and sack coat. Anthony had on a long-skirted, simple gray dress, a shawl, and a gray bonnet trimmed with pale blue ribbons that complemented her eyes. Stanton appeared out of the crowd, also in short dress and trousers. Bloomer greeted her and made the introduction to Anthony. Stanton was cordial but, distracted by her eminent guests and the thought of what her boys might have done to the house in her absence, she excused herself and rushed home.[177] She would later say that she liked Anthony immediately and should have invited her to dinner. But it might have been awkward to ask her and not the Bloomers. The next day, Bloomer and Anthony called on her, and "the way was opened for future intercourse and operations."[178] This was the most historic connection Bloomer would ever facilitate.

On June 12, the *New York Daily Tribune* devoted a page to praise of the new dress from a score of papers in a dozen states, headed by one titled "Bloomer's Turkish Trowsers."[179] The *Kentucky Post Boy* said that "this costume, call it Greek, Turkish, Chinese or

Hindoo . . . strikes us favorably . . . femininely graceful, convenient, tidy, and in harmony with the laws of health . . . the most beautiful our ladies ever wore."[180] Journalists began to converge on "Bloomerism" as the name for the trend, and as the term spread, it focused all the praise, blame, and debate on Amelia Bloomer. She had gone viral.

One widely reprinted column in a Boston paper claimed to report on an eccentric family that paraded the street in the new style, "Mrs. Bloomer in blue, long flowing ringlets, gipsey hat, rouged cheeks . . . little Bloomers all ditto. Mr. Bloomer made his appearance . . . a black hat worn jauntily on the left . . . dark checked Marseilles vest, frock coatee—skirt very short; Turkish pants, large check, front covered with pleats, very full in the legs and gathered round the ankle . . . black gaiter boots; small walking stick with the top in his mouth."[181]

Such images inspired a bewildering torrent of satirical columns, cartoons, and songs. A "satirical burlesque" was produced in Boston featuring Bloomer and Swisshelm as characters, titled "The Bloomer Rig, or the Revolutionists of the Nineteenth Century."[182] Most of these mentioned "Turkish" dress, and the heretical aspect seems to have inflamed critics. While to reformers it stood for personal freedom and social equality, to a conservative Christian, the wearing of Muslim dress could appear close to blasphemy and a symbol of depravity. Others would be offended by the idea that American women could only follow foreign fashions and would rename it "The American Costume," with the idea that the United States could adopt it as a unique national dress.[183]

Hundreds of letters poured into the little post office at Seneca Falls, some hostile, but most of them from women all over the country "making inquiries about the dress and asking for patterns," until it seemed that half the letters the Bloomers sorted were for Amelia. She printed some excerpts and wrote a general response in *The Lily*. At last, she had slips printed with a description of her clothes to send out in reply to inquiries.[184]

The attention amazed her. "We had no thought that our putting on a convenient and comfortable dress was going to raise such a breeze." But she tried not to let it disturb her and continued to testify to its comfort and convenience in the work of her daily life. "We are our own housekeeper and servant—we wash and iron, bake and brew, cook and wash dishes, make beds and sweep the house, &c." She quoted Helene Marie Weber, who wore male dress, and said if girls were raised in it, "we should see fewer delicately formed women, and none with overlapped ribs."[185]

More reports of the dress came from New York State, Boston, and Kenosha, Wisconsin. Many who hesitated to wear it everywhere still wanted it for work and walks. Women poured their hearts out to Bloomer in letters, grateful for her example. One wrote that she was alone in adopting the new dress where she lived, "all ridiculing me with as great a degree of merriment, as if I were a baboon or some other horrid creature . . . I never heard of you before, nor saw the paper of which you are editor, but I already love you and can bid you God speed."

Almost every paper she picked up seemed to have a column on the subject. Bloomer summarized and interpreted the national discussion for her readers and modeled her response to it, aware that they needed encouragement and support to make so radical a change, just as otherwise isolated people now find community online. To editors who accused "those who adopt it of all manner of bad things . . . we take it upon us to tell this class, one and all, that they are meddling with what is none of their business." But she also disapproved of women who "have overdone the matter, and got up a sort of fantastic dress, with cap and feather for the head . . . Let the material of the dress be as rich as you please, ladies, but do study simplicity in making it." She offered "patterns and full directions for making the dress" to anyone who sent her four new subscribers.

Demand for *The Lily* still increased. Bloomer ran out of April and May copies, ordered more from the printer, and reprinted her popular column on "the new costume" in her June 1851 issue.

Gifts arrived for her. A Boston publisher sent her his illustrated sheet on Jenny Lind, printed in gold. Fowler & Wells of New York City sent books on health and the rights of women. And she received an invitation to a festival of Central and Western New York editors and their friends, with a midday dinner, "on hydropathic principles" at the Glen Haven Water Cure, which she happily accepted.

On a beautiful June morning, she boarded the steamboat in Skaneateles with three women friends. Her friend William H. Burleigh, an agent of the State Temperance Society, greeted them and introduced the women of his family, all in short dresses. The steamboat chugged down the cool, clean waters of Skaneateles Lake for two hours to a collection of white frame buildings with porches facing the lake, surrounded by gardens and shade trees. Bloomer was less than two miles from her birthplace.

Dr. James Jackson and his assistant, Theodosia Gilbert, met them at the dock. Gilbert and about six other women there also wore the new dress. After a tour of the property, they were given a lavish hydropathic meal, low fat and without spices, and afterwards moved to a large parlor "where letters were read, toasts given, and speeches made."

When they arrived back at Skaneateles, the streets and windows were filled with people waiting to gawk at their short dresses. Boys giggled, but the rest only looked, and Bloomer traveled home in peace.

Word spread of the Glen Haven gathering, and the *New York Express* quoted a guest who said the women in the new dress "looked like owls or kangaroos." Editors fanned the flames of controversy with columns, reprints, and letters that called it a biblical "abomination" and the usurping of male dress. A Boston paper called it "clumsy" and "silly . . . the most ridiculous contrivance in the way of dress that has ever been introduced."[186] An editor in Missouri expressed his "disgust and contempt" and called the instigators "a few old maids and half cracked blue stockings."[187] Another in Georgia wrote that "This absurdity of dress may suit such Amazons as Mrs. Bloomer and her crew . . . Costume we know changes arbitrarily . . . But then those who change it must be beautiful, elegant, or powerful; they must be 'stars of fashion.' The wives and daughters of all the upstart Flunkeydom, with all the poets and schoolmistresses thrown in, will never be able to do away with a single curl; much less with the present graceful costume among ladies of true refinement."[188]

Some praise continued too. *Harper's New Monthly Magazine* printed a fashion column in its July issue with a romantic illustration of the "Turkish Costume" and no mention of Bloomer's name. "Dresses of prevailing immoderate length . . . are among the silliest foibles of Fashion; expensive, inconvenient, and untidy." They commended the new dress modeled on the "far more convenient, equally chaste, and more elegant dresses of Oriental women . . . the style is based upon good taste, and, if the ladies are in earnest, must prevail."[189]

Bloomer's new friend Mary C. Vaughan complimented her for "practicing as you preach . . . How comfortable you must feel . . . what a fall there will be in the price of whalebones, and hooks and eyes, when all the sex have followed your example." The money saved "will furnish us many a nice pair of French gaiters to show off our pretty feet, beneath the graceful fall of the Turkish trowsers."[190] She was not the first or the last to note that the new dress was cheaper as well. And Vaughan had come around to women's suffrage too, convinced by her desire for temperance legislation. Only months earlier, the idea had been "utterly repugnant" to her, but she told Bloomer she was not ashamed to change her mind.[191]

A New York City paper claimed that a man had been seen "in petticoats, and with a bonnet on." Bloomer replied that any man who disapproved of the new dress should do the same and see how they liked it. In any case, she said, "we pledge ourself . . . to protect you in your right to dress as you please." A Black woman was seen in Syracuse "in the Turkish costume, and a gypsy hat . . . presented her by some young men" as a joke, it was implied. Bloomer wrote, "It is not customary to show so much regard to the wants of colored women . . . We hope the dress was a good one, and we doubt not the pleasure derived from wearing it will make the lady truly grateful . . . May the young men be equally liberal to others."[192]

Her readers requested a portrait of her in the new dress, and she took the train to Auburn to have a daguerreotype made for the *Boston Museum* in exchange for a copy for *The Lily*. She also printed an engraving of "The New Costume" selected from a Boston paper, the best picture she had seen of it so far.

The Massachusetts *Lowell Courier* reported that a mill owner of that city offered a dinner to all the women workers who adopted the "Bloomer costume" on or before the Fourth of July. Several already wore it. Bloomer wrote: "We hail with pleasure the adoption of our costume by the working classes, for it is we who have an active part to perform in the drama of life, that need the free full use of our limbs, and all our vital organs." Many of the reform elite of Boston embraced the new dress too. A bride wore "an elegant white satin Bloomer" for her wedding, and the papers reported the details as if it were any fine gown.[193]

But Bloomer received letters from ladies who had worn "the short dress" once or twice, and after being laughed at, gave it up. "We can only say that these ladies are made of different stuff from us, or they would not be laughed out of their rights so easily." She recommended that no one put it on until they were firmly convinced of its benefits and their right to wear it. "We are as sensitive on this subject as any one, and our feelings have at times been deeply hurt by the remarks of pretended friends; but we are not to be frightened by ridicule."

"The dress" might dominate her mail and increase her subscriptions, but it was still an accessory to Bloomer's concern for women's health and freedom. She apologized for giving so much space in *The Lily* to dress. "There are so many of our readers who feel a deep interest in the matter, that we cannot well avoid giving it prominence. Then too, we are standing now altogether on the defensive, and must parry, or hurl back the attacks made upon us." But the worst threat to women's freedom, she told them, was still alcohol. She reported joyfully on the total ban of the manufacture and sale of liquor in Maine, which became known as the "Maine Law."

For July, she ordered an extra two hundred copies printed, thinking that would be more than enough, but she ran out again and increased her order for August in response. The wrapping and addressing work was becoming more burdensome, but she still could not afford help.

She was increasingly annoyed by people who sent her all the worst criticism of her. She tried to curb them by pointing out that she read fifty to a hundred papers a week and knew what they thought of her. But, she said, "if you have anything very funny to offer, walk up like a man and hand it to us."

One editor mocked the "effect of several sharp showers upon the new costume. The Turkish trowsers lost their graceful contour and flapped round the pedestal of the wearer like a wet banner round a flagstaff." Bloomer suggested that he next describe "how a woman looks and how she moves with three or four long dripping wet petticoats."

Women as far as Wyoming had adopted the new dress. Ohio papers reported that about two hundred women in Cleveland now wore it, and scores had appeared in it at balls in Akron and Toledo. A new ship, the *Viola*, in Brooklyn had a figurehead dressed in the "Bloomer costume." In the July Fourth parade in Hartford, Connecticut, "thirty-one beautiful young ladies, representing the thirty-one States, dressed a la Bloomer, and wearing wreaths of flowers, were the principal attraction."

Her picture in the *Boston Museum* was a disappointment. But the *Cayuga Chief* wanted one of its own and was willing to share the artwork, so she took the train to Auburn and stood for another daguerreotype. In anxiety, driven by the storm of public attention and wanting to publish her image in *The Lily* before the larger papers got to it, she wrote to Fowler and Wells of the *Water Cure Journal* to ask that they delay their planned illustration of her and to please use the one from the *Chief.* The sympathetic Wells wrote back immediately to reassure her.

And then the artwork was delayed. She apologized to her readers, reprinted a few hundred extra copies of the issue with the Boston picture for her new subscribers, and wrote more encouragement. "We learn from the papers, and from private letters, that in every state, and almost every section north, south, east, and west, many have adopted the dress . . . For ourself we should feel like a criminal condemned to punishment were we obliged to go back to the old style of dressing. Our whole wardrobe has undergone amputation."

A craze for the Hungarian revolutionary Lajos Kossuth was sweeping the nation, reinvigorated by his visit to New York City with his family. Bloomer printed a few articles about his wife and mentioned the new "Kossuth hats" created by "Mr Genin, the celebrated New York hatter . . . very light, and when elegantly trimmed are said to be very beautiful and becoming . . . Wish we had one of them."

Thinking about it, she decided to do more than wish, and she wrote to John Genin about a hat to complement the short dress. To her delight, a parcel arrived in the mail for her from that skillful self-promoter. It was flat and broad-brimmed, made of soft white beaver felt, with a plume and wide ribbons. She tied it on and admired it in the mirror—as Genin hoped, it was "just the thing."[194] She thanked him at length in *The Lily.*

Bloomer's engraved portrait arrived, and it was acceptable, if unflattering. She did not reprint the *Cayuga Chief*'s profile of her. "Modesty forbids," she said. "Like Byron," the editor, had written, she "awoke one morning to find herself famous." He told how *The Lily* came to be, with factual accuracy, and said it now had a circulation of eleven hundred and that Bloomer had "boldly—may we not say, nobly—spoken out for the ENFRANCHISEMENT OF WOMEN." He claimed that "the tyranny of Fashion" prevented general acceptance of the short dress. "Had the new costume been reported from Paris or London, and been adopted by gilded babies and titled prostitutes, it would have found its eager converts and admirers . . . But . . . an unassuming Lady in Western New York asserts her independence for her own health and comfort, and Lo! . . . The world stands aghast at the presumption."[195]

The *Cayuga Chief*'s picture of her was reprinted in papers as far as Germany. With its spread, the hostile press multiplied. Women's status was changing fast, with greater access to education and employment, property rights, and access to the press and the lecture platform. Anxiety about traditional gender roles and identities was building, and this distinctive new image of an "emancipated" woman in trousers became the lightning rod for the reaction.

Jane Swisshelm was now opposed. She wore the new dress a few times, condemned it as ungainly, uncomfortable, and indecent, and publicly criticized Bloomer for promoting it. Bloomer wondered how a woman in trousers could be more uncomfortable than a man and offered some tips on construction. Swisshelm claimed that she made a spectacle of herself when she bent down to pick something off the floor. Bloomer spent part of an evening with Dexter trying to work out what she meant, and in the end decided it was "silly twaddle." Even in long skirts, a woman would show her calves to anyone behind her if she bent from the waist, but that was why most of them squatted. She tried picking things off the carpet as she usually would, "twenty times in succession," and every time, her hem, cut to fall three inches below her knees, slid down and dropped to the floor. "But suppose a woman should show her under skirts a little, what is the harm? Do they never show them now, and in the streets?"

Swisshelm continued her assault on the short dress and called Bloomer's last reply to her "bitter." Bloomer denied it. "We replied with the earnestness with which we shall ever repel false accusations ... Yet we bear her no ill will." Their primary goals were still much the same, and Bloomer was tenacious in her relationships despite disagreements on lesser matters.

The secret to Bloomer's success, such as it was, lay in her open-mindedness, combined with her steadfast integrity and respect for the rights of others. She had strong principles and convictions, including honesty, and she treated everyone much the same, regardless of their status. And after a lifetime of practice in small, close-knit communities, she had learned how to hold her ground; counterattack as needed with confidence, logic, and humor; and greet the person the next day in front of everyone at the post office.

Reports of the short dress and trousers now arrived from California and Europe. At the same time, rumors circulated in the press that Bloomer had given it up. She told her readers, "We have not worn a dress more than four or five inches below the knee since last spring." She only had one long dress left, a "double gown," or reversible wrap dress. "Could we have foreseen what we should have to encounter by such a step—how our name would be bandied about from mouth to mouth—how much censure and ridicule we must bear up against—how great an excitement we should cause, not only throughout our own country, but the whole civilized world—we might have been deterred from the course we have taken. Our weak nerves could not have been sufficiently braced." Still, she had no regrets.

The scorn from the press continued. *Frederick Douglass' Paper* reprinted what his coeditor, Julia Griffiths, found a "very amusing article" from *Punch* on "Bloomerism." It called the new costume "a sort of shemale dress" and said the wearers resembled "overgrown school-girls." The author admitted the benefits of giving up corsets and padding, "but Bloomerist inexpressible affections, and mimicries of masculine garments, nether and upper, such, my friends, I take to be no more than dumb, inarticulate clamorings for the Rights of women, George Sand phantasms, and mutinous female radicalisms . . . here, I say, do we, with Bloomerism beneath us, bubbling uppermost, stand, hopelessly upturning our eyes for the daylight of heaven, upon the brink of a vexed, unfathomable gulf of apehood and asshood simmering forever!"[196]

Undeterred, Bloomer opened 1852 with a fashion plate on her front page. One figure wore straight trousers, a cloak, and a broad-brimmed hat, the other, a sack coat and bonnet. She suggested fabrics and details of construction. Winter had given her a renewed appreciation for her clothes, which were warmer, lighter, and did not collect mud and snow and "whip it upon the ankles."

1852 brought a minor new trend among the progressive women of Seneca Falls: haircuts. Stanton called short hair a luxury and wrote that Thomas James, the popular Black barber, "had a room neatly fitted up for ladies, where he will cut off the hair, and shampoo the head for the small sum of one shilling. It would delight all physiologists and lovers of comfort, to see the heaps of beautiful curls and rich braids that have fallen beneath James' magic touch, from the overheated aching heads of about one dozen of our fair ones." Bloomer did not join them but defended their choice and added, "this is not confined to the wearers of the short dress, as some may suppose,—the majority of those thus shorn still adhering to the draggling skirts." They had started to develop individual style in tandem with their individual opinions, to a degree they would not have imagined a few years before.

Though Bloomer still lived a relatively private life in a rural village a day's travel from any significant city, she entered the new year as a figure of international notoriety. But she was not always credited for her work. A Boston paper reported that *The Lily* was edited by "the daughter of Judge Cady of the Supreme Court, and wife of Senator Stanton of this State." Bloomer flared up. "We are not the daughter of Judge CADY, nor the wife of Senator STANTON. We are the wife of our own husband whom we would not exchange for half a dozen Senator STANTONS; and although he is neither Judge or Senator at present we expect he soon will be, and then in the estimation of some we shall be of much more importance than now."[197]

She printed a column on "Woman's Wages" and commented on the new steam-driven sewing machines that allowed one factory girl to do the work of six. What was to become of the other five girls, Bloomer asked. "Already have employers ground their wages down to the lowest farthing, and now they propose throwing them out of employment entirely . . . there is nothing left for the women of America, but to press into the trades and professions." She learned that the factory women of Lowell, Massachusetts, had established the Lowell Bloomer Institute in September. She was honored and printed their manifesto. "It is a cheering sign of the times, to see women banding themselves together, for the mental elevation, and improvement of each other, and of their race, and we see in it an indication of a 'better time coming.'"

There was a special election that summer. The women of Seneca Falls attended the political debates "by scores and hundreds," and,

Bloomer told her readers, "what is more strange still, the men consented to it... some even volunteered to stay at home that their wives might go!... Probably the good treatment they received, was owing to the absence of the ballot box. What 'become of the babies' during the meetings we are unable to say; probably they behaved very well at home, seeing mother was to be gone only three hours to hear a speech; but if she had been going to deposit a vote, and been gone half an hour, there would no doubt have been great suffering among the children."[198]

Two more women's rights conventions were held, in Akron and in Worcester. Bloomer and Stanton were unable to attend but sent letters. Bloomer told them how the cause of temperance had led her to women's rights, and her thoughts on education, employment, and property rights.[199]

Temperance was enjoying a mild revival in Seneca Falls. The Daughters of Temperance distributed a petition for a state alcohol ban to the legislature, and Bloomer printed it in *The Lily* with the letter from the committee, with the comment that they should petition for suffrage first. A daughter of temperance criticized her for calling women's temperance societies futile. She misunderstood, said Bloomer. She approved of them for building social bonds and educating their members. "But... for twenty or thirty women to get together—the majority perfectly inactive and silent, while two or three take the lead and go through certain forms, and pass a few resolutions... has no more effect to stop the liquor traffic than the mewings of so many kittens would have."

A Woman's Temperance Convention was held in Albany. Bloomer and Stanton again sent letters. It was embarrassingly small, but they elected Mary C. Vaughan as president, and Susan B. Anthony and Dr. Lydia N. Fowler (no relation to the publisher Fowler) as secretaries. Anthony and Vaughan were appointed to coordinate temperance women across the state. The *Temperance Star* printed their proceedings but condemned them as women out of their sphere.[200] In the next issue, the editor apologized for mentioning the convention at all. In that case, Bloomer wrote, she should apologize for reporting on the men's convention, "for they say it was nothing more nor less than a MAN'S RIGHTS Convention."

Despite the backlash, the trousers had helped to make *The Lily* remarkably influential, and the opposition was countered by what felt to Bloomer like an equal or greater wave of encouragement and excitement.[201] But she also felt the strain of this overheated year of constant work and publicity. Her teeth were loose and painful, and she was considering having them pulled.[202] When the abolitionist Harriet N. Torrey sent her a letter of encouragement, saying, "May you live as many lives as a cat; and may each life be lengthened out to three score years and ten," Bloomer thanked her, "but we pray to be excused from the very long life she asks for us, unless the world becomes better, and we are relieved from our present laborious duties."

She still wished she could publish the same amount of content in two issues per month. But to do that, she would have to double her subscribers again or raise the price, which, as ever, knowing her audience, she did not want to do. But for the first time, she did not hesitate to continue *The Lily* for another year.

CHAPTER 8

Female Conventions

On the blustery Tuesday morning of April 20, 1852, the second annual Woman's Temperance Convention convened in the third-floor auditorium of Rochester's Corinthian Hall. Anthony would later call this "the most magnificent auditorium west of the Hudson," a Greek-inspired monument to high European culture. Two Corinthian columns backed the broad curving stage, and windows sixteen feet high filled the room with natural light in good weather. On this dark, wet day, the gas chandeliers and two lily-shaped brackets at each end of the room had been lit.[203] Frederick Douglass's newspaper office was across the street, and the next Fourth of July, he would deliver a famous speech in this hall. Later that month, Jenny Lind would sing here. But this morning, it was less than half-filled with four or five hundred rustling women, many of them in the new costume, for the founding meeting of a new Woman's State Temperance Society.

This time, Amelia Bloomer did not send a letter. She sat on the stage in her best short dress and trousers, made of silver-gray silk, with a turban instead of a lace cap, looking over the audience to the twelve-foot-wide window at the back of the room as rain streamed down the glass. She was almost thirty-four, and for the first time in her life, persuaded by Susan B. Anthony, she had accepted an invitation to speak.

Anthony called the meeting to order. Elizabeth Cady Stanton was appointed president, and Mary C. Vaughan, who turned out to be a vibrant woman with strong features, glossy black braids, and a dimple in her chin, was made one of the five vice presidents. Bloomer and Anthony were elected secretaries. Letters were read, and Stanton made the first address in her black satin short dress and matching trousers, accessorized with white linen cuffs and collar, a gold pin, and freshly cropped hair.

In the afternoon, the convention was opened to the public. The hall, which could hold 1,800, quickly filled with damp people, talking and laughing and shaking water out of their clothes. From the stage, Bloomer could see only a few vacant seats left in "the vast sea of heads." Order was called, and Anthony read resolutions. In the middle of her presentation, Frederick Douglass walked in and found a seat.[204]

The first three resolutions passed without discussion. The fourth denounced legislators and knowing bystanders as more guilty than rum sellers. A man objected. Bloomer stood to comment. A rum seller "was regarded as an immoral man, and we could expect nothing better from him. He was also legalized and could show his authority. The moral man, who condemned the practice in his heart, and still did nothing to oppose or prevent, had no such excuse."

After some argument on this, and more discussion of amendments, it was time for Bloomer to take the lectern.

Hundreds of sophisticated reformers and journalists waited to hear her, educated people who had heard, or who were, the most celebrated speakers of the day. They knew of her through the press. Some might condemn any speech by a woman.

After the initial applause, Bloomer apologized for her inexperience and expressed her fear that she would not make herself heard in such a large hall, before she looked at her manuscript, looked up, and in a clear voice began her forty-minute speech.

"This is an era in the temperance cause which calls for the earnest labors of all true friends of humanity. . . . A feeling akin to contempt has swelled our hearts when we have heard those who have all power in their own hands, so laud the influence, and call for the aid of feeble, powerless woman." But now she believed that women had a role to play. "If we would have freedom," she said, "we must strike for it, and the time for action on our part has fully come."

What should that action be? To win a voice in government, "a right wrongfully withheld, which we should not lightly yield." But for now, urging men to vote the opinions of their women was still worth the attempt. And sympathy for abusive drunkards should be exchanged for rejection of them and support for their wives.

Bloomer took a radical step farther. "Drunkenness is good ground for divorce," she said to the hundreds of listening faces before her, "and every woman who is tied to a confirmed drunkard should sunder the ties; and if she do it not . . . the law should compel it—especially if she have children." A bill had passed the state's House that could make this idea into law, and even if it did not pass the Senate, it would be brought up until it did pass. She called for consistency in action and ended, "if we faithfully perform our allotted task the crown of victory will be our reward; for God will surely defend the Right!"

A journalist reported that she was "distinctly heard and highly applauded throughout."

The following day, Bloomer went home, possibly because she had other work or her symptoms flared. In her absence, the business committee recommended *The Lily* to the women of New York and instructed the finance committee to pay Bloomer enough to publish their proceedings and print extra copies. At home with the speeches, letters, and notes piled on her desk, she edited an eight-page special double issue and composed her editorial describing the new Woman's State Temperance Society.

A week later, she returned to Rochester to sit for another daguerreotype, this time at the request of the prominent photographer Edward Tompkins Whitney. She was more self-conscious than she had ever been before, not only because of her dress but because she was so often described in the papers; her slight figure, her small feet and hands, her somewhat yellow and aged skin tone, her "sweet" voice.[205] She wore her new hat, with its plume and broad ribbons, and Whitney had her lean on a pillar, still in her coat and gloves. She was surprised and pleased with the result. For once, she thought, she looked "quite handsome." He presented her with a copy in a gilt case lined with etched red velvet, a genuine treasure.

Afterward, her Rochester friends invited her to the common council meeting on liquor licenses. She had never been to a government meeting before. It overflowed the courtroom. It began with the presentation of letters from "over two thousand men, and four thousand women, against the granting of licenses," and statistics showing the crime, poverty, and public expenses caused by the liquor traffic. A minister testified on the suffering caused by alcohol, and Bloomer glanced at the impassive faces of the council as he spoke. Her friends whispered to her that the majority supported the liquor trade, and there was little to be hoped for from them, even though all the arguments that evening were firmly in opposition. The sight refreshed her awareness of the reality of the obstacles they had to overcome.

As *The Lily* gained subscribers, its demands on her time and strength grew. Bloomer still did all the work of it herself. She still ran her home, cared for children, and worked long hours in the post office. Her health worsened, but she tried to work through it. All her rewards were in activity and relationships, and so much was happening. It felt impossible to say no to any of it.

Many letters arrived in support of the Women's State Temperance Convention. Bloomer's speech received several positive reviews. There was some horror at the resolution in favor of divorce and some laughter at the very idea of "Female Conventions." Susan B. Anthony wrote her first letter for *The Lily* and promised a plan for auxiliary societies. Several interested people sent ten dollars to become life members of the new society. Bloomer emphasized to her readers that the membership fees would benefit women and be managed by women. Men had "struggled hard at the formation of the Society, to get into office, but we thought best not to trust them at present."

The society appointed Bloomer, Susan B. Anthony, and Gerrit Smith as their delegates to the annual meeting of the State Temperance Society in Syracuse that June of 1852, but it seems Smith did not attend. When Bloomer and Anthony arrived at the Temperance House hotel in Syracuse at dusk in their short dresses, they walked through a piazza filled with male delegates.

The next morning, as they prepared for the meeting, a servant informed them that a gentleman wished to speak with them in the parlor. They went downstairs and were greeted by the Reverend Samuel J. May, who Bloomer had never met but knew of as "a warm friend of the wronged and oppressed."[206] He was about twenty years older than her, a genteel progressive Bostonian and Unitarian and father to five children. He was also Louisa May Alcott's uncle, though this summer she was only fourteen.

They sat down together in a quiet corner, and May informed them that some of the most conservative clergy among the delegates were "terribly shocked" at the idea of woman delegates and threatened to withdraw from the meeting if Bloomer and Anthony were admitted. To avoid conflict, some moderates had sent May to ask the women to withdraw. But he did not pressure them. He stated the facts and told them to do as they pleased.

They thanked him and said they would take their places at the meeting, credentials in hand.

"If the meeting decided we had no right there, we would submit, but we would not be 'backed off' without the trial." May accepted this. They were surprised by his visit, but it braced them for what was to come.

Shortly after they entered the hall and took their places on the platform, a man on the opposite side stood up, turned his chair around, and sat staring straight at them, "with all the impudence of a boor." They decided he was "an ill-mannered, ungentlemanly fellow" and turned their attention to the meeting.

Bloomer's friend William Burleigh read the annual report. In it was a sentence that acknowledged the new Woman's State Temperance Society as a "useful auxiliary." When an officer moved that it be adopted, a man near him jumped up. Bloomer recognized him as "Mr. Impudence of the morning." He was the Reverend Dr. Mandeville of Albany. He announced his "unqualified condemnation" of the women's society and began to rant. Bloomer was a little stunned by his speech, which was "characterized by more venom and vulgarity than it had ever before been our fortune to hear." He continued to denounce all women who left their homes to take an active part in the cause. He called them, and specifically Bloomer and Anthony, a "hybrid species, half man and half woman, belonging to neither sex" and said that dress reform and women's rights "must be put an end to—cut up root and branch." If the convention approved the women's society and accepted their report, he would resign. With that, he picked up his hat and strode out of the hall, not to be seen again.

The meeting disintegrated into chaos. "Amid the confusion of 'Mr. President!' . . . 'Order!' 'I have the floor!' 'I will speak, right or wrong!' from at least half a dozen voices at a time," Bloomer could not tell whether their report was accepted or not.

In the midst of this, calm as ever, Anthony stood to address the chair. But before she could say three words, she was called to order on the grounds that women had no right to speak. In the midst of "a storm of applause on one side, and insult on the other," she stood for a minute but sank to her seat when she realized she could not be heard. The president lost his patience and threatened to quit the chair, but this only created a brief lull.

The conservatives would not budge. The liberals fought to be heard. One "succeeded in keeping the floor a few moments, and spoke ably in defence of woman." A journalist present wrote that, in response, "such thundering applause shook the chamber, as we are not used to." At last, the gathering appealed to the chair to decide. He said that their constitution, and the invitation to the meeting, seemed to allow women's participation, but "there were no female societies in existence five years ago when this society was organized . . . he therefore considered her inadmissible."

Bloomer and Anthony were exasperated. Perhaps the society's founders had not expected the participation of women, but women's temperance societies had absolutely existed all over the state five and ten years earlier. Regardless, they were still not allowed to speak. The liberal men appealed the decision. The chair favored the conservatives. At last, Mandeville's motion was voted on and won, though since delegates had not been required to identify themselves to avoid the presentation of the women's credentials, it was possible that nondelegates had voted.

Some of the liberal men, including Reverend May, refused to give up. They secured the Wesleyan church of Syracuse, and just before adjournment, they announced that "Miss Anthony and Mrs. Bloomer would hold a meeting in the evening."

There was plenty to discuss and rejoice over at supper. Both women had attended many "political, temperance and woman's rights meetings, but never before . . . one where all these were combined and jumbled up together." Sympathizers dropped by to comfort them, "thinking we must feel hurt, and crest-fallen. But we needed not sympathy . . . we knew that the proceedings of this day would add more strength to woman's cause than all the praise and commendation that could be bestowed upon her."

Bloomer and Anthony walked to the Wesleyan church with their friends. A large crowd followed them, almost twice the number the church could hold. Men officiated, but everyone was allowed to speak, and "the best feeling prevailed . . . after the excitement and intolerance of the afternoon" the "cordial interchange of sentiment was truly refreshing." Anthony offered the four resolutions of the women's society, and after a respectful discussion, all were adopted unanimously. Bloomer was invited to speak; she made a few remarks and excused herself due to her bad health and the late hour. To close the meeting, Charles Wheaton, an officer of the state society and a friend of John Brown, sang "The Lament of the Widowed Inebriate," which to Bloomer was "truthful and touching, and caused the eye to moisten with sympathy." Afterward, the progressives were pleased to learn that the conservatives' evening meeting had been "nearly deserted."

But the battle was not over. The next morning, the state meeting reconvened. Delegates from the more liberal New York City Temperance Alliance, supported by other temperance groups, "proposed to combine their organizations with the State Society." The old conservative faction blocked them. Bloomer contrasted their "obnoxious behavior" with the "gentlemanly and dignified" conduct of the alliance delegates, who insisted that one united organization would be more politically effective. Another resolution was proposed to invite "all Societies of every sex, color, kindred and tongue." The opposition insisted that including women would make them ridiculous and "impair the influence of the Society," and this resolution was blocked as well. The meeting ended "with a show of good feeling, but in reality, with heart felt dissatisfaction on the part of many if not all."

The use of the words "ladies" and "women" in certain contexts at this time was similar to how they would be used by later feminists. The word "lady" was associated with delicate, euphemistic femininity that glossed over their abilities and needs. Many women's rights advocates still used "ladies" in polite social contexts, but "Woman's Society" had a stronger ring than "Ladies' Society." When Bloomer used the word "woman," she was making a political statement.

"At no time during the whole of the proceedings" she told her readers, "did a woman claim a seat there, or attempt to speak," except when Anthony tried and "got no further than 'Mr. President' . . . We could not have believed it possible for two women to give such a fright to a score of clergymen, and cause such a tremor and turmoil of passion . . . especially as we did nothing more than walk quietly into the house and take seats. A few more such scenes will have the effect to make women believe they really are of some consequence."

Anthony's speech at the chapel was published in several papers. John Thomas, Frederick Douglass's assistant, wrote a report of the meeting for Douglass's paper that mirrored Bloomer's and said, "We have never . . . in all the meetings we have ever attended, (and we have attended many rude and disorderly ones,) attended one so rude and disorderly as this. . . . Indiscretion and want of principle, and it seems to us of common sense, will pretty effectually close up the life of the N.Y. State Temperance Society."[207]

The reports of the conservative men's behavior at the state meeting convinced many doubters of the need for women's societies. There had been debate at the women's convention in Rochester, Bloomer told her readers, over whether they should join the men's state society. "Others objected to this on the ground that women would not be received as equals in that Society . . . the result proves that it was a wise decision. As that body in their self-conceited wisdom have repudiated woman . . . she is not bound by any rule of action which they may lay down for her, neither will she cower before their frowns." She called for founding auxiliary women's societies across New York. "If men will cooperate with women in these, well; if not, let women work alone. But if composed of both men and women, let woman's be the controlling power, or let it be shared equally."

Anthony reported to Bloomer that she and the other lecturing agents had visited at least six villages and towns to hold large temperance meetings and that "the people manifest much interest in this new movement of woman." With new leadership, and access to publications that facilitated discussion and the spread of information, the women of the state were educating and organizing themselves.

Bloomer's advocation of divorce for the wives of confirmed drunkards at the Rochester conference produced another swarm of letters and editorials. She reasserted that alcohol was the cause of most crime and that drunken parents produced "vicious, imbecile, and idiotic children." But she also claimed that the offending resolution only meant separation, not a legal divorce that would allow remarriage, to avoid violating the teaching of Jesus, who only approved of such in cases of adultery. She advocated for a woman's right to custody of her children and "her own person and earnings. . . Grant this, and few women will care to enter a second marriage, so long as the wreck of a former husband pollutes society with his presence."

With no legal recourse, and convinced of their moral position, more women used violence to stop liquor sales. One smashed up a barroom in Wayne County, New York. In Cincinnati, a woman "severely horse-whipped a man" who often invited her husband to grog shops. Bloomer praised them. "We do not pretend to say what we would do should we see our husband led on to destruction, but we hope we might have courage to defend our own rights, and his, with such weapons as would most surely do the work." When another woman destroyed a rumshop after the owner ignored her pleas to stop serving her abusive husband, her community hired an attorney to defend her. The rum seller, who had once been arrested for illegal sales, withdrew his charges and paid her costs. One journalist hoped that even more women would act similarly, to which Bloomer said, "AMEN."[208]

In 1852, for the first time, the new Forest Lodge of the Good Templars in Ithaca admitted six women as equal members with the men. When a lodge was founded in Seneca Falls, Bloomer joined. She became an active member and, later, an officer.[209]

But her health continued to fail under the strain of her new endeavors. At last, in the sweltering heat of mid-August, she agreed to let Dexter open her mail and forward anything he could not answer, packed up her papers and pens, and moved to Dr. Hamilton's Hydropathic and Analytic Asylum in Rochester.[210]

She published *The Lily* from her room at the asylum, and as usual, she was frank with her readers. "Those who do not know us suppose us to be a great stout 'amazon;' and those who have seen us ... taking so active a part in the business and pleasures of life, have not dreamed that all this was done with an aching head and feeble frame ... it is so common for women when they are not well to give up to gloomy forebodings, and useless complainings, and to be helpless and inactive, that for one to take an opposite course, and seek relief in activity and bustle it cannot be realized that they are really sick ... it is the desire to be better fitted for our present and future duties, that has induced us to ... try the effects of Dr. Hamilton's skill in patching up our broken-down, drug-ruined constitution."

While at the asylum, she did not entirely seclude herself. She went out to a meeting in Elmira to discuss the creation of a new state vocational school for young adults, to be called the People's College. A paper reported that she and Stanton had been there, though Stanton had been home in Seneca Falls. The two women were often yoked together in the press, even when, as on this occasion, only one had been present. The four agents of the Woman's State Temperance Society met there too, and Bloomer went to their first meeting and heard Susan Anthony speak before she left.[211] They told Bloomer that they were welcomed everywhere, "partly because of the novelty of a woman speaking," and partly because total abstinence was more popular again. Anthony had attended a "monster gathering" in Albion and held a women's meeting afterward. Many men turned up, and she told them "to appreciate the privilege which woman permitted them to enjoy—that of remaining in the house and being silent lookers on." She was there for the women, with their "thoughtful faces—faces that spoke of disquiet within, of souls dissatisfied, unfed."

Temperance meetings were not the only gatherings in which women were attempting to integrate themselves. In response to her query in *The Lily* regarding whether women would be welcome at a journalism convention in Rochester, the new editor of the *Geneva Courier*, Winthrop Atwell, wrote that "no one could object to a seat by the side of 'sister BLOOMER,' yet . . . we should protest against sister Anybody 'speaking in meetin.'"

"Just as we suspected," Bloomer replied. "There are 'old fogies' among editors, as well as among the clergy. . . . Although we should enjoy the fun mightily, we think we will not attend the convention; for we have too much respect for ourself to take a seat by the side of such an ungentlemanly, little souled man."

Atwell read this and melted down. But Amelia never read much of his "rage and indignation" that summer because Dexter intercepted several issues of the *Geneva Courier*, which both of them thought had declined in quality anyway, and used them to light the fire in the post office.[212]

In early September, there was a three-day National Woman's Rights Convention in Syracuse. Bloomer's health kept her in Rochester. Stanton signed the invitation, and this time, instead of sending a letter, she wrote a speech and resolutions to be read by Anthony. Bloomer later read with interest the discussion of whether the convention should have its own newspaper.[213] After a discussion of funding, they tabled the idea.

Bloomer returned home at the beginning of October, mentally and physically refreshed, though not entirely recovered. But there was a dangerous outbreak of cholera in Rochester, and this would be a busy month. Seneca Falls would host the People's College meeting to discuss the creation of the school, followed by the Woman's Temperance Convention. And there was election season. "Our other half deems our assistance of so much importance one might suppose the result of the election depended very much upon our faithful performance."

The organizer of the People's College meeting was anxious that the "Women's Rights Ladies" would derail it. They did not, but they did ensure that the word "person" would be used in the college rules so that all people would be admitted and taught together, regardless of race or gender. This experiment in vocational education, rooted in organized labor, would become a seed of the land-grant college system.[214]

The next morning, Bloomer got a few hours of work in before walking over to the Wesleyan chapel for the Women's State Temperance Convention meeting. Stanton presided, and it was well attended, with delegates from eleven counties present. About fifty women had on the short dress and trousers, including the famous Lucy Stone. Bloomer was delighted to meet so many women that she knew through correspondence, but Stone made the strongest impression on her. Bloomer found her "a talented lady, and a beautiful speaker."

One resolution, which would forbid "voluntary association with him who uses, or him who furnishes intoxicating liquors," met with resistance. One woman said that it "invaded our social relations too far. Many were connected in their family relations, with persons engaged in this traffic." Strong arguments were made in favor, and it passed, as did the others. Lydia Ann Jenkins offered another: "That we will go by the hundreds, if not by the thousands, at the coming of our next legislature and present a petition for the Maine Law, at our own hands." This was promptly adopted.

Around this time, Bloomer finally read one of the *Geneva Courier's* venomous editorials. Atwell wrote: "Mrs. BLOOMER . . . goes in for opposing the men at a fearful rate. She must be rather a hard customer in domestic argument."

"Yes, that we do," she wrote. "We 'go in for opposing the men' at any and all rates, when they so far forget their duty as to enact and sustain laws which oppress and cruelly wrong both women and themselves! . . . As to 'domestic arguments' had we been so unfortunate as to have been tied to so narrowminded a man as is Atwell of the Courier, we should have been a 'hard customer;' for we never would submit to his petty tyranny. Thank Heaven! such has not been our fate! If the Courier is particularly interested in the welfare of our other half we suggest that he make inquiries of him about what sort of a 'customer' we are."

In response, Atwell raged that the "female reformers" of Seneca Falls "not only put on the trousers, but they cut short their beautiful hair, and talk politics like a book!"

"That is true," Bloomer wrote. "Very many of our ladies, of all classes and ages, have taken a fancy to enjoy the luxury of short hair, and have submitted their beautiful locks to the shears of JAMES, the barber. They have it 'shingled' close, and as fast as it grows out cut it off again . . . As to politics, the women of this town are pretty well 'booked up' on that subject . . . And what may appear still more strange . . . our men . . . seem to enjoy talking common sense matter to sensible women, quite as much as the simpleton who presides over the Courier would to talk nonsense to simpering, silly ones."

Atwell claimed that Bloomer reported "nearly fifty women" at the People's College meeting "had on the 'unmentionables.'"

She replied, "We said no such thing. We saw no ladies at the People's College meeting or elsewhere with 'unmentionables' on, and but three or four who were dressed in short skirt and trousers; but at the Temperance Convention the number thus dressed was estimated as high as fifty. Put on your spectacles next time you read The Lily, neighbor."

The Whigs lost the election. This meant that the Bloomers would lose their positions in the post office as soon as the official dispatch arrived to nominate their replacement. With this in mind, they prepared the office for their successor and continued their work meantime.[215]

Bloomer would have to abandon her women's reading room along with her post office job. But that spring, Stanton had started a series of evening discussion "pic-nics" held in parlors. A few men attended and were sometimes called on to lead, but it was mostly a women's group, inspired by those of Margaret Fuller. The goal was intellectual development through discussion of texts, with an effort to "systematize thought" and answer "the great questions. What were we born to do? How shall we do it?"[216] They ended with music, and sometimes dancing, and Bloomer was usually home by ten. The discussions in the post office had been more organic, but the intellectual rigor of Stanton's gatherings had its advantages. And after the last few years, the women were braver now, willing to express their opinions in mixed company, and argue for them too.[217]

CHAPTER 9

Famous Speaker, Famous Spectacle

For her January 1853 issue of *The Lily*, at the start of her fifth year in publication, Bloomer had at least two thousand subscribers and more signing up all the time. For comparison, Ralph Waldo Emerson's magazine, *The Dial*, never reached three hundred subscribers, Frederick Douglass's the *North Star* got to about four thousand, and the largest daily in New York City, the *Tribune*, had about two hundred thousand. She was still at the bottom end of the scale, but nothing close to this success had seemed possible in her anxious first months of publication.

After her speech at the 1852 Women's Temperance Convention, she began to receive offers for paid speaking engagements. Thanks to the new income, Bloomer could at last embark on publishing four pages twice a month in a larger folio format. She held the annual price at fifty cents and commissioned a new masthead from a woman engraver in Elmira, whom she praised as an example of all the women entering professions. She paired this with a story from Lucy Stone of her visit to a cabinet shop in Massachusetts, where she was "surprised to see two women at work." She asked one if she liked it. The woman said she did. "'To be sure,' said she, 'it makes our hands larger and harder, but I had rather have a hard hand with ten shillings a day in it, than a soft, delicate hand with two shillings a day.'"[218]

Still, Bloomer's ambivalence about her life as a newspaper editor and publisher never left her. "No chance seems left for us to

escape; and that same invisible hand seems leading us forward—
almost against our desires. We would there were a dozen such
papers where there is but one now, but we would also that other
hands and heads than ours had the direction of them." One more
would appear in February, when Paulina Wright Davis would start
a monthly paper for women called *The Una*. It was a dollar a year.
The Lily was still fifty cents.

But she turned this editorial toward inspiration. Sadness at the
persistent injustice of the world increased her sense of purpose and
was mixed with joy at "the signs of progress which we see around
us" in temperance, abolitionism, and "the uprising of the women
of our country to . . . demand their rights . . . It is a source of joy to
us to know that *THE LILY* has . . . called into being new thoughts,
new hopes, new desires and aspirations and strengthened and
encouraged wavering ones."[219]

Before Christmas, Dexter had invited Amelia's supporter, the
famous phrenologist and publisher of the *Water Cure Journal*, Orson
Fowler, to give a lecture series and read heads in Seneca Falls.
Despite her initial skepticism, the scientific aura of phrenology
took them in, as it did so many white intellectual reformers of their
time, and regardless of whether they agreed with all of the ways
in which it was interpreted and used to divide and dehumanize
the human race, it appealed to them, as many such "readings"
do, with the promise of better self-knowledge. Fowler agreed to
fit them in the first week of the new year and advertised in his
Phrenological Journal that in the next volume, he would publish
"biographies, portraits, and Phrenological developments of many
distinguished individuals," including Horace Mann, Ralph Waldo
Emerson, Gerrit Smith, Lucretia Mott, Abby Kelley Foster, and
Amelia Bloomer.[220]

Amelia sat patiently as the polite fingers of Mr. Fowler searched
over her scalp and forehead while his phonographer took down his
words in rapid shorthand. "You have a brain of only average size,"
said Fowler. "You are very energetic and forcible, liable to go beyond
your strength and take upon yourself more than you are really able

to do . . . everything must be done in a hurry, when you walk you run." Bloomer felt things intensely, he said, had strong loyal attachments, made friends easily, and enjoyed social life. "Combativeness is large; you are quick to resent and quite apt to feel the full force of opposition, and you readily meet difficulties and dangers, in fact the more opposition you have, the more courageous are you." Her digestion was not good—again, no news there. Wealth did not interest her. She was a sympathetic, generous, ambitious person, devoted to the common good, good with business transactions, and—a strange twist—overly susceptible to the opinions of others.

Dexter's was less complex. Fowler repeatedly called him adaptable, as well as kind, unselfish, healthy, witty, an analogical thinker, sensitive to criticism, and diffident. He recommended higher self-esteem to both of them.[221]

The women's petition for the Maine Law to ban liquor in New York State was circulating, and Bloomer received over fourteen hundred requests for petitions. If they each were returned with a hundred signatures by the Albany meeting on February 21, she said to her readers, "what an expression of popular feeling would it present to our rulers! . . . Divide your villages into districts, and appoint a committee who will take each their part, and call upon every woman for her signature. Pass no one by without giving her an opportunity to sign."

Bloomer not only had agreed to handle the petitions, she also printed and sold the Woman's State Temperance Society's tracts and accepted submissions to a contest for a new tract, written by a woman.[222] This additional labor was in part repaid by the lecturing agents, who distributed copies of *The Lily* across the state and signed up new subscribers. They often consulted with her and Stanton when they passed through Seneca Falls.[223]

The women's society planned a preparatory meeting for the end of January. Bloomer printed the call for delegates from the auxiliary societies and assured any hesitant women that the train fare would be halved for those attending the meeting and could be paid by the societies. If they felt timid about traveling alone, male delegates could accompany them.

She continued to answer letters about dress reform and to attack her opponents in *The Lily*. Reverend Marsh wrote in the *Journal of the American Temperance Union* that it was "unfortunate that these Ladies hold in such painful remembrance the discussion in the State Society at Syracuse." Those discussions were not about them, he said, but "a constitutional question of the State Society. . . It would almost seem that they hope for gain of some sort from the cry of persecution."

Bloomer could not let this attempt at historical revision go by. "Those discussions did relate, not only to the Woman's Society, but to its delegates then on the floor of that meeting . . . the remarks of Mr. Mandeville were in many respects personal. . . . Deliver us from such 'friends!' . . . We will do Mr. Marsh the justice to say that he acted throughout the whole meeting at Syracuse, in a cool and gentlemanly manner . . . But after the question was up he felt bound to sustain his party, right or wrong."[224]

Atwell of the *Geneva Courier* had backed down. Bloomer did not. In an editorial, she wrote, "It is said that a smart application of the 'birch' sometimes has a salutary effect upon naughty boys. We judge this to be true in the case of the editor of the Geneva Courier; for no sooner did he feel the smart of our 'keen two columns article' of a month or two ago, than he becomes for the time being as gentle as 'a sucking dove.' Hear what he says of THE LILY: 'That delicate Lily published by "MRS. AMELIA BLOOMER" Seneca Falls, is a curiosity in its way . . . but full of rich, racy things, and well worth double fifty cents a year.'"

On February 20, Bloomer traveled to the women's temperance meeting in Albany with the collected Maine Law petitions. When she arrived at the packed Baptist church, she found Mary Vaughan and asked her what the plan was for presenting the petitions to the legislature. There isn't one, said Vaughan, it was left up to us as the committee on petitions. They found some sympathetic state representatives, asked them about proper procedure, and recruited the traveling lecture agents Emily Clark and Attilia Albro to join their committee.

The next morning, they attended the first hour of the meeting and then slipped out a back door. They walked ten minutes along State Street to the capitol building with a large, two-handled basket filled with about six hundred petitions—all that had arrived in time for Bloomer to bring with her—each rolled up, neatly labeled, and tied with a ribbon.

The legislature was still held in the old capitol building, despite complaints about its size and lack of grandeur. It looked much like Bloomer's old Presbyterian church in Seneca Falls, with the porch and high Greek columns in the front, though with a larger volume of plain brick building behind them. At the statehouse door, they were met, as arranged, by the handsome Hon. Silas M. Burroughs. He escorted them to seats within the bar of the House, returned to his own seat, and made a motion to permit them to present their petitions. Several journalists reported the reactions of the representatives.

> Mr. Hastings trusted the request would not be granted. It would be setting a bad precedent.
>
> Mr. Miller hoped as ladies suffered most from intemperance, that this request might be granted.
>
> Mr. O'Keefe, of New York City, said: "Sir, as this is a most extraordinary application, so let it meet with a most extraordinary reception. Let those high-minded, high strung and spirited women, who discard as worthless the antique dress of the Elizabethan age to glory in the modern habiliments of jackets and pants, let them walk down the middle aisle of this chamber, and with masculine stride, which so admirably becomes such feminine delicacy as theirs, present their petitions."[225]

Burroughs made no reply. Bloomer reported later that "Mr. O'Keefe is a young man, and like many other boy-men, imagines himself a great personage ... He no doubt thought himself on the popular side, and aimed to be very witty at the expense of the ladies.—But the tables turned against him, and he only gained odium where he looked for applause."

A large majority passed the vote to approve. Burroughs escorted the women to the center of the middle aisle with their basket, and Clark addressed the assembly. "We ask protection, that all that is sacred in the homes of the Empire State may not be considered of less moment than the $2,685,900 invested in the liquor traffic in this State; we ask you to pass a law entirely prohibiting the sale of intoxicating drinks, and we most respectfully but earnestly solicit the early attention of your honorable body to our petitions."[226] They passed the basket up to the clerk's desk and lingered at the bar for half an hour to receive the congratulations of members.

They returned to the Baptist church, where Clark took the stage and announced what they had done. An astonished "shout of congratulation" went up from the audience. "It was an unheard-of thing for women to do, and our reception augured success."

When she could be heard, Clark went on to say that "if the Legislature refuse to pass the Maine Law now," they would return the next year "with five hundred thousand petitions, instead of twenty-eight thousand." But that was the women's task. The men should vote "and see to it, that they elect such men as will do their duty without being importuned with petitions."

Bloomer spoke in the afternoon, and in the evening, they split into two simultaneous meetings, one in the church and one in the capitol. Hundreds were turned away from the church. Clark presided over that meeting and spoke. Bloomer called on the women to better themselves and take responsibility for their influence and actions. They had the moral right to the ballot box, but for now, they must convince the men to pass a Maine Law. The audience "remained very quiet and several times loudly applauded" her.

This convention exceeded Bloomer's hopes. It was a wonderful contrast with the brief, unreported gathering of "a small band" the year before. "How different the prospect! Men and women from all parts of the State . . . united in one common cause, and laboring for one common object . . . To us it was a happy time, a blessed meeting of kindred spirits—an era in woman's history never to be forgotten . . . Truly the past year has been one of great interest and importance."

But their petitions, collected with so much effort by so many, were once again ignored by the legislature.[227] A Maine Law in New York seemed unlikely this year.

Nevertheless, Bloomer's work continued. On the dark, rainy February morning after the Albany convention, Bloomer caught a train to New York City with Susan B. Anthony and the twenty-two-year-old Antoinette Brown. Dr. S. P. Townsend, the patent medicine and sarsaparilla king, had invited them to hold a series of meetings there, with the assurance "that every preparation would be made and we should be received by good audiences." The Fowlers of the publishing company would put them up.

They got into the dark and dirty city around two in the afternoon. Bloomer and her companions were struck by many women who seemed to "think nothing of holding their dresses *higher than the knee* and displaying drabbled and filthy petticoats . . . And yet, strange as it may appear, these city ladies . . . are ready to laugh outright at our more tidy and comfortable dress. Oh! How proud these sights made us feel of our much-loved attire."[228]

They were booked into the impressive new Metropolitan Hall; the Broadway Tabernacle, which was a progressive church downtown; and Knickerbocker Hall.[229] All three venues sold out, at twenty-five cents per ticket, each with a capacity between three and five thousand seats.

The Metropolitan, built but not finished in time for the Swedish singer Jenny Lind's United States debut, was in a similar style to Corinthian Hall in Rochester but on a much grander scale, with two tiers of balconies. The progressive editor of the *New York Tribune*, Horace Greeley, and his wife met them in the reception hall and accompanied them to the stage, where they sat with their host, Dr. Townsend, and other luminaries. After a prayer by Antoinette Brown, Bloomer was introduced. She wore dark brown changeable silk with flowing outer sleeves and tight undersleeves, the skirt and trousers trimmed with rows of black velvet, gaiters over her shoes, black lace mitts, and a black and cherry-red headdress. Her bodice, decorated with bands of black velvet and a diamond stud pin, was open over a white chemisette.

"From the earliest agitation of the subject of temperance down through the whole past course of the cause," she began, "woman has had a great and important part to perform in the great struggle for freedom . . . She has done all that the custom of the time permitted her to do. But it has been insufficient. And she has been guilty in submitting to the power of men." Women contributed to intemperance by allowing liquor in their homes and believing that reform was not their business. "Deliver us from such dead weights on society and on the spirit of Progress! None of woman's business, when she is subject to poverty and degradation and made an outcast from respectable society! . . . None of woman's business, when her children are stripped of their clothing and compelled to beg their bread from door to door! In the name of all that is sacred, what is woman's business if this be no concern of hers?"

At this point, the crowd burst into applause, and Bloomer rose on the wave. "None of woman's business! What is woman? Is she a slave? Is she a mere toy? Is she formed, like a piece of fine porcelain, to be placed upon the shelf to be looked at? Is she a responsible being? Or has she no soul? Alas, alas for the ignorance and weakness of woman! Shame! Shame on woman when she refuses all elevating action and checks all high and holy aspirations for the good of others!"

She continued into the theme of wives forced to support drunken husbands. "Public sentiment and law bid woman to submit to this degradation and to kiss the hand that smites her to the ground . . . Let her show to the world that she possesses somewhat of the spirit and the blood of the daughters of the Revolution!"

She spoke for an hour and "concluded her remarks amid long continued applause." Greeley wrote in the *Tribune* that this speech "marked out an entirely new field in temperance thought" by her focus on women.[230]

Bloomer was followed by Brown, Anthony, and Horace Greeley. At the end, over a hundred people crowded the rostrum, eager to meet and congratulate the speakers. Some were devoted to temperance, others just wanted to stare at them. It was a thrilling success, but she was glad to return to Mrs. Fowler's cozy parlor, having "passed through the ordeal unscathed."[231]

Outside, the streets of Manhattan were often a painful experience for Bloomer. There were rich and poor in Seneca Falls, but the scale of the contrast here brought tears to her eyes. "What is all the grand display, the gay equipage, the gorgeous show of the wealthy, while the poor hapless victims of bad laws and a corrupt public sentiment meet you on every hand?" Her hosts brought her to the Tombs, an infamous and corrupt prison slowly sinking into the swampy ground of the Five Points slum downtown, where they toured the parts of it suitable for ladies. After this and a visit to Sing Sing, Bloomer introduced prison reform as a new topic in *The Lily*.

Though they planned to return home after the Metropolitan meeting, more invitations drew the three women into a lecture tour. They traveled up the Hudson, speaking mostly to large audiences. Bloomer was home in a week, but at the end of March met the other two women again for meetings in Brooklyn and Buffalo. They sold out a hall of a thousand seats in Buffalo and extended for two more evenings. Many women came to visit them where they stayed, and Bloomer wrote that "we hear from all the same expression of feeling ... 'We must have the Maine law; what can we do to obtain this law?' ... All feel that the only way in which women can do anything effectually in this cause is through the ballot-box."[232] Their hosts gave them a tour of the sights, "but to me," Bloomer told her readers, "all cities are alike, and I see little to admire in their high brick walls and dirty streets."[233] She was glad to return to Dexter, village life, and her "quiet sanctum."

These tours demonstrated that they had become famous speakers, and famous spectacles. Bloomer knew that many people only wanted to inspect her dress and trousers up close.[234] But she was pleased to find that "a woman can travel from one end of our State to the other in this dress without annoyance; and though she may occasionally hear a passing remark . . . there will be nothing to make her feel uncomfortable . . . Even in the City of New York, where it has been said a woman could not appear so attired without being mobbed, we have freely walked the streets, and been as respectfully and courteously treated . . . there is about as much self-respect and civilization existing among the New Yorkers as with people in the country."

A Pennsylvania woman wore the short dress in defiance of her church and converted several others. A paper called them "fearless dauntless women who dare to do right" and quoted one who said, "When you hear that I have given up the short dress you may know that I am *dead*."[235]

But others were already discouraged, and the tide of opinion was beginning to turn. The *New York Tribune* blamed the cloth industry: "Liberty, individuality, tasteful vanity in female dress might be pleasant," but it would cut fabric and notions sales by "fifty per cent . . . To our certain knowledge multitudes of ladies in this city were busy in getting ready their Bloomer rig, and only waited for the sure success of the thing to appear in public. But the trade took the alarm. It was only to tip the wink to the rude boys at the street corner and the thing was done . . . The old fogies kept low and bided their time. They knew that most of our liberty is rhetoric, and that the many are the prey of the few."[236]

Stanton was pregnant again and still tied to home, though her fame as a writer had spread. She renamed her "pic-nic" gatherings "The Conversational," and Bloomer continued to attend. At one of them, Stanton read an "address to young girls," in which she discussed the importance of good education and financial independence and warned against social conformity. Bloomer admired it and published it in *The Lily* for March 1, 1853. It would be Stanton's last direct contribution to *The Lily*.[237] On March 4, Bloomer set off for another speaking engagement in New York City. She took the train to Albany, spent the night with friends, and arrived at the Fowlers' house midday, in time for a good dinner "already steaming on the table." With practice, and the improvements in rail service, she enjoyed travel now. "I have always felt very timid about going very far from home without a 'protector,' but I have as yet seen nothing to be protected against."

Antoinette Brown and Susan Anthony met Bloomer in the city for their engagement with the Sixteenth Ward Alliance at Knickerbocker Hall. They spoke to a large and attentive audience, and the following Monday, they met at the Broadway Tabernacle to form another auxiliary society. Bloomer found the New York City women interested but hesitant. "There are good temperance women enough here, but they have not yet drank in the truth in regard to their right and duty, to come boldly forward."

That night, so much snow fell on the city that Bloomer woke to the sound of sleigh bells in the street. But strong sun melted much of it off, and the women went to the Greeleys' that evening for a literary party. Most of the guests blurred together for Bloomer, but she remembered the journalist Charles A. Dana, the writer and historian Mrs. E. F. Ellet, and the poets Alice and Phœbe Cary, who were about Bloomer's age and whose work she admired.

The evening dress of the poet sisters shocked Bloomer. They wore fashionable gowns with "arms bared to the shoulders, and the neck to the armpits." Since it was a chilly night, they also wore four-foot boas around their necks and kept readjusting them over their naked shoulders, an indecent and silly spectacle to Bloomer's eye. She knew that her short dress might look equally wrong to them, but their display of skin still repelled her. "However . . . it was their appearance that displeased me, rather than their conversation or manner," she told her readers. "Tastes differ, that was all, and I was not used to seeing women in company half-dressed."

The curious attire wasn't the only quirk of the night. The subject of spiritualism came up, and Mr. Greeley, with his earnest bespectacled round face and balding head, stood between his two parlors and pointed to a table between the front windows. "I have seen that table leave its place where it now stands, come forward and meet me here . . . and then go back to its place without any one touching it, or being near it." But Bloomer had attended a spiritualism debunking lecture and demonstration two years earlier in Geneva, and she retained her skepticism.[238] If the dead want to talk to us, she wrote, "why do they not do so directly, like honest sensible spirits, instead of through such low mediums, and in so unsatisfactory and groveling a manner?"[239]

Eccentricities aside, Bloomer told her readers, "We had a very pleasant social evening, notwithstanding all were strangers to us. We find kindred spirits in Mr. and Mrs. Greeley, who fully endorse the principles we advocate."

At home again, Bloomer was disturbed by an appalling portrait printed above a long flattering article in the friendly *Phrenological Journal.* "A very large, grave, elderly woman, with our name under it ... It is really too bad for one to be represented as more ill looking than they really are—especially when they are far from handsome— and then sent all over the world for people to look at." The *Journal* agreed with the *Cayuga Chief* that it flattered her, to which she said, "Well, we will not dispute it—but this only confirms our assertion that it does not look like us."

Her critics continued to assert that her family life must be a nightmare. Bloomer wished they would "investigate the matter and devise some plan of relief for our poor suffering husband and 'five children.' Ha, ha! we should like to see the workings of our 'gude man's' face as they offered words of condolence and sympathy, and hear the kind and unruffled tones in which he would thank them for their tender solicitude and politely bid them return and bestow equal care on their own domestic relations."[240]

Long after the Bloomers expected it, the dispatch arrived announcing Dexter's replacement in the post office by J. T. Miller, whom they had replaced four years earlier and whom Bloomer, as "Ida," had once scorned as a temperance hypocrite. She was disappointed to see Fuller praise Dexter and disregard her in his *Courier* notice of the change. "Mr. Fuller ... probably thinks with some others that 'man and wife are as one, and that one the husband' ... Well, ours is not the first instance where woman's services have been unacknowledged and unappreciated, and probably will not be the last."[241]

With this lucrative position at an end, Dexter began to look around for his next enterprise. Amelia was relieved to have one less. "Our experience while in office has confirmed our faith in woman's entire capacity and fitness for such business . . . Our greatest regret in leaving the office is that it must pass back into the hands of men exclusively."

But rather than protect her health by accepting this reduction in her workload, Bloomer refilled the space with public speaking engagements. She gave a speech for the Good Templars of Seneca Falls, perhaps the first she gave in her home village. It was a rainy Tuesday, but the church was crowded, and Fuller wrote, "she ranks among the foremost of the woman lecturers, as she certainly excels most of those we have heard."[242]

In New York City, on May 12, a planning meeting of temperance men was held in the lecture room of the Brick Church on Beekman and Nassau streets in Manhattan to discuss a "grand World's Convention" during the World's Fair in the fall. Bloomer was not there, but she had signed the credentials of the seven women delegates: Lydia Fowler, Mary S. Rich, Emily Clark, Susan B. Anthony, Mary C. Vaughan, Lucy Stone, and Abby Kelley Foster. Once again, the conservative men were shocked by their presence, and the liberal men threatened to resign if women were excluded. After a verbal battle, the substantial progressive faction once again withdrew to another venue and organized an alternative Whole World's Temperance Convention. In their absence, the conservative men insulted them and referred to the disgrace of "women in breeches."[243] Bloomer printed Mary C. Vaughan's report of the proceedings and Lucy Stone's speech.[244] She was not surprised, but she had hoped for better after the obvious shift toward the women in Syracuse the previous summer. The "old fogys" seemed to be in denial. "Whether men will or no," she wrote, "woman will make herself heard, and her power felt on the temperance question."[245]

CHAPTER 10

Expediency and the Break

Bloomer published her June 1, 1853, issue of *The Lily* a little early so that she and Dexter could travel up to the Woman's State Temperance Society meeting in Rochester that day. She was grateful for the additional support. After certain conversations with Susan Anthony and Antoinette Brown that spring, she knew there might be a battle.

Corinthian Hall was filled to capacity with an anxious and excited audience. Some were there for the cause of women's rights, some to laugh at the odd clothes and radical speakers, and some were there for temperance alone. On the platform, among many others, were Stanton as president, Dr. Lydia N. Fowler and Emily Clark as vice presidents, Anthony and Vaughan as recording secretaries, and Bloomer as corresponding secretary.

Stanton gave a forceful opening address. "It has been objected to our Society that we do not confine ourselves to the subject of temperance, but talk too much about woman's rights, divorce, and the Church. . . . Let it be clearly understood that this is a woman's rights society." Low gasps and uneasy mutterings were heard from parts of the audience. This was not a unanimous sentiment.

Next came reports on the achievements of the society over the past year. Special notice of *The Lily* was made as the only temperance paper "under the control of a woman . . . Its editor having held during the past year the office of Corresponding Secretary of our Society, the Lily has naturally become the organ through which the action of the Society has been made known to the public."[246] As far as Bloomer was concerned, this was not the central mission of *The Lily*. Whether or not the executive committee had plans to co-opt it, she retained sole editorial control.

Someone proposed an amendment to allow men as officers. Another committee was elected to consider this, including Bloomer, Vaughan, Anthony, Douglass, and Stanton.

Bloomer thought that giving men power in the women's society was a terrible idea. She understood the point, and she too wanted to see women and men work together as equals. But she did not think they were competent yet. Seated at a table with the committee, she evaluated her position.

In her view, by their training from birth, most men would dominate a conversation, and most women would let them. Stanton and Anthony were exceptions. Stanton had a rare degree of education, intellect, and confidence, supported by family money and connections, and she had little compassion for those she regarded as less enlightened than herself. Anthony was from a radical Quaker family and was an experienced administrator and reformer. But most women were more like Bloomer, raised in authoritarian homes, and many had less support than she did, as dependents in conventional families, with no connections, no money, and little education or confidence. Even the better off still had much to learn, like Stanton, who still did not understand parliamentary procedure. The men were objectively more qualified for leadership. But if women were to organize themselves, form arguments, and stand their ground in debate, they would have to learn by doing these things in a supported environment, as Bloomer had. Bloomer understood that *The Lily* and this society controlled by women were vital educational and networking opportunities, not simply political instruments. But her influential friends disagreed.

Stanton and Anthony were the promoters of this amendment, supported by their friend, the brilliant and eminent Frederick Douglass. He was Bloomer's age, a Black man born and raised in slavery. He had overcome, and still contended with, worse obstacles than those Bloomer had faced to educate and free himself, and to build his career as one of the greatest reformers of the century. He was occasionally sensitive about his lack of formal education, but he did not sympathize with Bloomer's point of view.

Anthony, Stanton, and Douglass presented two resolutions that Bloomer could not support. One was to allow men to hold offices in the society. The second was to change its name from "The Woman's" society to "The People's."

Bloomer explained her opposition to both. "Knowing the minds of the people to a great extent throughout the State in regard to the Society," she told her readers in *The Lily* afterward, "we could not feel that such a change was desirable, or wise—and we trembled for the result, should the advocates of this new measure persevere."

She suggested that they could organize a new society on their own terms and "let all who would, come into it." But they said no. "Nothing short of bringing the present Society on to their proposed platform would suffice." This was probably influenced by the fact that it was already established, had two thousand members, and had $1,761 in its treasury.

The committee split over these two resolutions. At the vote, Anthony, Stanton, and Douglass won the majority. Bloomer and those who agreed with her wrote a minority report to present to the convention along with the resolutions. She remained convinced of her position, but she also felt willing to stand by the society however it went. And, because of the threat to her friendships and the stability of the organization, she determined to stay out of the public debate.

In the afternoon, after the treasurer's report, the convention decided that male members could vote on all questions. More business was conducted before Anthony read the majority report of the constitutional revision committee and stated the position of the minority.

Antoinette Brown, with her deep blue eyes, simple dress, and graceful dignity, argued for making men equal members on ethical grounds. Emily Clark disagreed. After a year as a lecturing agent, she thought "that the power of the Society lay in the fact of it being a Woman's Society." Anthony said that she "had always felt ashamed" that men were members but not allowed to hold office and said she had met many people who agreed with her, as had another lecturing agent who was not there. The other agents present—Albro, Clark, and Vaughan—said they had the opposite experience. Vaughan recognized the principle of equality but also that their supporters statewide had signed on and donated to a women-controlled organization, and that if men could be elected to office at this early stage of the movement, women would lose that control. "Expediency," she stated, defined as "the good of the cause," demanded that this change should be delayed. After a charged discussion, the topic was tabled until the next morning. They spent the evening arguing the question of divorce. Temperance had hardly been addressed.

In the morning, there was much anxious talk in various parts of the auditorium. After some debate about process between Dexter and Douglass, Mr. Stebbins presented the minority report and spoke at length. If they called it a "People's Temperance League," "everyone would assume it was led by men," and he believed it would be. "The management will go to those who have the experience." He thought they should not be a women's rights organization and made the bizarre claim that no temperance society in the state barred women from voting. In any case, he and another man agreed that all donations had been given to a women's society and were not transferrable.

Stanton asked Douglass to clearly restate the question at hand. He did and commented that the minority had dominated the floor. He was called to order. Anthony said "the men" were trying to take too much control. "We think if they would be quiet awhile, we can defend ourselves pretty well." Douglass sat down. Bloomer took this opportunity to comment that the effect of allowing men to hold office was "foreshadowed by the conduct of the men in this convention."

A woman said that this was a temperance society and too many other issues were being dragged in. A man said he thought the women "should work on alone for another year ... we could not have all that was right at once." Dexter, concerned by the developing conflict, said he was afraid the society would dissolve if they could not settle this question. He suggested a compromise: some offices could be open to men, but the controlling power would remain with the women.

Stanton said she could agree to this, and that "the presence of a minority report need not lead to a schism in the Society." She was willing to abide by the decision of the majority. In an attempt to smooth over this conflict that threatened to dominate the convention, Douglass moved to table the proposed amendment, which was agreed. They moved on.

That afternoon, to Mary Vaughan's surprise, she was elected president over Stanton by three votes. Douglass, indignant, held up a slip of paper. He said it was one of many circulating the hall: a printed joke "ticket" or preprinted ballot with a list of preferred candidates, including Vaughan for president. Similar "tickets" were distributed by political parties and others to voters at elections before the federal regulation of ballots in the twentieth century.

In this context, it seemed ridiculous and was met with general laughter. Dexter said he "hoped no one would vote the printed ticket unless they liked it ... for his part he was glad ... as it would save him the trouble of writing a long list of names." A few must have cast a suspicious eye at him for this. But it was not clear who was responsible.

Anthony was elected recording secretary. But with direct reference to Vaughan's earlier statement, she said that by electing Vaughan, the society had opposed women's rights in favor of political "expediency." Because of this, she declined the office.

Vaughan called her to order "for engaging in personal remarks." Douglass thought that there was a misunderstanding. The decision on their proposals had not been made, it had been tabled, he said, and he hoped Anthony would not decline. Dexter started to say something, but Anthony interrupted. There is no use of wasting words, she said. My soul is not in this society, and there is no reason why I should keep my body here.

Douglass moved that "the best thanks of the Society be tendered to Miss Anthony." All were in favor. Amelia Bloomer was reelected corresponding secretary. Stanton was elected first vice president. She aligned herself with Anthony and declined. Dr. Lydia N. Fowler was elected instead. Stanton gave up the president's chair to Vaughan. A resolution was unanimously passed to thank her. "We honor her sentiments, love her as a sister, and will ever hail her as a fellow worker in this cause." And with that, Stanton and Anthony resigned from the Woman's State Temperance Society a year after helping to found it. The schism was complete.

From Stanton and Anthony's perspective, they were the radicals for wanting to open up the society's offices to men and redirect its mission. At the same time, they now advocated "educated suffrage," with a test to determine eligibility, not universal suffrage. And in wanting their skillful male friends to take leadership positions immediately, they favored political expediency of a different kind.

Bloomer said more than once that this disagreement did not affect her friendship for Stanton or Anthony, though she was not sure they felt the same at the time. Still, she had acted according to her conscience and they to theirs, and there was not much more to be said.[247]

After the convention, the Bloomers took a refreshing day trip to Niagara Falls on the train. Back at her desk, Amelia composed a double number of *The Lily* to accommodate the convention proceedings and wrote a long editorial. She explained that though she knew of the plan to change the society, and some writers said she had been an open opponent, only a handful of attendees knew her thoughts on the subject, and most there assumed she had sided with Stanton and Anthony.

But to make herself clear: "The Society was not organized as an equal rights Society, but as a Woman's Temperance Society." When men could respect women as equals, she would welcome them to the leadership, but the events had shown they were not ready. "It does seem strange to us that any liberally disposed person can ask women to surrender the control of their Society into the hands of men at the present juncture of affairs ... those who advocate this surrender, claim to be in favor of women's rights, while several of those who urged women to keep the power in their own hands, were of the conservative stamp." Some promoting the change had told her that "we shall have just as much power—it will be just as much a Woman's Society as before; while we accord to men the *right* they will have too much *gallantry* to ever accept office. This is not in accordance with our views of right, or with our ideas of an equal rights society ... We cannot say to our brothers, we accord you the right to hold office in our Society, but shall think you *mean* if you accept it."

She regretted that the "noble and talented" Stanton was no longer president but was glad that Vaughan had gained the opportunity. She was still troubled that "anything should have been introduced to throw dissension into our ranks" and that so little time had been spent on temperance.[248]

Another surprise awaited the new leadership of the society. It seemed that Anthony had drained the treasury without the approval of the underconfident treasurer, Mrs. Alling. There was not much left to pay Bloomer for printing.[249]

Frederick Douglass wrote in his paper that Stanton and Anthony had wanted to make the society's constitution "consistent with the principle of human equality ... On the other hand, strange to say ... the world renowned Mrs. BLOOMER, whose name has been supposed to represent the most ultra ideas of the equality of the sexes, was for keeping the men out of office." He said that Bloomer, Vaughan, and Clark wanted to stack the offices with "ladies of their own particular opinions" and claimed they said that "women's rights ought not to be talked of on their platform." And the joke tickets demonstrated that there had been a plot to replace Stanton with Vaughan.[250]

The persons behind those printed candidate lists were still unknown. Many were opposed to Stanton and Anthony's shift toward women's suffrage, criticism of the church, and advocacy for divorce. They might have thought that Vaughan would refocus the society on temperance alone.

Three weeks later, the National Convention of Colored People was held in Rochester, with a hundred delegates from all over the country. No white people were admitted, and Bloomer used this in her reaction to Douglass's column. "The man who contended so strongly for the right of men to hold office in the Women's Society, and share in the control of its affairs—Frederick Douglass, who when he found he could not carry his measures felt himself called upon to denounce those who presumed to differ in opinion from him, and to misrepresent and traduce their motives . . . opposed white men taking part in a Colored Convention! And why? . . . He felt that the whites had advantages over the blacks, and that if admitted to their meeting they would do all the talking." But that if the Black men were "thrown upon themselves, they would act freely and gain strength and confidence for the discharge of whatever duties may devolve upon them. What Mr. Douglass failed to see in the case of the woman, he saw clearly in that of the blacks. The cases are precisely the same." If Douglass read this, he did not respond in his paper.

Bloomer was still an officer in the mixed-gender Good Templars. She and Dexter were appointed delegates from their lodge to the first annual state meeting in Ithaca, where they were hosted by Judge Amasa Dana and his wife, Mary Speed Dana. Bloomer was glad to "see *women* there, on a perfect and entire equality with their brothers." She was invited to speak twice, and she told her readers that she was "the first woman who has ever spoken publicly in Ithaca. Some fears were entertained by friends as to the result, and we were cautioned about talking woman's rights—but of course we could not help spicing in a little. We are happy to say that nobody was alarmed by our remarks. Either owing to the interest felt in the subject, or some other cause, the audience failed to discover the 'long ears, and cloven foot.'"[251]

Stanton and Anthony did not attend. They and Douglass remained committed to temperance, but it was not a primary cause for them.

Bloomer continued to accept invitations to speak on temperance and women's rights and was warmly received.[252] For July Fourth, she agreed to give a holiday oration on temperance at the village of Harford. On the ferry, she ran into Mary Vaughan, who was on her way to do the same in Speedsville. It was a beautiful day for the ride down the lake, and the women talked to two legislators who had promoted the Maine Law in the State Senate. At Ithaca, Bloomer's hosts met her with a carriage and drove her the last eighteen miles. Bloomer was escorted to the outdoor stage by women in the new dress, and she spoke to a crowd of over fifteen hundred, who listened to her "with the most earnest attention, and judging from their countenances the novelty of hearing a woman talk was lost in the interest excited by the subject."

That evening, she gave another lecture on how unjust property, labor, and family law multiplied the evil effects of intemperance on the lives of women. The next morning, her new friends drove her to Homer, where she stopped for her midday dinner. It was her first visit since her family moved away. She took a stroll to look for her childhood home, "around which clustered many fond recollections. We had no one to guide us in the search, but the impressions left on our mind at six years of age were so strong that we could not be mistaken. The place was soon found. Though much altered it still retained enough of its former likeness to enable us to identify it, after an absence of twenty-nine years ... to us and ours has Time brought much of change, and somewhat of sorrow; yet upon us personally has his hand rested lightly."

Deep in thought, she walked back to the hotel. Word of her visit had spread, and family friends were gathering to welcome her. They congratulated her, shook her hand, and asked if she would stay and give them a talk. She agreed. Her Harford friends said goodbye, and her Homer friends escorted her to the red brick mansion of William Sherman and his pleasant family.

When she took the pulpit at the Presbyterian church that evening, the house and gallery were "densely filled with an intelligent and attentive audience." The next morning, a committee asked her to stay and speak another night, and she agreed. After that, she caught the early morning stagecoach for Glen Haven, an easy two-hour ride from Homer. Dr. and Mrs. Jackson welcomed her, and she rested there for two days, though she agreed to address the residents one evening and also accepted an invitation to speak in the tiny village of Scott, four miles away, to a surprisingly large audience. Again, the hosts wanted her to stay on, but she was ready to go home. Mary Vaughan wrote to report a similar experience with her holiday oration and subsequent invitations. It seemed to Bloomer that fifty women temperance lecturers in the field would not be too many.

In her accumulated mail were several letters from young women asking for a job or assistance in finding typesetting work. She did not have a printing office, and the *Courier* did not employ girls, but she wrote a paragraph to encourage them in *The Lily* with reports of women who had rapidly learned the type cases.

Not only had the women's temperance society lost Stanton and Anthony as members, Bloomer had also lost them as contributors. Still, she always had more good submissions than she could print. Her worse problem was her health, which was collapsing again. And she had two conventions to attend in New York that September.

On July 21, Bloomer returned to Glen Haven for a few weeks. Doctor Jackson prescribed her the usual water cure routine, and to "write *very* very VERY little." She tried, but she would not suspend *The Lily*, and she slipped away to her bedroom to write articles and letters. And she went out to speak in Homer again on two successive evenings.[253]

She enjoyed the cold water cure itself very much, as not everyone did. At regular intervals every day, she plunged and showered and was wrapped in wet sheets. "Chills and shivering I know nothing about, but come out of it all in a glow of heat, and greatly refreshed."

After the first week or two, she found a better writing spot. Half a mile along a shady road from the Glen, there was a narrow winding side path that led down to the verge of the cliff, and there in the shade of the hemlock trees was a comfortable seat and a writing table with a view of the broad blue lake vanishing to the north between high sloping hills. She worked there, with the sound of the birds above her, the wind in the trees, and the waves against the rocks below. At a distance, she could see people fishing, which seemed cruel to her, and little rowboats full of patients. The sound of their oars and laughter carried to her across the water.

She found time for recreation between her treatment and her work. She had always been nervous of small boats, but at the Glen, she got bored and did not want to seem fearful, so she allowed another patient to persuade her. Once she was out on the water, she loved it. Soon, she was rowing herself back and forth across the lake for pleasure and exercise. One day, she joined a party of patients to row to a bowling alley, a German innovation. She was not good at it but had fun.

On another day, she joined two acquaintances to row up the lake to Staghorn Rock, which would later be understood as a fossilized coral reef. At the base of a large slate bank was a solid limestone formation half a mile long that appeared to be made of petrified animal horns and antlers. It was difficult to dislodge them, even with a crowbar, but Bloomer broke off a few samples to take home and give to a school. A geologist had theorized that it was some kind of insect formation, but she told Dexter, "To me it is a great mystery, and the greatest natural curiosity I ever saw." Afterward, they rowed down to a little cove and had the picnic provided by the Glen: white and graham biscuits, graham crackers, tea cakes, and blackberries. "A supper was never eaten by any of us with a better relish or more true enjoyment." Before them, the lake was glassy and calm, and the sunset reflected crimson, scarlet, and gold on the water.

She could have stayed until winter, but she had conventions to attend. On August 20, she returned to Seneca Falls, dealt with some work, packed her lecturing dresses, and caught the train to New York City.[254]

The two-day Whole World's Temperance Convention and the four-day World's Temperance Convention were held at Metropolitan Hall in New York City, one after the other. Bloomer attended both. Once again, she stayed with her friend Mrs. Fowler, along with Susan Anthony, Antoinette Brown, and her contributor Frances Gage, who had made the trip from Missouri. Gage had become a good friend, but they had never met before, and Bloomer was glad to shake hands and connect the name with this long, strong Yankee face, with high color in the cheeks, sharp eyes, and smooth dark ringleted hair shot with gray.[255]

The Whole World's Temperance Convention was first. It had been organized as an inclusive alternative to the World's Temperance Convention after the planners rejected the seven women delegates. About a thousand people attended, with delegates from twenty states, Canada, and Europe.

In his opening remarks, Thomas Wentworth Higginson said, "Let it be understood, once for all ... this is not a Woman's Rights Convention—it is simply a Convention in which Woman is not wronged." Later, on the cover of her copy of the proceedings, Lucy Stone wrote, "This was virtually a Woman's Rights Convention."[256]

Bloomer found it a heartening event, full of "peace and harmony." Afterward, she gave a temperance address at the women's convention at the Broadway Tabernacle. A hostile journalist called that convention "THE LAST VAGARY OF THE GREELEY CLIQUE," a boring "assemblage of rampant women ... unsexed in mind all of them ... Are there to be no more children? ... It is almost needless for us to say that these women are entirely devoid of personal attractions ... They violate the rules of decency and taste, by attiring themselves in eccentric habiliments, which hang loosely and irregularly upon their forms, making that which we have been educated to respect, to love, and to admire, only an object of aversion and disgust."[257]

Bloomer, in her eccentric habiliments, made time to visit the Crystal Palace exhibition and a vegetarian banquet at Metropolitan Hall intended for six hundred guests, but attended by only three hundred, mostly women. The meal was late, and none of it was well made, with only lukewarm water to drink. But there was music afterward and good speeches until ten.[258]

In Seneca Falls, Bloomer wrote up the conventions before she packed to leave on a multistate tour, this time with Dexter, who was looking for a new business. They went overnight to Cleveland for the National Woman's Rights Convention, stayed with old friends, and explored the town. It gave Bloomer an impression of "health and comfort" with its broad streets and shade trees and many beautiful large buildings under construction. She gave several lectures in the area and spoke at the convention.[259] Before it ended, they left for Mount Vernon, Ohio. Amelia had an invitation to lecture there, and Dexter had an appointment with the owners of the *Western Home Visitor,* a literary family paper with a reformist slant and a circulation of about four thousand. On first impression, Mount Vernon seemed like a pleasant town twice the size of Seneca Falls.

After that, they traveled south for another of Bloomer's lectures, and then to Columbus. They toured the Ohio Penitentiary, the Asylum for the Blind, and the Deaf and Dumb Asylum, where she met students with "bright happy faces and sparkling eyes" and watched a lesson, fascinated by the rapid communication between the teacher and students through "finger motions." Bloomer spoke on temperance and women's rights to large audiences and met with the secretary of the Ohio State Temperance Society to discuss organizational concerns. She wrote, "I am well pleased with Ohio thus far, yet I have seen nothing sufficiently attractive to win my affections from my native State, and my own dear home."

From Columbus, the Bloomers went up to Detroit via a steamship from Sandusky, which they boarded at night. It was terribly crowded, and everyone made beds "on the floor, and on the sofas, and all lay down in their clothes to get what rest they could. Black and white, old and young, were all huddled together in a hot unventilated room. It was a beautiful moonlit night," but too cold to stay on deck. Toward the end of the night, they sailed into a dense fog and went aground twice before reaching the city, where the Bloomers stayed with friends for two days. "I am agreeably disappointed in Detroit—it is much pleasanter and more finely laid out than I had supposed it to be." She gave a lecture to another good audience and left the next morning for Chicago in another fog so thick that the gaslights of the station were still burning when their train left at 9:00 A.M. They were informed that it was not simple fog but smoke from the burning marshes near the city. Twenty miles later, they left it behind, and all could see the beautiful autumn colors of the countryside as they passed the occasional log cabin or farm, until they reached the shore of Lake Michigan and traveled parallel to it. Through the trees, "by the light of a nearly full moon, we occasionally caught a glimpse of its quiet and silvery expanse."

She had worse opinions of Chicago and Milwaukee, both rising new cities but both saturated with alcohol. The German and Irish immigrants who made up half of Wisconsin were in strong opposition to a proposed Maine Law.[260] Once home, she rested for a week but was soon back at work on *The Lily,* lecturing in nearby towns and catching up on the news and her three weeks' landslide of mail.

Several Maine Law candidates ran for New York State offices this year, and even temperance men who disapproved of women speaking on a public stage asked them to persuade male voters. This had worked well in Michigan, and Bloomer approved. If men disagreed with the women's choices, she wrote, they should remember their claim that women could vote through them. The Whigs saw their entire ticket elected, and a majority were Maine Law men.

At the end of 1853, Dexter made the decision that many Easterners made at this time: to move west. He purchased an interest in the *Western Home Visitor* in Mount Vernon, four hundred miles from Seneca Falls. They would move there before the end of the year. Amelia would contribute to that paper and have access to their modern printing shop for *The Lily.*

Their marriage was grounded in equality, but it does seem that this was Dexter's idea. Amelia's parents were still alive, and in this move, they would leave behind their home and almost all their friends and family, including Amelia's niece, Jennie, her dear dead sister's daughter, now almost four years old, "a little cherub, who still lives and bears her name—a bright, intelligent being, on whom we have bestowed much of hope and love."[261]

In her editorial announcement of the move in her December 1 issue, Amelia told her readers, that "we, as a true and faithful wife, are bound to say in the language of Ruth 'where thou goest, I will go.'" *The Lily* would continue, and maybe it would be better.

Friends, we pray you let not our change of location affect
our intercourse with each other . . . We feel that it matters
little in what part of the vineyard we are placed, so we but
improve and cultivate to the best of our ability the part
assigned us. And this feeling bears us up under the heart-
sorrow occasioned by the sundering of the many ties that
bind us . . . We bid farewell to all with an aching heart.

Yet our grief . . . is mingled with hope for the future.
We prefer to look on the bright side of every picture . . .
So we will dash aside the tears, and school our heart to
bear with fortitude this the greatest sorrow ever laid upon
us; believing that it is for our interest to take this step,
though it be so agonizing to part with those we love.[262]

If she thought or felt anything else about this decision, it is
unrecorded.

When Seneca Falls learned of the Bloomers' plan, the Good
Templars organized a public meeting and banquet at Union Hall to
see them off. Isaac Fuller announced in the *Courier* that "although
we disapprove of some of the measures advocated in the *Lily*,
we part with it and its worthy editor with sincere regret . . . Mrs.
Bloomer has had the entire direction of it, both editorially and
financially, displaying talents and business qualifications possessed
by few of the gentler sex and which but few of her friends were
prepared to see her exhibit. The ability and energy with which
the *Lily* has been conducted have attained for it a circulation of
over four thousand copies in different parts of the Union, thus
giving to our enterprising village notoriety which it would not
have otherwise obtained."[263]

Between four and five hundred people came to the farewell
banquet. Five long tables were loaded with beautiful food twice,
for two seatings. Speeches and toasts followed, and, as always,
resolutions were made, this time to thank the Bloomers and wish
them well. The furniture was moved to the walls, the dance band
struck up, and the party went on until late in the evening.

In the morning, Bloomer rose, dressed, lit the fire, started breakfast, and looked around her beloved little house. It would all have to be sorted, then discarded or packed.

She could not attend the meeting of the executive committee of the Women's New York State Temperance Society that December and sent her resignation as corresponding secretary. The meeting gave her a vote of thanks and appointed a replacement.

Whether Bloomer saw this move as a welcome or unwelcome retreat from what had become a very public life, we have no indication beyond her writings in *The Lily*. She had always been torn between public life's attractions and rewards and her physical limitations. At the same time, she could continue her work almost anywhere if she chose. It seems clear that Dexter was both following his own ambitions and the curiosity about the West that he had felt since he was a boy, and that he wanted to remove his wife from the centers of reform that had so consumed her life in recent years. The move may have seemed like a rational choice if Amelia could put aside the pain of separation from home. As always, she did her best.

CHAPTER 11

A New Field of Labor

Dear Ohio! Land of beauty;
    Land of generous cheerful toil;
    we pray thee, to "The Lily,"
    Kindly welcome to thy soil! . . .

Make it not a tender house-plant:
    Always to be watched with fear—
    (Lest it faint, in frost or sunshine.)
Nursed and petted all the year.

Let it feel, as does the tall oak,
    Summer's heat and winter's snow.
Give it culture, give it freedom—
    Let it have a chance to grow

    —Frances D. Gage, "Appeal for The Lily"

Mount Vernon, Ohio, was a vibrant small town on the Vernon (now Kokosing) River, fifty miles northeast of Columbus and one hundred miles southwest of Cleveland. It was known for foundries, Johnny Appleseed, and a branch of the State Bank of Ohio. In 1853, it had four newspapers, and *The Lily* would become the fifth.

Ohio was much less progressive than New York. In moving there as a married woman, Bloomer had lost her legal property rights. But she and Dexter did not expect to stay.[264]

They returned to Kenyon House, the large Italianate brick hotel near the public square downtown, where they had stayed on their last visit. It was December and cold, but Amelia lay awake listening to the sounds of drunk men and boys hooting and yelling in the street below. All day, and most of the night, crowds of them stood around the doors of rumshops, blocking the sidewalk. When she went out, she was irritated by their "offensive breath, staggering gait, idiotic stare and silly expression." Even some of the men who came to pick up their newspapers at the offices of the *Western Home Visitor* showed "unmistakable signs of intoxication." There were four temperance societies in Mount Vernon, but, she wrote for the first Ohio issue of *The Lily*, "there is fault somewhere, and necessity for action, both on the part of temperance men, and city officers."[265]

She and Dexter were working together again, now on the second floor of the Kremlin Building. Dexter was editor and co-owner, with Ethan A. Higgins, of the *Visitor*. Higgins was about ten years younger than the Bloomers and had lived in Ohio all his life.[266] Amelia lent her famous name as a contributor and assistant editor to the *Visitor*, as well as publishing *The Lily*.

She greeted her new readers in an editorial. It was safe to assume they knew her name. "What I have been in the past, I expect to be in the future—an uncompromising opponent of wrong and oppression in every form, and a sustainer of the right and the true." Her first article for them was "Woman's Right to Employment."[267] Her second was in reply to yet another set of "Golden Rules for Wives" in an exchange paper. "Faugh on such twaddle! 'Golden rules for wives'—'duty of wives' . . . Why don't our wise editors give us now and then some 'golden rules' for husbands, by way of variety?"[268]

Her first priority was still her own paper. She spent about $150 on fresh new type and a new masthead from Buffalo.[269] Using these on Higgins's steam-powered press run by a team with only two newspapers to publish, instead of the old hand press of the *Courier* in Seneca Falls, which was often taken up by job work, gave *The Lily* a professional "new dress" that made her proud. But there was still one more improvement she hoped to make. She made inquiries and began to interview women typesetters.[270]

Any fears she had about losing readers in the move were quickly allayed. Dexter would write that her list grew to six thousand subscribers, though all other statements leave it at four thousand.[271] But though she felt optimistic about her work, she felt personally bereft, "a stranger in the midst of strangers . . . And yet we do not regret coming hither. There is a wide field of labor here opened before us, and it is our purpose, if life and health are spared, to enter into, and improve it to the best of our ability."

Invitations to speak arrived, more than she could accept. On January 9, she took a slow train fifty miles south to Zanesville, through "wild, mountainous and rocky" country, with stops at every little hamlet. Gentlemen on the train, intrigued by her dress, asked where she was going. When she told them, they said they doubted she could accomplish much in such a conservative town.

It did not appear promising when she arrived. A cloud of coal smoke from its seven iron foundries hung over the town, and as soon as she stepped out of the train and inhaled, Bloomer experienced "an unpleasant and choking sensation." She took an omnibus straight from the station to the hotel, where she was warmly greeted by the proprietors and her host, Jesse Atwell. Everyone treated her with kindness and respect. Atwell took her aside and informed her that a local temperance society planned to give her a set fee while they pocketed the balance of the house. He told her to dismiss them if they approached her, since she "could just as well have the whole."

It was not the first time she had to advocate for equal pay. She later wrote that around this time, she spoke to a group that told her afterward that "no lecturer, unless it was Horace Mann . . . had drawn so large a house and put so much money in the treasury." When they asked what they should pay her, she said, "You say I have done as well for you, and even better than did Horace Mann, pay me what you paid him and it will be right." They seemed surprised, "but seeing the justice of my demand, they paid it without a word."[272]

In Zanesville, she spoke on "Woman's Rights" to an attentive overflow crowd. Atwell invited her to give a second lecture, but the annual Convention of the Ohio Woman's State Temperance Society opened the next day in Columbus, and she caught the train there the next morning.[273]

At the convention, the famous Mrs. Bloomer was welcomed and elected to the familiar office of corresponding secretary. She was surprised at the small gathering and that "many prominent women whom we expected to see, and who should have been in attendance . . . to have aided, counseled, and strengthened the more shrinking and less capable ones, were absent."[274] The defeat of the temperance candidate for governor had discouraged them, and their leading temperance newspaper had gone under. Many felt they should give up, "that the people may drink of the terrible cup of intemperance to its very dregs."

Later, she confronted this sentiment in *The Lily.* "We have also sometimes felt like yielding up the contest . . . and thus leave our opponents to reap the full extent of the evils we combat, but then the solemn question comes up, IS IT RIGHT?"

She stepped in. Their resolutions seemed weak to her, and she offered a series of her own that declared temperance a priority over party politics, that a Maine Law should be put to a state referendum, and that since women could not vote, men must accurately represent them. All were unanimously adopted. Within a day or two, she led a delegation to the state capitol to present a petition for statewide liquor prohibition.[275] There, she stepped aside for the convention president, Mary T. Conner, who presented the petition. The Senate voted to lay it "on the table, and to have it printed." This was no guarantee of anything, but the women had made themselves heard, and they felt encouraged.[276]

She would continue to alternate newspaper work and traveling lecture work through the summer, taking short trips around Ohio and Indiana, all of which went well. She and Dexter helped found a Good Templars lodge in Mount Vernon, the second in the state.

Both became officers, and the weekly meetings became a good source of social life for them.[277]

At times, she still addressed questions of dress and gender. "Male Bloomers" was a phrase that had popped up here and there since the moral panic of 1851 to describe various real and imagined gender-nonconforming men, including those who adopted Turkish dress, cross-dressers, and kilt-wearers. Most recently, it had been used to refer to "the Man in the Shawl," a new trend that in a few years would describe President Lincoln himself. Articles disparaged such "female-minded males."[278] Bloomer was consistent in her response. "There is a class of men who seem to think it their especial business to superintend the wardrobes of both men and women ... with all the importance of authorized dictators." She disliked the shawl and considered it bad for posture because wearers had to grip it and often hunched their shoulders to keep it on, "but if worn at all, men have the same right to it that women have. If they find it comfortable, that is enough; and no one has a right to object to their wearing it because women wear shawls." Both men and women wore sack coats; "must either dispense with this comfortable garment because it is worn by the other?"[279]

Women were increasingly involved with journalism and newspaper publication across the country. The *Cincinnati Gazette* had hired a team of women compositors who were, "after only two week's experience, beginning to be quite expert and useful." The paper predicted that in "another year several hundred females will find profitable employment in this new field."[280] Early that spring, Bloomer put her principles into practice once more and hired Charlotte W. Lundy from New York, a widow with three months of experience, to set type for *The Lily.*

All of the existing employees in the *Visitor* printshop were men. The Bloomers openly discussed Lundy's hiring in front of them, including the plan for her training by Higgins and the experienced printers, and no one indicated disapproval. But once Lundy arrived and began work, the male employees soured. Bloomer described her as an "agreeable intelligent ladylike woman" around twenty-five years old, with "great energy of character."[281] She was still a woman in a traditionally male workplace. Dexter and Higgins acted as a buffer most of the time, answering her questions as needed. Bloomer was unaware of any trouble until one day, when both of them were out, Lundy stepped into Bloomer's office to ask how to indent a piece of poetry. Bloomer had never set type herself and told her to go into the other room and ask the men. Lundy returned within a few minutes. They had refused to advise her.

Bloomer walked into the shop. She asked for an explanation and was met with a wall of resistance. "All hands, with the foreman of the office as leader, avowed their determination not to work in an office with or give instruction to a woman. And, further, they said they had drawn up a paper to that effect which had been signed by all the printers in town. The foreman also defied us to find a printer in Ohio who would give instructions to a woman." Since she could not talk sense into them, she left them to their work and considered her options. She was not their direct supervisor. She knew that she would side with Lundy, and she knew that Dexter and Higgins would support her. But she would have to let them do the talking.

When Higgins came back to the office, she informed him of the problem, and she told Dexter when he returned the next day. The two men went into the printshop and "held a long conference with their workmen, telling them it was not their intention to employ women to set the type of the *Visitor*, but that Mrs. L. would remain and work on the *Lily*, and that they should expect of them that they should give her all the instructions she might need in her work. If they would do this willingly and cheerfully, well; if not, they might consider themselves discharged." They would not allow their staff to determine *The Lily*'s employment policy. In response, all the men quit.

Lundy wrote to the *New York Daily Tribune* of this incident. They did not print her letter but summarized it, made jokes about the false gallantry and drunkenness of printers, and wrote that "she must not complain if she experiences some of the trials and annoyances which reformers have encountered before her. She is treated no worse than a male negro would probably be, and 'women and n——' have of late been growing too saucy and aspiring, and will have to be reined in a little." But they claimed to be glad that Lundy's coworkers had not "succeeded in breaking down or bluffing off their new competitor" so far.[282]

In the midst of this conflict, Lucy Stone arrived in town on her lecture tour and chose to speak on "Woman and Her Employment." Bloomer much appreciated her supportive influence. "Her words were like soothing oil on the troubled waters. It seemed as though an overruling Providence had directed her steps hitherward to allay the excitement and to subdue the angry feelings, to plead the cause of womanhood . . . and she was in a great degree successful."[283]

Higgins and the Bloomers soon found three more women typesetters and three new men, including a journeyman from Columbus. Amelia moved *The Lily*'s typecases into the *Visitor* office, and from then on, they all worked together, as Bloomer wrote, "peaceably and harmoniously. It does our heart good to see the happy change which has been wrought in the office by the attempt to crush woman's efforts in her own behalf. The moral atmosphere has been purified, and superciliousness has given place to friendly and cheerful intercourse."

On May 1, 1854, the governor of Ohio signed a ban on liquor sales. In New York State, as hoped, another Maine Law passed the legislature, but, to the indignation and grief of the temperance community, it was vetoed by Governor Horatio Seymour, who had promised to sign it during his campaign two years earlier. Bloomer reported that the veto was "celebrated by the liquor party with firing of cannon, bonfires and illuminations, with shouts of rejoicing and drunken revelry. The devils in hell must have rejoiced, while the angels in heaven must have wept, over the scene." A Daughters of Temperance society sent the governor thirty small pieces of silver, representing the payment Judas received for betraying Jesus.[284]

At the end of May, Bloomer traveled back home to Seneca Falls. She wrote to Dexter, "Would that you could see face to face the friends of old, and receive the hearty grasp of the hand which would meet you at almost every step, and above all that you could gaze with me upon our dear cottage home which we took so much pleasure in improving and beautifying . . . I can hardly realize that it is not my home still, that I should not if I passed within find everything as of old, and you to welcome my return."[285]

But it was only a visit, and soon she was on the familiar train station platform again. She went to Utica for the annual meeting of the Woman's State Temperance Society. It was well attended, and the crowd was energized by Governor Seymour's veto. Bloomer was added to the business committee and made an honorary vice president. One of the agents told her that she had lectured 114 times that winter.[286]

In Ohio, a married woman's property bill was reported in the State Senate, with language that would give women freedom of movement, equal rights to custody of their children, and inheritance rights. Another bill proposed to strike the words "white male" from the state constitution, giving Black men and all women the right of suffrage. No action was taken on either of them, but, Bloomer wrote, "this is the first report, so far as we know, made in any legislative body, in favor of granting to woman the right of suffrage . . . we consider this an encouraging evidence of the increasing liberality of public sentiment."[287]

The new liquor law was being enforced in Mount Vernon, with arrests and fines of anyone found drunk in the streets. On her return, Bloomer found that the night was now quiet in the center of town, as she had wished for on her first night there.

Mirroring her experience of the spring, there had been a walkout of journeymen from the office of the *Philadelphia Daily Register* after the publisher hired two women typesetters to work in an office on another street. Bloomer reported that "the men said they acted in obedience to a resolution of the Printer's Union . . . that they would work for no man who employed women to set type, no matter whether employed in the same office with them or not. A chivalrous set of men truly! And as noted for their courage." The publishers kept the women and let the protesting men go. The men threatened violence, and several were arrested and fined on charge of conspiracy. "Let not women be discouraged by such hostile manifestations on the part of men," Bloomer wrote, "but rather let them press forward till they break down every barrier which is raised to obstruct their advancement."[288]

In Maine, Olive Rose became the first woman in the nation elected to political office, as register of deeds for her county. She won 73–4. In Penfield, Ohio, Adeline Swift was elected town supervisor, though she was disqualified afterward for being a woman. In her speech to her constituents, Swift reemphasized her support for equal rights, temperance, and abolition. She listed great women leaders of Europe and "the best talent enlisted in our cause. With such women as Mott, Davis, Bloomer, Rose, Foster, Hunt, Nichols, E. Oakes Smith, Gage, Severance, Stanton, Rev. Antoinette Brown, Lucy Stone &c. . . . and a host of others too numerous to mention, we cannot fail of success."[289]

Frances Gage wrote to Bloomer from Iowa, where she was speaking on temperance in the eastern half of the state. She called it "as beautiful a country as my eyes ever beheld . . . all of life that is desirable, except a railroad, and that is staked out and begun . . . permit me to say here to your readers, that if they are . . . resolved to emigrate, they will find Iowa upon the route I have traveled, possessed of attractions which must soon fill it to overflowing with the best people in the land, and if they want a place, they must speak quick. The immigration is immense . . . The Iowa Code is so strong against drunkenness, and so kind to woman, that dram drinkers and the tyrant don't choose to come here. Ho! for Iowa, then, beautiful, sun-lit Iowa!" Though, she said, "I have not seen a woman in Iowa dressed in 'Bloomer.'"

Bloomer answered, "Secure the farm . . . and when we learn its whereabouts we may locate ours along side of it."[290] Another move seemed wise. Waves of cholera had swept Ohio, and the fear of it rose again that summer with hundreds of deaths reported in Chicago, Detroit, and smaller towns. Gage assured Amelia that in Iowa, it affected mostly immigrants.

In early July, Dexter sold his interest in the *Western Home Visitor* to Higgins, who planned to move it to Columbus. Though they were not sure how much longer they would be in Mount Vernon, the Bloomers still cultivated friendships there and one day drove out to a village with about twenty other Good Templars to found a new lodge. It was a lovely, cool day for the fourteen-mile carriage ride through an attractive stretch of farmland. But on the return home, Bloomer experienced "a severe attack of one of those terrible headaches which have so marred the happiness of our life, and which by the time of our return completely prostrated us and rendered us an unfit companion for the pleasant friends who bore us company."[291]

In September, Dexter set off on a tour of the West by himself, as far as western Iowa and the Nebraska Territory. After a few weeks, Amelia received a letter from him that said he had decided on Council Bluffs, Iowa, on the Missouri River, and had bought a house there.[292]

In 1854, Council Bluffs was a frontier town three hundred miles from any railroad. This meant limited and slow mail service. Local newspapers were printed on handpresses and distributed by stagecoach. None had the circulation and reach of *The Lily*. It is almost certain that Dexter knew that with this move, Amelia would finally have to give it up. And with travel so difficult, any lectures she gave would have to be close to home.

For him, this was a historic opportunity. A land rush had started, and he was experienced in government contract work and in real estate investment and sales. This move promised to be an exciting adventure for him, with new opportunities for wealth and a political career. And with any hope, it would return Amelia to a quiet life in a dry climate, where perhaps she would finally regain her health. She still felt guilty when she could not accept an invitation, though lecture tours exhausted her. Doctors recommended rest and less writing, but her commitment to *The Lily* and her reform work grew with their success. The move to Mount Vernon had made little difference. This time, they would move out to the farthest edge of the farthest Western free state short of California, "in anticipation that many years would elapse before the excitements that had surrounded them would be able to reach them again."[293]

Though the prospect of less work appealed to her, and though she supported Dexter's ambitions, without him, Amelia would never have chosen to move so far from her loved ones and the centers of reform.

In late September, with Dexter still away, she visited Richmond, Indiana, to meet with Mary Birdsall, secretary of the State Woman's Rights Association, to discuss the sale of *The Lily*. She gave a few lectures and organized two new lodges of Good Templars while she was there. Temperance and women's rights organizations seemed to be thriving in Richmond, and major railroads connected it with the other urban centers of the nation. It seemed like a secure home for *The Lily*. Birdsall was her first choice to take it over, but she had a baby and hesitated to commit.[294]

After less than a year, Paulina Davis was too ill to continue *The Una*. The annual Woman's Rights Convention in Philadelphia debated whether to start a new paper but decided they could not afford it. Bloomer seems to have missed the news about Davis, or not taken it seriously, for she wrote to ask if she might be interested in merging the profitable *Lily* with *The Una* for five hundred dollars: two for herself and three "to pay the expense of sending the paper to such of my subscribers as are entitled to one or more numbers next year."

By late October 1854, Dexter had crossed the Missouri River into the Nebraska Territory and, after a short exploration, looped back to Iowa via Omaha. An Omaha editor reported that Dexter looked "hale and hearty, and seems to enjoy the ride across the prairies admirably" and offered to take him hunting. Amelia thanked him for his hospitality in *The Lily*, but on behalf of her animal-loving husband, she wrote that the editor would have to "adopt some other plan . . . for his guest knows nothing about handling a gun."

Bloomer learned that Clarina Nichols of Vermont was moving to Kansas with her family, which gave her more hope that friends might join them in the West. "May they be prospered in their doings," she wrote, "and may they live to see Kansas declared a free State."

In November, with Dexter still not home and time running out to place *The Lily* with a new publisher, she went through her accounts. She had not heard from Birdsall or Davis, and she wrote to Davis again with a cheaper deal. She was now less concerned about money than providing for her subscribers. But a few days later, Birdsall wrote to say yes.

After almost two months away, Dexter returned to Mount Vernon the third week of November and told Amelia the details of his choice. She began to wrap up her business. She advertised her type for sale, and in her final issue, December 15, she printed the new prospectus for *The Lily*, listing Mary B. Birdsall as editor and proprietor and herself as corresponding editor. There would be no break, and the price would stay the same. With *The Una* discontinued, Bloomer informed her readers that *The Lily* was now "the only paper published devoted to the elevation and enfranchisement of woman . . . Let there be a general rally to its support, so that it may not be said that we have not a single paper devoted to the advocacy of Woman's Rights."

Next came the packing, and one last printer's delay before she could mail her last issue. She imagined how her four thousand readers would soon read that she was on her way to become "a simple housekeeper among the bluffs of the far off Missouri."

A year and five days after their arrival, the Bloomers said goodbye to Mount Vernon, where, Amelia said, "we have felt like strangers making a brief sojourn in a strange land among strange people—ever looking forward to the time of our departure." They visited friends in Columbus and Cincinnati and went to Seneca Falls. Every time she passed her old cottage, now occupied by a stranger, Bloomer felt as if she had only dreamed of Ohio.

The New York winter was off to a bitter start, with temperatures as low as -26°F. In the snug house of a friend, Amelia wrote a reflection for *The Lily*. "'Oh! how cold!' is groaned out by thousands of poor suffering human beings, who are crouching in wretched hovels and rickety garrets, without means sufficient to purchase a load of wood or a loaf of bread, and without employment whereby they can earn a dollar." The Third Annual Fancy Dress Ball was coming up, with costumes available for rent for eight or ten dollars. Another ball was planned as a benefit for the poor. A new relief society had been organized, and an industrial school for poor children, though, said Bloomer, "the root of the evil will not be reached. People are ready to apply a remedy to the results, while they overlook or neglect the cause."

The reelection of abolitionist William H. Seward to the United States Senate was the topic of conversation everywhere they went. "The utmost efforts were made to defeat him, and his election is regarded as a triumph of freedom over slavery—of right and justice over oppression and wrong . . . The next question of importance is the Maine Law." The temperance movement was continuing to gain political traction. Michigan, Indiana, and Ohio had passed or were considering prohibitory liquor laws.

From Seneca Falls, they traveled up to London, Ontario, to spend Christmas with friends. Bloomer was invited to speak on women's rights and temperance there, but the Methodist church would not allow the first topic, so she gave it to a large audience in the town courtroom. In her letter to *The Lily*, she commented that "temperance is regarded by the over pious ones as a subject so much more sacred than that of Human Rights."[295]

After Christmas, though it was a stormy January, Bloomer continued her lecture tour to Indianapolis and Lafayette in Indiana, then on to Cincinnati, as well as many smaller towns, until in one Ohio village, she had to cancel her lecture and take a few days off to rest. Some of the audience had traveled eight miles to hear her. "It grieved me sorely to disappoint them, but I was really too sick to lecture." She had to cancel the next one too. "This is, I believe, the first instance that I have failed to fill my appointments."

Her health and the weather relented long enough to allow her to give one promised lecture and to travel with Dexter back to New York. They would stay and visit with loved ones until their departure for Iowa in mid-March, timed for the spring thaw of the Missouri River.

As to how Bloomer felt about this move and the end of her years at the helm of *The Lily*, we have only the words of her final editorial.

> We need rest and relaxation—or at least a change of occupation; and feeling thus we learned without regret that the beauties of the western prairies, and the prospects of their growing cities had been sufficient to induce our "gude mon" to locate in the young and thriving State of Iowa.
>
> We have dearly cherished The Lily, and we have been greatly cheered by the daily evidence we have had of the good it was doing. This has encouraged us to go forward, even when we were nearly fainting over our self-imposed task. And did circumstances favor it, we should probably labor on ... But The Lily ... must not be allowed to stand in the way of what we deem our interest. Home and husband being dearer to us than all beside, we cannot hesitate to sacrifice all for them.

But she would not be "retiring into obscurity," and would still address her readers as a corresponding editor. "After the middle of January our Post Office address will be Waterloo, N. Y., until the middle of March; after that time our friends will address us at Council Bluffs City, Iowa."[296]

CLOCKWISE FROM TOP LEFT

Amelia Bloomer—Howland, NY. *American Phrenological Journal* 17 (March 1853): 52, Library Company of Philadelphia, accessed October 16, 2024, https://digital. librarycompany.org/islandora/object/digitool%3A68297; Elizabeth Cady Stanton with her sons Daniel and Henry, 1848. Elizabeth Cady Stanton Trust; Rev. Antoinette Brown. Oberlin College Archives, RG 323, Class of 1847 file; Susan B. Anthony, age 28, 1848. "Photograph of Susan B. Anthony," RBSCP Exhibits, accessed October 16, 2024, https://rbscpexhibits.lib.rochester.edu/items/show/392. University of Rochester Libraries, Rare Books, Special Collections and Preservation.

Henriette d'Angeville (1794–1871) dressed to climb Mont Blanc, 1838. Bibliothèque de Genève; Elizabeth Smith Miller, 1851. Carrie Chapman Catt Papers, Manuscript Division, Library of Congress; Jane Grey Swisshelm. Minnesota Historical Society; Clarina Nichols. Kansas State Historical Society.

TOP Dexter and Amelia Bloomer. Courtesy of Council Bluffs Public Library.

MIDDLE Possible portrait of Bloomer's niece Amanda "Jennie" Snow and her father. Courtesy of Seneca Falls Historical Society.

BOTTOM, LEFT *Lucy Stone, head-and-shoulders portrait, facing right,* between 1840 and 1860, Library of Congress.

BOTTOM, RIGHT Abby Kelley Foster. Alfred M. Hoffy, Robert M. Douglass Jr., (photographers), *Abby Kelley Foster / by Hoffy; from a daguerreotype by R. Douglass Junr.,* ca. 1846, Philadelphia. Published at the Arch St. Gallery of the Daguerreotype, printed by Wagner & McGuigan. Library of Congress.

TOP *Seneca Falls, New York (upstream)*, Smithsonian American Art Museum. Museum purchase from the Charles Isaacs Collection made possible in part by the Luisita L. and Franz H. Denghausen Endowment.

BOTTOM *Seneca Falls, New York (downstream)*, Smithsonian American Art Museum. Museum purchase from the Charles Isaacs Collection made possible in part by the Luisita L. and Franz H. Denghausen Endowment.

J. L. Magee, "The Great Bloomer Prize Fight...," 1851, BIB ID# 535413 GIGI,
American Antiquarian Society.

"Our Fashion Plate," *The Lily*, January 1, 1852. Courtesy of the New York State
Library, Manuscripts and Special Collections.

Fashions for Early Summer.

LEFT "Fashions for Early Summer," *Harper's Weekly*, 1851. Author's collection.

BELOW "Glen Haven Water Cure, Glen Haven, New York," 1858, advertisement, Scott Cortland Co., Duke University Libraries Digital Collections, accessed October 16, 2024, https://repository.duke.edu/dc/eaa/B0186.

GLEN HAVEN WATER-CURE,

RIGHT Pantalettes for girls, in *Journal des Dames et des Modes*, July 15, 1821, Costumes Parisiens (29), Rijksmuseum RP-P-2009-4079-3, Gift of the M.A. Ghering-van Ierlant Collection, accessed October 16, 2024, http://hdl.handle.net/10934/RM0001.COLLECT.510801.

BELOW "Woman's Emancipation," engraving, *Harper's New Monthly Magazine*, August 1851: 424.

Halloo! Turks in Gotham, 1851. Library of Congress, accessed October 16, 2024. https://www.loc.gov/item/2008661791/. Text reads: "Mrs. Turkey having attended Mrs. Oaks-Smith's Lecture on the Emancipation of Dress, resolves at once to give a start to the New Fashion and in order to do it with more Effect, she wants Mr. Turkey to join her in this bold Attempt." Their baby is also wearing Turkish dress and smoking, a vice associated with Turks.

Pl.17.

BLOOMERISM IN PRACTICE,

The morning after the Victory.

Mrs. TURKEY reposing on her laurels, waiting for breakfast.— Mr. TURKEY mending his coat-tail. Enters Master Turkey crying: „ Oh Ma ! Breakfast will never be ready, for Biddy says: „She wants to do like Missus, and won't cook anymore, sez she!—" (First disappointment—)

A. Weingartner, "Bloomerism in Practice: The morning after the Victory," print, ca. 1861, *Digital Commonwealth*, accessed October 16, 2024, https://ark.digitalcommonwealth. org/ark:/50959/9880w895c. Description reads: "Mrs. Turkey reposing on her laurels, waiting for breakfast. Mr. Turkey mending his coat-tail. Enters master Turkey crying: 'Oh Ma! Breakfast will never be ready, for Biddy says she wants to be like Missus and won't cook anymore sez she!' (First disappointment.)" Mrs. Turkey's smoke ring reads "For President Mrs. Turkey!" The Black servant's protest banner reads "No More Massa & Missus," the white servant's reads "No More Basement and Kitchen." The boy's reads "No More Papa & Mama!"

A Minard, the able and faithful Miss Martineau who had laboured the boys' reading. The Martineau's Norval.

OPPOSITE Amelia Bloomer, daguerreotype by Edward Tompkins Whitney, Rochester, April 29, 1852. Courtesy of Seneca Falls Historical Society.

THIS PAGE, TOP LEFT Mathias Keller, "The New Costume Polka," sheet music cover, 1851. Author's collection.

THIS PAGE, TOP RIGHT Mary Brose Tepe. R. W. Addis, *Marie Brose Tepe, Civil War nurse and vivandière...,* photograph, accessed October 16, 2024, https://www.loc.gov/item/2021630920/.

THIS PAGE, BOTTOM Masthead for *The Lily, National American Woman Suffrage Association Records: Subject File, -1953; The Lily. - 1953,* 1851, manuscript/mixed material, Library of Congress, accessed October 16, 2024, https://www.loc.gov/item/mss3413201744/.

ABOVE Illustration from a temperance pledge, ca. 1841. Thomas S. Sinclair (lithographer), published by James Porter, photograph, Library of Congress, accessed October 16, 2024, https://www.loc.gov/item/97503997/.

LEFT "Student's Calisthenium at Vassar," *Scribner's Monthly*, August 1871: 345.

"Ladies' and Misses' Bathing or Gymnastic Suit," *Harper's Bazaar* VI, no. 30 (1873): 455. Hathitrust, accessed Oct 16, 2024, blob:https://babel.hathitrust.org/ec015224-9223-4f63-9cdd-e0c391c0a183.

CLOCKWISE FROM TOP LEFT

Lizzie Bunnell Read, from *A Woman of the Century: Fourteen Hundred-Seventy Biographical Sketches Accompanied by Portraits of Leading American Women in All Walks of Life*, ed. Frances Elizabeth Willard and Mary A. Livermore, 1893; *Frances Dana Barker Gage, -1884, half-length portrait*, n.d., photograph, https://www.loc.gov/item/2005678060/; *Portrait of Annie Savery*. State Historical Society of Iowa, Des Moines; Dr. Mary Walker. C.M. Bell, *Walker, Dr. Mary.*, between 1873 and ca. 1916, photograph, https://www.loc.gov/item/2016713273/.

CLOCKWISE FROM TOP LEFT

Mary Livermore. Chicago History Museum, ICHi-051132; Amelia and Dexter Bloomer in front of their house in Council Bluffs. Courtesy of Seneca Falls Historical Society; Lizzie Boynton Harbert, from *A Woman of the Century: Fourteen Hundred-Seventy Biographical Sketches Accompanied by Portraits of Leading American Women in All Walks of Life*, ed. Frances Elizabeth Willard and Mary A. Livermore, 1893; Arabella (Belle) Babb Mansfield. Courtesy of the Iowa Department of Human Rights, Iowa Women's Hall of Fame; Mary Coggeshall. University of Iowa, Libraries, Iowa Women's Archives.

THIS PAGE, TOP George Simons, "Omaha Indian Village," Council Bluffs Public Library, accessed October 16, 2024, https://archive.councilbluffslibrary.org/items/show/4484.

THIS PAGE, BOTTOM George Simons, "Steamer Omaha," Council Bluffs Public Library, accessed October 16, 2024, https://archive.councilbluffslibrary.org/items/show/4487.

Library Special Collections, "Council Bluffs in 1851," Council Bluffs Public Library, accessed October 16, 2024, https://archive.councilbluffslibrary.org/items/show/4315.

Victoria Woodhull speaking on behalf of a suffrage delegation. *Washington, D.C. The Judiciary Committee of the House of Representatives receiving . . .*,1871, photograph, accessed October 16, 2024, https://www.loc.gov/item/2004670399/. The woman speaking is identified as Victoria Woodhull in the text of the accompanying article (p. 347).

CHAPTER 12

Ho! For Iowa!

O n his solo tour of the West in 1854, when Dexter first got off a stagecoach in Council Bluffs in front of the Pacific House hotel, he thought he "had gotten into a very rough looking place." It had taken him five days to travel three hundred miles on dry roads from the nearest railroad station in Davenport.

The United States conquered land farther and farther west, driving out and massacring the Native peoples and confining them on government-controlled reservations. Between 1847 and 1855, Congress granted almost sixty-one million acres of land to white veterans of every war in the nation's history and their heirs. It also legalized the transfer and sale of land warrants. This opened up a huge market for speculation. Warrant brokers in the East supplied land agents in the West, who purchased warrants cheaply and sold them on a standard one-year credit advance, or "bond for deed." Speculators snapped up much of the land and resold it at a profit before the end of the year, some to settlers, much of it to other speculators.[297]

This was Dexter's new choice of work. Like most white people, he regarded the conquest of the land and genocide of its peoples as natural and inevitable. The sufferings of Native people might inspire the Bloomers' pity but not their outrage.

Council Bluffs was still a small collection of roughhewn buildings in the prairie by the broad, brown Missouri River, with one unpaved central road that petered out into footpaths through tall grass and sunflowers. After a poorly attended Protestant service that Sunday in a small room with a few benches and a crate for a pulpit, Dexter went to the Mormon Tabernacle in the afternoon. He found the sermon interesting, the more so because the Smith family had lived near his father's house for a time. He had a clear childhood memory of hearing Joseph Smith tell "of the appearance of the Angel and of his finding the golden plate from which the Book of Mormon was written."[298]

He explored the area. Lovely valleys among the bluffs were covered in bushes and cottonwood trees or grass and flowers, not the dense hardwood forests that had confronted settlers in his home state. Dry, warm winds swept across land free of disease-breeding marshes and swamps, and bushels of scarlet-gold wild plums were sold in the market.[299] Native people were visible around town, but the Omaha had recently signed a treaty to cede their land and move north to a reservation.

One day, while returning to Council Bluffs from Omaha, Dexter saw "a small white building . . . near the foot of the sloping bluffs." It was well away from any street or fence, a two-room unfinished frame house on blocks with a clear view over the prairie to the river. He found the owner and bought it for $250 down and $300 the following May. The man promised to finish it by then.[300]

February 1855 found the Bloomers in Amelia's sister Elvira's house in snowy Waterloo. In the parlor where she and Dexter had been married, Amelia read in the papers how heavy storms had blocked the railroads in and out of Chicago for a week and made roads impassable. Steam engines froze, and at least one trainload of passengers burned benches for warmth and raided the freight for food.[301] Iowa might be only a few days from New York in June, but in winter, it would be another matter. On the positive side, a Maine Law passed the Iowa legislature, though, as always, enforcement would be the next question.

Her women's rights friends in New York continued to speak and write and lobby, with Anthony as their leader.[302] In March, Bloomer went to the first women's rights meeting ever held in Waterloo.

The harsh winter lingered, and the distant Missouri River stayed frozen later than usual.[303] Dexter lectured in Seneca Falls on "The Great West" in hopes of convincing people to follow them out to Iowa.[304] Bloomer ventured into the cold three evenings to give double lectures in Cayuga County on temperance and women's rights. She would have given four but again had to cancel the first one due to illness, and Dexter gave her audience his description of Council Bluffs. Their host, Martha Beatty, reported on the talks to *The Lily* and expressed her concern for Bloomer. "Oh, for more such women in the field . . . But I fear unless the balmy atmosphere of our western prairies renovates her health, it will be long, if ever, ere we see her face, or hear her earnest tone for woman again."[305]

On March 20, the Bloomers set out for Iowa with a niece who was traveling to Illinois. After visits to relatives in Buffalo and Chicago, they caught the train to St. Louis.[306]

The railroad carried them through "vast prairies . . . in an almost unbroken condition," and they often saw deer and other wildlife from the windows. At St. Louis, they learned that the Missouri River was still too low for steamship navigation as far as Council Bluffs. They could wait or go back to Keokuk, nearly two hundred miles north, and take the stagecoach. Rain seemed imminent, so they found a hotel and paid a visit to Amelia's dear friend Frances Gage, who welcomed them joyfully and insisted that they stay with her and her family.[307]

The Gages had moved to St. Louis from Ohio two years earlier. It was "a much finer city" than the Bloomers expected, almost twice the size of Chicago. But it was Bloomer's first time in a slave state. "Outwardly there is little evidence of its existence here, yet it exerts an influence upon society which is felt to the very core . . . one word of condemnation of a system so unjust and barbarous, would mark me out as an object worthy of the severest censure and punishment." The Kansas-Nebraska Act, passed the year before, had sparked violence over the question of slavery in neighboring Kansas.

But the city election during their stay "was a temperance triumph." There had been an election riot the year before, but this year, the mayor closed the grog shops and told mothers to keep their boys in at night. The town was so calm, Bloomer heard a man say that "women might have gone to the ballot box and deposited a vote, with perfect propriety." Temperance was making gains nationwide. Liquor prohibition finally passed in New York, and it passed in the Nebraska Territory, and a referendum was underway in Iowa.[308]

Bloomer took advantage of the travel delay to organize a successful women's suffrage meeting with Gage. It was met with some insults and condemnations, but, Gage wrote to Birdsall, "such things only made more talk and discussion, which is all we want."[309]

At the end of the week, the Bloomers decided to leave their furniture to be shipped after them and take a boat seven days up the river west to St. Joseph, and then a stagecoach. They booked a stateroom in the elegant new *Edinburg*.

Onboard, there were at least a hundred other passengers in the cabin and many more on deck. Bloomer gathered that about fifteen states were represented among them, and not in a positive way by some, who, she thought, must have been raised "in the back woods." She had rarely encountered anyone, especially women, with such rough manners. Many of these frontierspeople appeared much as Mark Twain would later describe the Missourians of his youth, and Bloomer had a moral struggle with her distaste. "Naturally they may have warm hearts, kindly feelings and a fair share of intellect; but circumstances are against them." She could not regard them as social equals, "yet we should strive to better their condition, and by our courteous bearing endeavor to stimulate in them a desire for improvement and a reaching after better things."

Snags and sandbars frequently brought the *Edinburg* to a sudden stop or startled the passengers with a crash and scrape as the hull struck an underwater log. The boat following them stove a hole in her side and had to unload and return to St. Louis for repair.

For part of the trip, an enslaved Black woman of about twenty, visibly ill and in the custody of her master's agent, traveled with them. Bloomer learned that she had been sent to be sold in New Orleans but was declared unsound due to advanced tuberculosis and was being returned. The agent took her off the boat at Independence. "Poor thing!" wrote Bloomer. "Her chains will soon be broken; but how much she has yet to suffer ere then none can tell."

Bloomer was invited by the captain and some passengers to give her lecture on women's rights, which she managed to make heard over the noise of the boat's machinery. The next evening, a dance was organized. The passengers were shy, but Bloomer was bored and needed exercise. She led the way, and "others soon followed me upon the floor, and evening passed off pleasantly."[310]

At St. Joseph, a small supply town for migrants heading west, they found they had just missed the stage to Council Bluffs and were stranded for two days at "a very ordinary" hotel. High winds kicked up clouds of dust, and Bloomer caught a cold. The evening of their departure, she was visited by two men with a petition inviting her to give a women's rights lecture. They claimed they could collect an audience in an hour. Bloomer did not see how that was possible, but she agreed. "I had never yet refused to proclaim the new doctrine of woman's rights when I found people anxious to hear." She ran upstairs to tell Dexter and change into a lecturing dress. But before she could get the trunk straps undone, they were startled by a "great outcry and ringing of bells on the street." Enslaved men were sent out with dinner bells to announce the lecture, and when Bloomer arrived at the courthouse, it was full of people eager to see the first "woman agitator" to visit St. Joseph.

After her lecture, they hurried back to the hotel. Bloomer had just taken off her hat when she was called down to the parlor again. The same two gentlemen wanted an encore the next day. This time, she refused. "At two o'clock on a rainy morning, feeling tired and sick," she boarded the stagecoach for Council Bluffs.[311]

After dozing on and off until morning between Dexter and the window, Bloomer woke up enough to evaluate the other passengers. She was, as she expected, the only woman on the stage. They were nine inside, mostly young men, wedged three to a bench for two days and a night, with occasional breaks to get out and stretch, find a privy, and eat. One man turned out to be

Kit Carson, the legendary American frontiersman. "Having heard much of him we eyed him with a good deal of interest and curiosity, but saw nothing remarkable about him except his clothes, which were of buckskin, fringed around the bottom, wrists and collar, a style entirely new to me."

The last of the other passengers got out at the Nebraska ferry. On their fifteenth wedding anniversary, Sunday, April 15, 1855, the Bloomers arrived in Glenwood, and for the first time, Amelia set foot on Iowa soil. It was a beautiful day, and the countryside was green and gently rolling. They decided to walk ahead while the stage changed horses, and they stopped in a lovely grove to enjoy the scenery and eat a picnic lunch until the stage caught up with them.

At Council Bluffs, they took a room at the Pacific House, and the next morning, they walked over to see their little house. The walls were still bare lath, and it had no kitchen. Dexter found the owner, and when the plastering was done, Amelia alone signed the deed to complete the purchase.[312] Women could own property in Iowa.

As usual, her fame preceded her. Three days after their arrival, the *Council Bluffs Chronicle* reported that she "still pertinaciously adheres to the wearing of the *reform* costume, which has gained her a worldwide notoriety."[313]

After two weeks, their furniture had still not arrived, and one of their trunks contained grafted fruit tree seedlings and shrubs that had started to sprout. They moved into their house with a borrowed table and two chairs. Standing in the front doorway, Bloomer could see across three miles of fresh green "bottom land" to the river. Clear streams flowed through it, and hundreds of cattle grazed on the grasses and wildflowers. She saw birds and a few wild elk. On either side of the valley were the yellow marl bluffs, between 50 and 250 feet high. In the evenings, the elk would walk up past her house to sleep on top of the bluff.[314]

They bought a used sheet-iron stove and some dishes, and Bloomer made up their bed on the plank floor. Dexter built a rough board kitchen and laundry room onto the back, which flooded every time a hard rain sent water sheeting down the bluff. It was uncomfortable, and embarrassing when people visited, but Amelia knew that it was temporary. And she soon realized that many of her neighbors were in similar situations.[315]

In May, two weeks after their move, she wrote to Mary Vaughan and told her how strange it felt to have nothing to do but keep house "after the many and various duties devolving upon me for the last six or seven years ... I have commenced life as it were anew."

About the time the Bloomers moved in, a group of Pawnee set up camp on the top of a bluff nearby. They spoke "tolerably fair English" and visited the Bloomers often, but after about a week, they said goodbye and set off west. Bloomer told Vaughan, "There is something interesting to me in these children of nature and I almost regretted their departure ... Their parting from their old home and the graves of their fathers is said by those who witnessed it to have been exceedingly interesting and pathetic. The women and the aged men wept, and the stout-hearted warriors could ill conceal their emotion of tenderness and affection." Her sympathy for them was not deep. Women could buy property in Iowa, she told Vaughan, and she hoped they would take advantage of the opportunity.[316]

The minister of the storefront Congregationalist church invited Bloomer to a ladies' church fundraising meeting. They elected her president, and another newcomer, Sophia Douglass, first director, "thus putting their affairs into the hands of two Episcopalians."[317]

In the evenings, Bloomer walked up to the top of the bluff behind their house to watch the sun set over the plains beyond Omaha and breathe the sweet evening air. There, she imagined "the day when this wild bottom will be filled with the hum and stir, and thronging multitude of a large city and these bluffs covered with elegant residences, and tasteful retreats from the turmoil and activity that will reign below."[318] In bed at night, on the floor, she listened to the sounds of animals and insects, the wind in the grasses, and the creaking boughs of the cottonwood trees.

Council Bluffs now had almost two thousand inhabitants and three hotels but no sidewalks. Most new houses were log cabins sided with cottonwood boards, and most roads were footpaths.

Bloomer enjoyed it all "vastly." She took long walks and got to know her neighbors. There was little social hierarchy. Everyone knew everyone else, went to the same church, and "joined in the same festivities."

After supper one night, with Dexter out at a railroad planning meeting, Bloomer sat at their one table to write, with a lamp lit and the front door open to the transformed prairie view. "The tall dry grass of last year's growth on this land is on fire, for about half a mile in extent, and the flames sweeping off towards the river are devouring everything in their path . . . The whole country round is illuminated by the bright flames, which dance and crackle as they sweep on their course, while the columns of white smoke, rising high in the heavens, set off by the dark horizon, which forms the background beyond, add greatly to the beauty of the scene."

Sawmills and brickyards supplied the rapid destruction and development of the prairie. "Gardens are being fenced, trees planted, streets opened and graded . . . The city is extending out on the bottoms towards the river." The settlers believed that those rich lands were "high and dry, and in no danger of being overflowed."[319] They hoped to be the terminus of the first railroad across the state within three years, which would continue out to California until Council Bluffs became the center of the nation.

There was still no rain, and the Bloomers' well went dry. They carried in water for their own needs, but their New York plants died under the hot sun or were bitten off by rabbits.[320] Dexter found an office and advertised himself as an attorney, counselor, and land agent. By the end of June, he had listed over a hundred lots suitable for businesses and farms.[321]

Back East, Lucy Stone was married at last to Henry B. Blackwell, brother of the famous Dr. Elizabeth Blackwell. Like the Bloomers fifteen years before, they had the word "obey" omitted from the service, and they appended and published a "protest against the laws of marriage." Stone remained "Miss Stone." There was a predictable uproar about this in the papers. Bloomer enjoyed Gage's defense of them in *The Lily*. Their feelings on the subject were much the same, and Bloomer wrote: "Yes, I am glad Lucy is married, and glad they made a protest."[322]

The Iowa state ban on liquor sales was to go into effect that July. Bloomer wrote in favor for the local paper and praised the editor's opposition to horse races.[323] They reprinted her column describing Council Bluffs for *The Lily*, which also acted as an advertisement for Dexter's land agency and her own wish for friends.[324]

A week before the end of June, Bloomer's household goods arrived—two and a half months late. She joyfully set aside her writing to plunge into the hot work of "the unpacking, and the stowing away, and general turning upside down and confusion of various articles," followed by "hanging paper, putting down carpets, setting the furniture to rights, and getting things generally in living order."

Bloomer was invited to give the Fourth of July oration at a town 120 miles east of Council Bluffs, but she could not face the trip in the heat.[325] On the holiday, she woke at dawn to the familiar boom of cannon. She dressed with a sense of "joy and thankfulness for all the many blessings which have been bestowed upon us as a people." In the morning, she and Dexter attended festivities in Glendale, where they had first arrived together, and learned that it was still known as "Hang Hollow" by some because a murderer had been hung there. People pointed out the limb of the gallows tree.

At midday, they crossed the river for a dinner with some state officials in Omaha. By the time they got to the Douglass House, the speeches were over, and a lavish table was laid under a bower of tree branches next to the hotel. But despite the new prohibition law, "liquor flowed freely."[326] Bloomer had not been part of such a scene for fifteen years, and her holiday mood sank into horror and pity as she watched men and women drink alcoholic toasts, and a drunk young man babble dull nonsense for over an hour at the speaker's stand. Later, she wrote, "those now in power are anti-temperance, pro-slavery, Administration, Douglas Democrats, and little is to be hoped or expected from that party in favor of morality and human rights."[327] They returned to the sober celebration in Council Bluffs, but her sadness colored her evening.

It is unclear when Bloomer realized that two of her distant cousins had moved to Omaha two weeks before herself. Charlotte Kennedy Turner was married to the wealthy businessman Charles Turner, and her sister Hannah would become Bloomer's close friend.

All the New York and Ohio conventions and meetings for fall were announced in *The Lily*, with long lists of the names of her old friends.[328] She wished she could join them, but it was too far, and she resigned herself to following them in the papers.[329] But then Mary Birdsall in Richmond became ill, and there was a gap in the arrival of *The Lily*.[330] Bloomer depended on it now, as her more isolated readers always had. She had found no equivalent community in Council Bluffs. "I judge that the Spirit of Reform does not dwell here ... With one or two exceptions ... there is an absence of interest in subjects affecting the rights and happiness of humanity—among the women especially." There were almost no traveling lecturers or concerts and limited access to new books, and she missed her wealth of exchange papers and meetings. She had to hope this would all improve with time, and with the railroad.

Sympathy in letters from the East did not help. She appreciated being remembered, but she often felt most isolated after reading a friendly letter. "But I would not have my friends think of me as sad and lonely in my chosen retreat—for I really am not. Some sad hours I have had ... and I have then sighed—not to return—but that I ever wandered away." But when she got back to work, or went for a walk, or paid a visit to a new friend, "such feelings speedily pass away, and I am happy and contented."

Still, there was much to adjust to in her new home. The nearness of the slave state of Missouri hovered over her. When an article in the *Council Bluffs Chronotype* recommended a "female academy" in St. Joseph, Missouri, she wrote to counterrecommend the State University in Iowa City, which educated the sexes together and where the soil was not "cursed with slavery."[331] The literal fruit of that soil was in the market at Council Bluffs too, the only apples and peaches available, though there were also cheap bushels of local wild plums.[332] She dried apples and made preserves and pickles, familiar tasks she had done almost every year since childhood.

One "prominent woman" told Bloomer that she opposed women's rights and that she believed that if women could vote, "there would be more women than men vote against the Maine Law." Bloomer found that hard to believe. "If such is the case with the women here, this place is an exception to the rest of the world." The new law meant that no new liquor licenses had been issued in Council Bluffs, but there were still drunkards in the streets. The Sons of Temperance had a new chapter in town but only allowed women as "visiting members," so Bloomer refused to waste her time on them. Not even in church had she heard anything in support of temperance or the state liquor ban. She was not optimistic about enforcement.[333]

By the end of August, she had been proven correct. The liquor trade in Council Bluffs continued, and men told them it was pointless to complain because the constables opposed temperance and chose the juries. But if she had to start over again from scratch with temperance, women's rights, and all she most valued, she would.[334]

October came, with "cool frosty nights, [and] warm sunny, golden-hued days." After the first frosts, the Bloomers had lit their heating stove, "but now fires are again put out, and the evenings are so warm that we sit with doors and windows open."[335] Controlled burns on the prairies scented the air with smoke. Horse races and runaway teams endangered pedestrians and smashed carriages and coaches.

Native people were more numerous in the streets and in their autumn settlement along the river. One day, while Bloomer sat sewing indoors, a shadow darkened her window. "On looking up, I saw the faces of two Indians pressed against the glass." They gazed around her room and left. She was glad they did not come in. She still found them "friendly and harmless" but no longer enjoyed trying to talk with them, called them "filthy and disgusting," and disliked "their begging propensity." That afternoon, they came back and stole two pickling melons from her kitchen steps. They did not return, though "a number" were camped not far from their house. "They have no tent, but their fire is blazing brightly, and as I sit writing, their singing and laughter is clearly borne upon the wind to my ears."[336] As their settlements by the river grew, their drums and songs at night alarmed the white settlers until, a local paper said, they reported them to the marshal "as a nuisance, and soon had the pleasure of seeing their camp on fire, and the natives on the march for other quarters."[337]

Bloomer was busy preparing her home for winter and missed her old life less. She wrote less too, "for now that I am not jagged up by the printers calling for copy . . . I feel a growing disinclination to write at all." She still believed in her causes, but she needed rest and had more immediate distractions.[338]

Small steps in introducing the Yankee culture of the East were being made. An Iowa grand jury gave Bloomer a pleasant surprise by indicting several Council Bluffs citizens for selling liquor, gambling, and horse racing.[339] A new literary society for both men and women began to host lectures and debates. She attended a debate on women's suffrage, which attracted a full house, though the arguments, all by men, struck her as naïve and uninformed. When they finished, Bloomer stood up and replied to what she could in the ten minutes allotted. The three male judges decided against, 2–1, and then an appeal was made to the audience, who reversed the decision.[340] They invited her back to lecture on the subject.

She and Dexter helped found the Frontier Lodge of Good Templars, and Dexter spoke to the literary society on "Self-Culture." He emphasized the need for good schools and better access to books and newspapers and edifying lectures, and he recommended that everyone develop their writing and speaking skills.[341] The discussion question for the next meeting was: "Resolved: that there can be a justifiable cause for war."[342]

Amelia gave a Thanksgiving evening address on temperance in the Congregational church, her first speech in Council Bluffs. Despite freezing weather and a "hop" at the Pacific House, the pews were full.[343] The *Chronotype* editor praised her and hoped she might speak next on women's suffrage, with the caveat that he was noncommittal on that issue himself.[344] She did so at the end of the month to a good crowd at the receptive literary society.[345] "Had the people there assembled had the power of deciding the question, we should have had our rights guaranteed us at once. I find there is quite a strong feeling among women here in favor of our cause, though they are silent on the subject unless there is something to call out an expression of opinion."[346]

Shortly after Christmas, she received an invitation to repeat her talk before the Nebraska legislature signed by twenty-five of the members. She accepted, and the date was set for January 8, 1856.[347]

It was a bitter winter, and the cold was often fatal to the poor. People trotted through the streets when they had to go out, so bundled up in shawls, blankets, and buffalo robes they could not be recognized. The day before Bloomer was to speak to the Nebraska legislature, the temperature dropped to twenty-three below.[348] But, at 7:00 on the appointed evening, she arrived at the statehouse in Omaha, calm and prepared, and shed her heavy outer garments to reveal an elegant and simple long-skirted gown. No observer commented on her clothes.

General William Larimer, an abolitionist and Whig from Pennsylvania, escorted her through the crowded house to the platform, which was so packed she "hardly had elbow-room." Larimer introduced her in a "silence so profound that one could almost hear a pin drop."[349]

As she laid out her arguments, she saw "that they were telling upon my listeners."[350] It is a principle of all free government, she told them, "that the *people* rule; and as *all* the people must be subject to the laws, all should have a voice in their formation . . . Deny to any class in community the right to be heard at the ballot box, and that class sinks at once into a state of dependence, of civil insignificance, which nothing can save from subjugation, oppression, and wrong . . . The enfranchisement of woman . . . will place society upon a higher moral and social elevation than it has ever yet attained."

She later reported to *The Lily*, "I was listened to with the most absorbed interest to the end . . . Then came great applause."

The editor of *The Nebraskian* wrote that he thought "all persons of candor . . . will at least acknowledge that she is certainly a most pleasing and logical speaker, and that she handled the subject with great ability . . . we think she is very much of a *gentleman*."[351] The *Chronotype* reporter said, "we watched her closely, and saw that she was perfectly self-possessed—not a nerve seemed to be moved by excitement, and the voice did not tremble . . . She delivered her lecture in a pleasing, able, and, we dare say, eloquent manner that enchained the attention of her audience for an hour and a half. A man could not have beat it."

Another wrote that he found her arguments "unanswerable . . . Mrs. Bloomer, though a little body, is among the great women of the United States; and her keen, intellectual eye seems to flash fire from a fountain that will consume the stubble of old theories until woman is placed in her true position in the enjoyment of equal rights and privileges. Her only danger is in asking too much." The image of reform renewing society as fire renewed the prairie would have pleased her.

To her astonishment, General Larimer drew up and introduced a bill to grant women's suffrage in Nebraska. Many women attended the heated discussion. It passed, 14–11, and was sent to the Legislative Council, and then, as often seemed to happen, they ran out of time. Bloomer was later assured by members and by Governor William Richardson "that the bill would undoubtedly have passed had a little more time been allowed them."[352] A local correspondent to the *New York Tribune* said that "This is probably the nearest approach to a realization of the principles of our Women's Right's advocates, that has ever occurred."[353] Another wrote to the *New York Times* that some members talked about resigning "rather than sit one day longer with such a set of 'woman's rights fanatics.' Many voted for it doubtless in jest."

In the midst of the conflict, four of Larimer's opponents presented him with a petticoat as a symbolic insult, "over which there came near being a general melee." This gesture often included forcing the legislator to put it on, but they did not go that far. It was enough. The bill was dead, and so was Larimer's legislative career in Nebraska.[354]

"He is a true Woman's Rights man," Bloomer wrote to *The Lily*, "and for his efforts in their behalf is entitled to the thanks and the gratitude of the whole sex." Though the bill failed, "to their honor be it spoken, the House of Representatives of Nebraska gave a decision in favor of granting to women equal, civil and political rights with man!"[355]

The petticoat insult of that session rankled her. Not long after, she read of a similar one in Quincy, Iowa, in which twenty women made the same gesture to a senator who dodged a fistfight with a visiting Kansas colonel after calling him a traitor. She wrote a column for the *Chronotype* on "Petticoat Presentation."[356] It was bad enough "that men were willing to dishonor the mothers who bore them and the wives they have chosen for life-companions, by thus selecting their garment as the most fitting badge of cowardice, of meanness, of treachery . . . when woman imitates them in wrong doing, and desecrates her own garment to so bad a use, it is doubly to be deplored."[357]

As the Whig Party splintered into Northern and Southern wings over the extension of slavery into the Western territories, a coalition opposed to the extension of slavery came together in the new Republican Party. The Bloomers joined it. This year, Dexter became a city alderman and an editor of the *Chronotype*, now the first Republican paper west of Des Moines.[358] In January, Bloomer and Sophia Douglass held a successful fundraising fair and supper that paid for the floor and pews of the new Congregational church.[359]

That month, there were "tremendous snowstorms" across Iowa. It was the worst winter in years.[360] But in Council Bluffs, there was just enough snow for sleighing, and by the end of the month, the storms had cleared and the days were cold and bright.

Bloomer gave two more lectures in February.[361] Each month, *The Lily* arrived, looking much as it always had. One interesting column discussed the traditional legal rights of Seneca women. The Seneca required a two-thirds majority of mothers to agree to any treaty, said the author, while white women could not expect their government to listen to them at all.[362] Bloomer ended her formal corresponding editorship for *The Lily*, but she continued to write for it. She wrote up her experience with the Nebraska legislature and her lectures in Council Bluffs, which were probably her last for the winter. "The field for such labor is not very extensive here. The country is sparsely settled, and the facilities for travelling tedious . . . and besides I do not wish to engage in the business very extensively, as neither my health nor home duties will admit of it."

CHAPTER 13
The Domestic Sphere

New stores opened in downtown Council Bluffs, and by the spring of 1856, common luxuries became available to Bloomer once again: dry goods, hardware, housewares, clothing, medicines, and books. Two new temperance societies took over a large hall and held regular evening meetings. Dexter helped organize a Union Sunday School for the churches. He bought the lot next to their home, ploughed and fenced a new garden, and filled it with fruit bushes, vines, and trees. He built an addition to their house so that they now had a real kitchen, a spare bedroom, and a dining room. But rainstorms still occasionally sent floods of water into the back of the house, once enough that it poured through the kitchen door and covered the floors with mud.[363]

It was about this time that Bloomer gave up her short dress and trousers. She was thirty-eight years old. She wrote to a friend about the decision. She wanted to make new friends in her new home and "felt at times like donning long skirts when I went into society, at parties, etc." The high winds often turned her short skirts over her head and shoulders in the street, but she had "persevered ... till after the introduction of hoops. Finding them light and pleasant to wear and doing away with the necessity for heavy underskirts ... I gradually left off the short dress ... I felt my influence would be greater in the dress ordinarily worn by women." She still liked the short dress, especially for work, and everyone in Council Bluffs had treated her with respect when she wore it. But now she felt it was more important to fit in.[364] Hoops were not without controversy; many critics complained that they gave ludicrous volume to skirts, and without underskirts, women were in more danger of flashing their drawers. But they were an accepted, Paris-endorsed fashion.

Despite this change, the fame of the trousers still pursued her. In August 1856, *The Lily* reported on the National Dress Reform Association's first annual meeting. Bloomer was listed as a vice president, though she did not attend.[365] She did write a response to an article that claimed that *The Lily* was founded to promote hydropathy, abolitionism, and dress reform, and that Stanton had been the editor and had abandoned the short dress.[366] "I cannot remain silent," she wrote. *The Lily* was a temperance paper by and for women. Stanton wrote on temperance at the beginning and "never, at any period, or for any time, had the least control over the paper," and she had stopped writing for *The Lily* well before Bloomer sold it. Bloomer did not consider herself a great writer, "but after all the hard labor I have gone through establishing and sustaining The Lily for many years, and after all the censure and odium I have borne on account of my dress, I am not willing to be deprived of what credit rightfully belongs to me or to have it supposed that . . . I have been only a willing instrument in the hands of others."[367]

In the summer of 1856, a family arrived in Council Bluffs that would alter the Bloomers' lives: Joseph and Eliza Lewis and their seven young children. They arrived as part of a Mormon handcart company of poor converts brought over from Europe and organized by their church leadership to walk twelve hundred miles to the Utah settlement.

Joseph Lewis was a small disabled man raised in poverty. Eliza was pregnant and in poor health. Their land journey alternated between blazing heat and terrible thunderstorms that turned the roads to slick, ankle-deep mud.[368] They had no tent, and at the Iowa City camp, Eliza gave birth in the rain, on the ground. One week later, they set off again for a town north of Omaha, a 250-mile, eleven-day walk on starvation rations, the children all sick with malaria and scurvy. At Florence, the company met to decide whether to go on. It was dangerously late in the season, and a returning missionary urged them to spend the winter there. About a hundred, including the Lewis family, stayed, and about four hundred continued with their leader, James Willie, toward the mountains.[369]

Lewis rented a small, uninsulated house in Council Bluffs. That winter, as much as six feet of snow fell. Charitable women, Bloomer among them, helped keep the family alive, but Eliza died of typhoid in the spring. The charitable women offered to take the children, but at this point, Lewis refused.

When Mary Thomas, the new coeditor of *The Lily*, asked Bloomer for more regular contributions, Bloomer replied after some delay. She apologized for her silence and blamed it on the extra work of spring and "so poor health as to oblige me, much of the time, to refrain from all mental and physical labor."

Dexter built a stable and bought a pony and a sporty open carriage called a phaeton. Amelia learned to drive and began to take herself out for drives in the country as well as on errands.[370] Dexter ran for mayor in 1857 but lost.[371] In August, he and Amelia and other members of St. Paul's Church held a ceremonial laying of the cornerstone for their new building.[372]

In September 1857, Bloomer traveled east. She visited friends and family in St. Louis, Chicago, and six towns in New York, all in cold, wet weather—an unpleasant contrast with the climate she had left behind. Everywhere she went, her loved ones were anxious and sad, preoccupied with the latest economic panic. On her return to St. Louis, she found she had just missed the weekly trip of the *Omaha* to Council Bluffs. She gritted her teeth and caught a train and another steamboat to Leavenworth in the volatile Kansas Territory to pick up the *Omaha* there. Some slave owners on board learned her name and insisted she argue slavery with them. "They seemed to imagine me a sort of second Mrs. Stowe, gathering materials for a book, and manifested . . . considerable anxiety to know what I would say about them." The debate was mostly civil, and she was glad when it was over.

In Leavenworth, she waited "two long lonely anxious days" at the Planters House, a hotel known as a pro-slavery headquarters. She was about to despair and find another way home when the *Omaha* arrived. She boarded with great relief and ran into some Council Bluffs friends who accompanied her on the long, jarring last leg "of snags and sand-bars." This whole journey, she would write to her friend Harriet Torrey, she found hotels and handled her luggage and "never once felt the need of a *Protector!*"[373]

Requests for autographs and information on reform dress still arrived in her mail. She answered one question about the dress reform revival, saying that she wished them well but felt the experiment had been done and did not see any reason why it would succeed now.[374]

Over the summer of 1857, the British Mormon migrant Joseph Lewis had continued to search for work. But the bad economy made decent jobs scarce, and that autumn, after Bloomer's return, he decided to give up his "six bright little children." Twelve-year-old Mary was adopted by a wealthy banker's wife. Four of the boys went to families who eventually launched them on good careers. The fifth, four-year-old Edward Philip Lewis, was adopted by the Bloomers. They changed his name to Edward Dexter Bloomer and called him Eddie.[375]

Bloomer was now thirty-nine. Their niece Jennie also came to live with them part-time, and Bloomer's transition back into the domestic realm was nearly complete. The energy and organizational skill that she had put into reform work now went to her immediate community and church. She housed and fed any clergy, lecturers, or reformers in need of a place to stay. Once, when Dexter was away, she was alarmed when her guest for the night, who was fleeing the guerilla war in Kansas, showed up at her doorstep "armed both with bowie-knife and revolver." But she took him in. She continued to apply her intellect to her reading and her religion and loved to debate clergymen. On one occasion, Dexter came home from his office at midday for dinner and was amused to find her arguing with a visiting minister over the breakfast table, "all preparations for dinner being forgotten."[376] She and Dexter both continued to give occasional lectures on cultural and social issues.[377]

That winter, she agreed to give a lecture on the education of women to benefit the Library Association in Omaha. Ordinarily, to get there, she would take a stagecoach and a ferry. But the river had frozen, and when she arrived at the landing on the Council Bluffs side, she found the ice breaking up. Her only option was a broad flatboat, poled across by a ferryman. The prospect frightened her, and she considered turning back. "But I remembered my engagement and saw a carriage waiting for me on the other shore; so, with many misgivings and assurances from the boatmen, I ventured on board and was landed safely."

Her lecture went well, and afterward, she returned to the ferry landing. The wind had picked up, and when she saw the state of the river, her heart "fairly stood still . . . I found it filled with great blocks of floating ice." The only boat willing to attempt the crossing was a skiff rowed by two boatmen. They agreed to take a man but refused to take her. "I thought of my danger . . . and I thought of husband and child awaiting me at home, and no one to care for them." Why could she not cross as well as the man? They said it was because women would get frightened and tip the boat. She said, "If I will promise to sit very still and not stir, can I go?" The male passenger argued for her, and she was allowed to get in. "I sat in the middle of my seat and held on to each side of the boat, and I am sure I never stirred a muscle or winked an eye or hardly breathed while those brave men guided their skiff over the tossing waves, which seemed to engulf us at times and anon bore us on their tossing crests. Soon we were safely over and landed, ready to take stage for home . . . and on my part resolved never to incur a like danger again."[378]

In February of 1858, Dexter made a less harrowing crossing to give a lecture on "Modern Discovery and Invention" to the Library Association. A reviewer said it was "tolerably written, and displayed a pretty fair knowledge" but was "not as instructive, nor was the elocution of the lecturer as good as that of his wife."[379]

By the spring, the economic panic was entrenched. Towns that owed money on railroad bonds suffered as the tax value of their land fell. Western expansion slowed and stopped. The value of the Bloomers' land investments fell too. [380]

In May, shortly before her fortieth birthday, Bloomer had the pleasant surprise of a letter from her friend Harriet Torrey. With Eddie hanging off the back of her chair and climbing up to sit on her shoulders, she wrote a long reply. Torrey asked if she loved the West. Bloomer replied that she loved it as much as she had expected. "So far as we now know, I shall spend my days here, and be laid to rest, at last, on one of the high bluffs overlooking the mighty Missouri, and the beautiful plains of Nebraska beyond." She still missed her old friends and her old work. "When I look back upon the years that have passed since the Lily sprang into existence, and see . . . what strides forward women have taken—I am astonished, and almost doubt its reality at times. In my present isolated and inactive position, the past and the part I have acted in it, seems almost like a dream."

An unpleasant shock arrived in the June 15 issue of *The Lily*. Her letter to Torrey was published in it, edited in ways that obscured and altered the meaning. After all the misrepresentations and ridicule, and the loss of her influence and community, to see her words distorted in *The Lily* seems to have made something in Bloomer snap. She wrote an outraged letter to Torrey and Birdsall that assumed the worst, and she mailed it.[381] Birdsall printed it.

To Bloomer, Torrey's version let readers imagine that Eddie was "one of the 'five children' whom our opponents credited me with a few years ago, and who received so much sympathy on account of being neglected . . . instead of letting my letter tell them that he is a little motherless, homeless, bright eyed rosy cheeked four year old, whom I rescued from suffering soon after my return home last fall, and who has ever since been a severe tax upon my time, patience, and needle. Did she wish them to believe the story of my neglected children true? Or did she intend to convey the idea that he was a son of my old age? Whatever her intention . . . she deserves punishment;

and as her ears are not within reach of my hand or my voice, I will expose her and tell what I think of her through The Lily. And I care not whether she likes it or not."

She turned on Birdsall next. "I have cause of complaint against *you* too, first, that you occupied so much space with a letter containing so little of interest to a general reader; and second, that after giving so much room, you did not demand the whole letter, and give place to it entire, just as it passed from my hand . . . Now I am done scolding and I feel better; but I will be revenged on Harriet by not writing her any more 'notes' very soon; so she will not have a chance to make fun of me to the readers of the *Lily* or place me in a false light before them."

From there, her letter turned to politics. She and Torrey had agreed about Eastern women's rights leaders ignoring the West. "I believe there is as much talent in the West as in the East, and it would be well for Western women to have conventions of their own and do their own talking, instead of relying on Eastern leaders to carry on the work for them."

Birdsall commented below that she had printed Bloomer's letter because she mistakenly thought it was complete.[382] No other answers have survived. This reaction may have been Bloomer's last contribution to *The Lily*.

Its last issue seems to be one from July 1859. As the months went by, Bloomer made inquiries, and she understood that Birdsall had ended it without warning or explanation and that her thousands of readers were left almost as perplexed and bereft as herself.

In August 1859, Council Bluffs had an unexpected visit from one of the presidential candidates: Abraham Lincoln. When his steamboat was stranded on a sandbar, Lincoln's visit was prolonged for three days, and he gave a lecture by candlelight at Palmer's Hall. He was a good temperance man and was known as a great political debater. The Bloomers attended, along with much of the town. The following evening, his friend William H. M. Pusey gave a public reception for him attended by hundreds of people, including the Bloomers and their new friends Grenville and Ruth Ann Dodge.[383]

Dodge would become an important figure in the Civil War, the construction of the first transcontinental railroad, and the genocide of Native peoples, but at this time, he was a surveyor, banker, and city councilman in the Bloomer's social circle.

Through the spring and summer of 1859, Dexter continued to serve on committees, run for offices, and add to his résumé. As president of the school district committee, he helped organize the Council Bluffs School District under the new state education act.[384] He was an active leader of the local Republican Party. In early October, he was nominated for county judge and defeated, as he had been for mayor and district attorney, and for nomination to the legislature.[385] But the party was gaining strength as tensions increased between pro- and antislavery factions.

The economic panic meant more desperate poor, and fewer citizens willing to share what they had. Bloomer did all she could, but she found the community response lukewarm. She had founded a benevolent society in April, but they struggled to raise funds, and after they were swindled out of the take of a benefit lecture, they regretfully disbanded.[386]

Eddie's older sister Mary was rejected by her adoptive family. The Bloomers took her in and gave her their family name. She was fifteen now, and Eddie was six. At home in New York State, Bloomer's father died, and her mother moved in with her sister Adeline and her family.

Overall, 1860 was a less eventful year for the Bloomers. In May, Dexter took on a law partner, William Kinsman, an adventurous young lawyer, teacher, and writer.[387] In November, Dexter won a seat on the local school board, and Abraham Lincoln was elected president—the first Republican to hold that office—after campaigning against the expansion of slavery.[388] This election was a general triumph for the Council Bluffs Republican Party over the Democrats, who had won almost every one before. When the outcome became apparent, the Republicans organized a "grand jollification, illumination, and procession."

It began peacefully. Bloomer and her Republican neighbors set bright lamps in their windows. Businesses were illuminated downtown, and bonfires in the snowy streets blazed up to the evening sky. "Anvil cannon" were set off, in which two anvils were stacked with a charge of gunpowder between them, firing the upper one high into the air with a boom that echoed off the bluffs. Republicans loaded a wagon with their brass band and decorated it with two large backlit transparencies. One read, "Council Bluffs redeemed—Lincoln's majority 34." The other displayed a scaffold with a noose hanging from it, with the words "For DisUnionists." As the band played, this display was drawn by eight yokes of oxen through all the main streets of the town, followed by a growing crowd.

Outraged Democrats retaliated by parading their own transparencies that featured attacks on the Republican candidates. Some threw bricks at the Republican bandwagon and destroyed the display. When the procession stopped downtown for a speech from a local official, Democrats groaned and shouted him down and threw "bricks, stones, pieces of burning wood, and blazing rockets into the crowd" to drive them away. Women's skirts were set on fire, and many people were struck and hurt. The sheriff, mayor, and marshal were all present but did nothing, being Democrats themselves.[389]

The tensions over slavery that had simmered all of Bloomer's life were boiling over now, and all the attempts by men to save the union by compromising on this foundational moral question of human rights had ultimately failed. The nation was cracking apart.

CHAPTER 14

War and *The Mayflower*

On the evening of New Year's Day, 1861, Dexter came home from work with the first issue of a new newspaper addressed to Amelia. *The Mayflower* had been founded by Miss Lizzie Bunnell of Peru, Indiana, and the last coeditor of *The Lily*, Dr. Mary Thomas. Below the blocky letters of the masthead, which were thickly adorned with little flowers, it read, "Devoted To The Interests of Women," an echo of *The Lily*'s old tagline. Annual subscription: fifty cents.

Bunnell's introductory editorial took Bloomer straight back "to the first of January just twelve years ago, when my little *Lily* first sprang into existence." That evening, when the children were in bed, she read every article and relived the six years of her editorship. "All this came crowding through my mind, forcibly reminding me of what in my quiet life here I had well nigh forgotten—that I had once been a public agitator of great moral questions deeply affecting the human race, and had helped to set a ball in motion, which had continued to roll."

She compiled a list of several hundred addresses, which she sent to Bunnell and Thomas with a warm letter of support. She gave the names of women leaders and other papers that had come and gone: "And last of all my pet *Lily*, like a tiny child deprived of its nurse, and tendered over to the care of strangers, languished and died, without so much as giving its friends warning of the fate that awaited it, or bidding them farewell." But she told them she could see it resurrected in *The Mayflower*.[390]

They replied with gratitude and printed her letter with a paragraph of praise for "this tried and true friend of women's interests." But, they said, *The Mayflower* was not the legal successor of *The Lily*, though they had tried to buy it two years earlier. Birdsall was willing to sell but not on reasonable terms. So on the basis of much interest and goodwill from *The Lily's* readers, they started a new paper, with no hard feelings.[391] They sent copies of this issue to everyone on Bloomer's list.

Around this time, Dexter was appointed as a receiver of federal moneys for the land office at Council Bluffs in a commission signed by President Lincoln. This position came with a substantial salary.[392]

Amelia continued to contribute sporadically to *The Mayflower*. In April, she wrote about a local school exhibition she had attended.

Three hundred people were there. Mary Bloomer and a friend sang a duet of "Columbia, the Gem of the Ocean," one of several songs vying to become the national anthem.[393] Seated in the audience, Bloomer, near her forty-third birthday, thought of her youth, when such exhibitions were dominated by boys "while the girls, or a few of them, read compositions in a low monotonous tone, scarcely a word of which could be heard or understood." But this evening, the girls "took the most prominent part and spoke so loud and distinct as to be heard throughout the house." She could see them all in the future, stepping into pulpits and upon stages "to give utterance to their own earnest heart thoughts, and to plead their own wrongs and demand their rights." Around her, people who opposed the women's rights movement "gazed and listened with approving smiles." This was a clear result of the movement, "and an acknowledgement of some of the rights we claim . . . the right to speak in public—the right to compete with man in intellectual attainments—the right of the girls to consider themselves as the equals of the boys, and to outstrip them if they can, in all that is noble and worth attaining."

These were spots of joy in the midst of gathering darkness and fear. Just before Christmas, South Carolina had seceded from the

Union, and other slaveholding states rapidly followed. The growing violence between the treasonous Confederate government and the United States became an undeclared war in April 1861. There was immediate work to be done to outfit regiments. Francis Gage and her family moved back to Columbus, Ohio, and *The Mayflower* reported that "all the day long . . . she may be seen cutting and slashing in the piles of military dry goods, preparing work for the busy needles of her fair battalions" while another woman ran the sewing machine, "and the clicking of steel sounds like the cocking of an army of revolvers."[394] But the war had not yet affected Iowa, and daily life went on strangely the same.

Near the end of June, Dexter went to a meeting to plan the annual Fourth of July celebrations. There was a new tension at the prospect of the holiday under civil war. Dexter recommended that they organize "a Union Celebration of the coming Fourth of July." This was controversial, but it was adopted after "considerable debate."[395]

Even in war, dress could still be a subject of controversy. A bishop in Ohio "forbade anyone with hoops on to partake of the sacrament." Bloomer responded in *The Mayflower* that though clergymen had forbidden ornamental dress in the past, "we never till now supposed they felt it to be their duty to peer underneath the outer dress, and decide what style of undergarments, or how many, should be worn . . . we regard the hoop skirt as a positive blessing to woman."[396]

But then Frances Gage said that army hospital nurses could not wear hoops, and Bloomer asked *The Mayflower* what the regulation dress was. She agreed that hoops made no sense in a sickroom, but neither did long skirts. Perhaps the short dress and trousers would be more practical? Bunnell said she had "never *admired* the short dress for women, but its superior convenience as a working dress cannot be disputed."[397] Gage thought dress reform was still needed everywhere. "Let every sensible woman . . . resolve that her *regulation dress* shall suit her condition, business or taste. A short dress in the garden . . . a hoopless wardrobe in the nursery or cook room, a graceful trail or long skirts in the parlor, and the same two inches from the pavement in the street . . . But we did not mean to say so much on this threadbare question."[398]

Later in the year, *The Mayflower* described a vivandière uniform worn by a twenty-year-old field nurse from Menomonie. "The Turkish costume, as near as I can judge," said the correspondent, "the same as sensible ladies favored a few years since as a national style."[399] Many women would find the short dress useful in the war, including Harriet Tubman, who, on her famous gunboat raid along the Combahee River, almost tore her dress off when she stepped on her skirts, and "made up my mind then that I . . . would have a bloomer as soon as I could get it."[400]

Bunnell asked Bloomer if she would write more often for *The Mayflower*. Bloomer replied that she had "little incentive, little time, and less inclination to write for the press." She listed nine other women who she thought should be writing more. "But perhaps I should not complain. Undoubtably they are all otherwise engaged, and . . . their love of woman's cause is swallowed up in their love of country. And it is not strange that it is so—for should the great calamity which threatens our country overwhelm us, all hope of the success of our cause will be crushed out." Advocates of slavery were no friends of women's rights.

Domestic help was still scarce and expensive, and Bloomer ordered a "Huffer's Patent Washing Machine," a big box with four legs, grooved washing boards in each end, and a central cogwheel with a crank handle that agitated the wash through the hot suds. A crank wringer removed most of the water, which sped up line drying. It was now possible to do washing days on her own schedule with only Mary's help, which felt extraordinarily liberating.[401]

By summer, Union families were fleeing Missouri into Iowa. In July, the Seventh Iowa Regiment set up camp near Council Bluffs. A company of soldiers trained in the shade in front of Bloomer's house, and after several mornings listening to them drill, she thought she "could step into the ranks and *'right about face'* as well as some of our raw recruits do." Dexter was still averse to shooting prairie chickens, let alone his fellow men, but at forty-five, he could reasonably stay home. Instead, he became president of the Union League of Council Bluffs and helped raise troops and funds.[402]

In a letter to Bunnell, Bloomer deplored the shortage of nurses. She fit most of the requirements herself, being over thirty, "plain looking," and of good character, but her poor health disqualified her, and her children and husband needed her. Instead, she helped organize a Soldier's Aid Society and was elected their president. They quickly collected money and clothes and set to work for the regiment.[403] Dexter's law partner, William Kinsman, enlisted.[404] Mary Bloomer made him and twenty-one-year-old Joseph Straight each a "housewife," or sewing kit, out of scraps, with ties made of ribbons she had worn around her neck—rather romantic gifts from a sixteen-year-old girl.[405]

The time came for Company A to leave for the front. Two days before their departure, at the golden hour of the evening, Bloomer presented the Soldier's Aid Society's silk regimental flag to them with a short speech. She warned them against vice and told them to make the women proud. "Our good wishes go with you, and we shall ever hold you in honorable remembrance; and when this important war is ended . . . we shall heartily welcome you back to your home and friends." Some of the new recruits wept.[406]

But the war was still far away. "African Ladies," Bloomer's next column for *The Mayflower*, covered a report from the explorer Dr. David Livingstone on the women of the "tribes of Upper Zambezia." They were leaders, could vote, and were consulted by men on all important decisions. Husbands lived with their wives' families and obeyed their mothers-in-law. Bloomer contrasted this with the common claim that "the United States takes the lead in showing respect and deference to woman." Mere etiquette, she said. In addition, like other advocates of women's rights in New York State, including Stanton and Matilda Gage, she had read how some Native women of the Americas were also "admitted to . . . councils, and their words . . . listened to with respectful attention . . . How many men are there in this country who would consult their wives . . . or be governed by their opinions? . . . And then the *voting!...* We should like to ask the Doctor whether he thought the African women were degraded by voting; and whether the men treated them with rudeness and insult for exercising that right." Mocking the racist assumptions of her time, she went on, "Can it be that the native African is more gallant and respectful to our sex?" Perhaps some of her countrymen should visit there and take lessons.[407]

After their regiment sailed down the river, Bloomer and her society raised funds for hospital supplies to make and send. Bloomer sewed and appealed for donations to the *Council Bluffs Nonpareil* and *The Mayflower*.[408] In October, they accomplished their goal of outfitting the regiment.[409]

She became fascinated by stories of women who joined the army in disguise. Many went months before being discovered. She did not support the right of women to serve, but she admired "the brave spirit which leads women to dare everything in a good cause." This was true for lesser pursuits as well. "Every now and then we read of some clerk on a steamboat, or in a dry goods store ... turning out to be a young woman in disguise." In Council Bluffs, a young man from the East, "good looking, well behaved, and highly respected," had worked in local stores for almost a year before he abruptly left town. A newcomer had recognized him as a young woman from Ohio. "He kept the secret until the lady had left ... Everybody was amazed ... I presume she still wears the male attire, and will change her residence as often as discovered. And there are no doubt many others acting the same part." She attributed this person's motivation entirely to the need for higher wages.[410]

Bloomer also composed a letter on Helene Marie Weber, a European women's rights advocate and farmer who dressed in male clothing.[411] Bloomer knew people who had visited her, and they had reported her as "lively and entertaining—a learned and true lady." Once again, she did not approve of Weber's choice of clothes but defended her right to wear what she preferred.

This might be the last article that Bloomer wrote for *The Mayflower*. The Civil War had put a large dent in its finances, and

Bunnell and Thomas had only partial success when they appealed for support. Bloomer and Lucretia Mott both sent donations, but it seems that most of the Eastern women's rights leaders did not respond.[412]

At the same time, Frances Gage wrote in her "Field Notes" for the paper, the war was stirring women up. In aid societies, they mingled across all social and economic lines, found common ground, and realized their own power to organize.[413] This became a new theme in *The Mayflower*. In the summer of 1862, an editorial suggested that the war might clear the ground for a freer nation. The "terrible butchery of our adult male population," though a source of intense grief, would "leave the feminine element largely in preponderance, and give women an opportunity for a more successful assertion of their rights."[414]

At the beginning of June 1862, Bloomer went east to visit loved ones. In Ohio, she visited Frances Gage and other friends and talked with John Brown Jr. Cleveland women had organized a state society with an office and clerks and a steamboat to collect and distribute supplies to Tennessee hospitals. Council Bluffs' efforts looked feeble by comparison.

By July 11, Bloomer arrived in "beautiful and thriving" Seneca Falls just in time for a benefit festival organized by the local Soldier's Aid Society. Long tables were loaded with flowers and food. Bloomer was most drawn to the dishes heaped with "large and luscious strawberries and cherries," which were not to be had in Council Bluffs, and she wished she could send a basketful to Dexter. She also wished her fundraisers were half so successful. At the end of July, she headed home.[415]

There was news of a proposed new women's rights publication, with writing from Stanton, Frances Gage, Lydia Maria Child, and others. The prospectus said that it was "strange, that women ... should have no organ in America" and asked for the support of "women throughout the country." This new *Woman's Journal*, with the motto "Equal Rights for All Mankind," would be a semimonthly sixteen-page paper, with subscriptions for two dollars a year. And it would not be much of a forum. Contributors would be required to "abstain from all personal discussion."

From the Western perspective, these Eastern reformers seemed either defensive of their status, oblivious of their sisters in the newer states, or both. Bunnell did not understand why they said women had no paper, "for the Mayflower has steadily . . . advocated the whole extent of the woman's rights doctrine." But she welcomed them and thought the cause would be best served by a paper in each state.[416] However, this was the last anyone heard of it.

Conflict arose between the existing Soldier's Aid Society, of which Bloomer was president, and a new one led by her "right hand man," Mrs. Deming. Until now, they sent funds and supplies where they thought best, including to the state sanitary agent, Mrs. Annie Wittenmyer, in Keokuk, a powerful organizer whom Bloomer very much admired. Wittenmyer had organized an unofficial statewide system of local aid societies to collect and distribute hospital supplies for the troops. The state then created an all-male Iowa Army Sanitary Commission, which attempted to commandeer the women's organization and its resources. In the spring of 1862, the commission began to pressure Bloomer's society to join it, and a local male commission member convinced several Aid Society members that they would get more recognition for their work as a branch of the men's Sanitary Commission. Bloomer watched as her society voted for this and elected Deming their president. She disliked the commission, in part because men held all the paid positions while women did the work. She was hurt by the change and disturbed by the passivity of the women and the highhandedness of the organizing man but felt it would be awkward for her to protest. But when the other women assumed the Aid Society funds now belonged to their new group, she set them straight. She sent the money to Wittenmyer and let the new society go on without her, though she still donated to it.

In February 1863, Wittenmyer wrote to Bloomer to ask why she had heard nothing from them for so long and telling her of the desperate need for supplies.[417] Bloomer wrote back and explained that she had no power anymore. She took the letter to Deming, who wished they could help, but the Sanitary Commission now controlled their funds. So Bloomer went to work. She brought the letter to the branch meeting and asked if supplies such as butter could be collected and sent instead of money.[418] She also appealed to the public through the *Nonpareil*. The Aid Society got permission to send supplies to Wittenmyer, though not money, and the Sanitary Commission promised them credit for these contributions. On March 16, 1863, they shipped their first three boxes of food down the river. After that, they made larger and larger shipments almost weekly.

Bloomer was frustrated with the jealousies and infighting of the ladies of Council Bluffs. She thought they could be doing twice as much and that Wittenmyer deserved better. "I have gloried in your courage, independence and ability, and have rejoiced that it is *a woman* that is doing so much . . . I have chafed at thought of our ladies here withdrawing from you and giving all their support and confidence to a society of men."

That summer brought several hard losses for the Bloomers and their friends. Frances Gage's beloved husband died suddenly in May while she was traveling.[419] Bloomer wrote to her with condolences.

In early June, word came of the death of Dexter's friend and business partner, William Kinsman, near Vicksburg. Before the battle, Kinsman instructed Joseph Straight that his "sword and watch and other things be sent to Mr. Bloomer" if he were to be killed. Dexter memorialized Kinsman at the opening session of the district court that July.[420]

On July 1, 1863, Bloomer's youngest brother, August, was killed at Gettysburg, along with 80 percent of his regiment, as part of the Iron Brigade. He was survived by his wife, Laura, and their five children, the eldest of whom was named Frances Amelia after her aunt. Bloomer's mother died four months later at the age of eighty-four. Bloomer wrote nothing about these events, but two more deep connections to her Eastern youth were gone, and she was parentless now. The distance no doubt complicated her grief at these losses, and she felt her own advancing age.

Lizzie Bunnell married a doctor and became Lizzie B. Read. *The Mayflower* would continue, she said.[421] After she moved to her husband's home in Columbia City, Indiana, she apologized for the recent decline in the quality of the paper and promised better.[422] Bloomer may have suspected this was the beginning of the end but, as usual, hoped otherwise.

A sanitary convention was called at Des Moines in November 1863 that was rumored to be a trap set for Wittenmyer by the State Sanitary Commission to discredit her in public, motivated by personal antagonism rather than the stated desire for increased cooperation. One woman warned Wittenmyer that she would be accused of mismanagement, including "waste of goods, embezzlement of stores, and reveling and carousing with the officers." Bloomer intended to support her admired friend but at the last minute was too sick. She scrambled to prepare a replacement, but the person failed to go. She wrote a profuse apology to Wittenmyer.[423] But her absence did no harm. At the convention, Wittenmyer defended herself energetically and had many supporters. To Bloomer's relief, she left with better standing than before, and she would soon resign to pursue her hospital work independent of the state.[424]

Bloomer was reelected president of the Soldier's Aid Society again, despite everything. She attempted to resign that winter. Her motion was defeated, but to her relief, the group also voted to become independent again.[425] In the end, the others recognized her skills and were persuaded of the need to control their own organization. Bloomer might wish to retire, but her belief in principled action was pulling her back into the public sphere.

CHAPTER 15

Reconstruction and *The Revolution*

As the end of the war neared, the peacetime reform movements waited in the wings. Bloomer could not predict the coming split between previous allies in the fights for temperance, women's rights, and the abolition of slavery. And she would not have imagined that she would step back onto any state or national stage. But her old world was about to catch up with her new one.

For the moment, domestic life and soldier's aid efforts went on in Council Bluffs. Dexter built a better kitchen onto the house and raised funds for the families of soldiers in the county. This year, he was appointed the government bond receiver and disbursing agent for Iowa.[426]

Bloomer's hopes for temperance in Council Bluffs were still frustrated. Several violations of the local liquor ban were tried at the beginning of 1865 but were dismissed because three juries disregarded the evidence. Popular sentiment made the law unenforceable.

Even with all her struggles, it seems that Bloomer had become one of the most successful aid society leaders in Iowa. In recognition of this, two days before the formal end of the Civil War, she was appointed one of two assistant superintendents of the Iowa department of the Northwestern Sanitary Fair to benefit the soldiers. The fair would be held in Chicago over three weeks that June. She was charged with devising a symbolic arrangement of the contributions

199

from Iowa and soliciting donations to support her plan. Bloomer threw herself into the job and was flooded with correspondence as she directed donations, answered questions, and managed the feelings of donors.

In the midst of all this, the dreadful news came: President Lincoln had been assassinated. Council Bluffs was overwhelmed with grief. Special assemblies were held, and businesses closed. The town was draped in black mourning, and people wept openly in the street.[427]

In May 1865, Anthony and Stanton organized a convention of the Women's Loyal National League in New York City to address the inadequacy of Lincoln's Emancipation Proclamation. It freed "all persons held as slaves within the rebellious states" but not those held in the four slave states that had not rebelled.[428] Bloomer was invited to this meeting by Anthony and again was unable to go. But she wrote them a letter that reflected her experiences in Iowa. Though most women there supported the soldiers, she said, many thought the war "should have been prevented by a compromise and long for peace on almost any terms . . . But there is a class of women who . . . have never believed we should have peace or great success until the doom of slavery was irrevocably sealed."[429]

The work for the sanitary fair exhausted Bloomer, and she sought medical treatment when she arrived in Chicago. Whatever doctors she found, combined with the change of scene, the sociable work, and the interest of the fair itself, were all healing to her, and near the end of the three weeks she spent working at the fair, she wrote to Dexter that she was enjoying herself and feeling "quite well."[430]

While Bloomer's group arranged their table beneath banners and flags in the cavernous Union Hall, trophies of the war arrived daily for exhibition. John Brown's rifle and the catafalque of Lincoln's coffin, draped in black velvet and heavy black tassels, were displayed. Some trophies were souvenirs of slavery itself, including an auction block. It was rumored that Jefferson Davis had been captured while wearing his wife's dress, and volunteers set up a wax figure of him dressed in a gown from one of the family trunks.[431] This time, Bloomer did not write about this particular mode of shaming men.

The fair itself was a whirl of activity for Bloomer and her team, who served customers and kept their table stocked and their booth attractive. There were many famous visitors, including the great hero of the war, General Grant. Grant had partly built his career on his understanding of the importance of supplies in war and asked to meet the women of the Soldier's Aid Societies. Bloomer lined up with the others to receive him and shook his hand for the first time.[432] Grenville Dodge was their mutual friend, and it is likely that the Bloomers met Grant again when he visited Council Bluffs.

At some point, it's unclear exactly when, *The Mayflower* went under. Lizzie Bunnell Read settled in Algona, Iowa, with her husband and started a weekly county newspaper. Stanton's favorite sister, Margaret, moved to Central Iowa with her family. Stanton considered joining her, and both of Anthony's brothers had moved to Kansas "in the John Brown days." Bloomer learned that Jane Swisshelm had started her third newspaper, *The Reconstructionist*, and wrote to congratulate her and subscribe. But after Swisshelm suggested Johnson was complicit in Lincoln's assassination, he fired her from her government job, and her printing office was attacked by an arsonist. She gave up and retired to Pennsylvania.[433]

In 1866, Bloomer's home life was breaking down. She never wrote directly about her adopted daughter, Mary, who was now twenty-one. It seems their relationship was difficult. As the eldest child of her birth family, Mary was old enough to remember their terrible journey, her dead mother, and her vanished father. In March, Dexter wrote in his diary that they "had trouble about Mary" and "all very unhappy. It is the bane of our household. The skeleton in the closet."[434]

On September 9, Amelia's seventeen-year-old niece, Jennie, arrived from New York to stay with them. Ten days later, Amelia's sister Adeline died, aged fifty-six. Bloomer wrote nothing that survives about these events, but she was forty-eight and deep in the losses and upheavals of midlife, with menopause perhaps adding to her destabilization.

After a previous boyfriend left town, Mary had been spending time with Joseph Straight, the young man to whom she had given her neck ribbon when he went off to war. Straight had a bad reputation in Council Bluffs, was in debt, and probably drank.[435] It is also possible that Mary was pregnant, but this is speculation. The first man wrote her a letter, and at that point, Dexter sat her down "and told her she must *now* choose between them. Mrs. B very much excited about it." He is cryptic about the reasons.

On December 15, Mary told Dexter that she was engaged to Straight, and he and Amelia had a long talk with her. Dexter was disappointed but respected her decision. Amelia was outraged. She did not want Straight in the house, and she refused to attend their wedding.

Dexter told Straight that he would rather see Mary "buried in the earth than married to him." But on Christmas morning, Dexter gave Mary away in a full church. "I could hardly keep from crying all the while . . . Mary immediately left for Ohio with her husband. I have been kind to her lately and do not regret it as I have loved her very much and it is hard to part with her." The next day, Dexter worked in his office, and wrote that it "seemed good to be alone. Everybody is talking about Mary's marriage and regretting it." A child of one of their friends would remember she often heard people say, "Isn't it too bad the way those children turned out, after all the Bloomers did for them?"[436]

In January 1867, the first railroad line from the East was completed as far as Council Bluffs, and a year later, a monumental iron railroad bridge across the Missouri to Omaha was complete, with a secondary road for pedestrians and horse-drawn vehicles and the conduit for the telegraph line to California. Council Bluffs was no longer isolated.

Amelia gave lectures that winter, and even the editor of the Democratic paper admired them: "just enough of sarcasm in them to spice them well . . . Her delivery was not strong, but perfectly distinct and rather agreeable."[437] Her health was still poor, but in May 1867, she made the long journey east to New York City to attend the meeting of the Woman Suffrage Association, where they elected her a vice president.[438]

In the spring of 1866, Anthony and Stanton had founded the American Equal Rights Association, or AERA, at the eleventh National Woman's Rights Convention. This was their first attempt at a national organization, and its mission was to win equal rights and suffrage for all, "irrespective of race, color, or sex."[439] All through 1867, the AERA campaigned for two referenda in Kansas that would potentially enfranchise Black men and all women. But their Republican friends believed that promotion of women's suffrage would prevent Black male suffrage and refused to support the AERA. In response, Anthony and Stanton joined forces with the flashy racist entrepreneur George Francis Train, who toured the state with Anthony for two weeks to support white women's suffrage. Anthony advertised their lectures as AERA benefits, to the horror of many members, including Lucy Stone. Kansas voted down both referenda anyway.

Afterward, Train funded the national women's rights paper that Anthony had wanted for years. It was the first since the demise of *The Mayflower*, and it began as a sixteen-page weekly. They gave it the unfeminine name *The Revolution*.[440] Bloomer subscribed as soon as she learned of it. She never needed to agree with everything she read.

Many of Stanton and Anthony's friends found their alliance with Train repulsive. But it is important to remember that Stanton and Anthony did not want universal suffrage but "educated suffrage, irrespective of race or sex." In exchange for his support, they dismissed Train's outspoken racism and considered the "negro question" obsolete. Stanton claimed that Reconstruction would "be completed by mid-summer."[441]

Though Stanton and Anthony had given up reform dress well before the war, they still printed articles in *The Revolution* defending it as a remedy for "health-destroying" fashions.[442] And here and there in the postwar crop of young women, the movement had grown strange new branches. Newspapers as far as Honolulu reported that at the May 1868 meeting of the AERA in New York City, there were three women reporters in startling dress. One, from Chicago, wore tight black silk trousers, a green silk double-breasted vest over a shirt, and a gray overcoat, or paletot, "which reached a little lower than her hips." At one point, she unbuttoned her coat, put her right foot up on her left knee, and continued to write, using her leg as a desk "with the utmost nonchalance." Another was dressed all in orange silk: baggy, knee-length knickerbockers, with flesh-colored stockings, below a loose belted tunic and a loose vest. The third wrote for *The Revolution* and was more modest, but still deeply eccentric, in a black gown with no hoops, an "immense Panama hat, dishevelled hair, green stockings, and prunella gaiters."[443]

At the meeting itself, Bloomer was reelected a vice president, along with Stanton, Frederick Douglass, Henry Ward Beecher, Frances Gage, Antoinette Brown Blackwell, and several others. The revered Lucretia Mott, now about seventy-five, was made president.

The 1868 presidential election, the first after the war, in some ways echoed the divide in the women's suffrage movement. There were two reluctant candidates: Republican war hero General Ulysses S. Grant and the Democratic governor of New York State, Horatio Seymour, who was one of the worst possible options from Bloomer's perspective, between his racist positions and his turncoat 1854 veto of the New York liquor prohibition bill. White fears of mixed marriages and Black equality were key issues in this campaign, and Seymour ran on the motto "This is a White Man's Country; Let White Men Rule."[444]

In 1869, the Bloomers were in the same little house at the foot of the bluffs, still with Eddie and Jennie and a public school teacher, Mary Bristol.[445]

After years of establishing himself as a pillar of the community, a vestryman, a successful lawyer and businessman, a leader of the county Republican party, and the president of the school board, with business and political ties throughout the state, Dexter again ran for mayor of Council Bluffs. A paper joked that he was known as "Mrs. Bloomer's Husband." But this time, he won.

They hosted almost every reform lecturer who passed through Council Bluffs. Bloomer remembered well what it was like to find refuge in the home of a welcoming friend after long journeys, dirty hotels, and bad food. Dexter wrote that their guests included Anthony, Stanton, Mary Livermore, Anna Dickinson, Frederick Douglass, and many others.

That winter, Bloomer wrote in the *Nonpareil* that she and other suffragists did not oppose Black suffrage but "manhood suffrage alone . . . We are willing to accord to our colored population all the rights of citizenship, but we claim them also at the same time for ourselves. White men have laid upon woman laws hard to be borne, and we can look for nothing better at the hands of the black."[446] The day before her letter was printed, the Fifteenth Amendment was ratified, giving Black men the legal right to vote.

The third anniversary meeting of the AERA was announced for May 12, 1869, in New York City, with many great speakers scheduled.[447] Bloomer was already planning a trip to Seneca Falls that spring and wrote to Stanton at *The Revolution*, "I have been retired from the world so long that it would give me pleasure to see and hear something once more." Stanton replied in *The Revolution*, "Shall be glad to meet our good friend again."[448]

Lucretia Mott resigned as president of the American Equal Rights Association before this convention because of Train's appearances at AERA benefits. She told Stanton and Anthony that she thought it had been a mistake to combine the abolitionist and woman's rights movements and recommended that the AERA disband. Not long after, Train and his money left *The Revolution*.

Bloomer traveled to New York City for the May meeting. She attended a reception for movement leaders at the AERA offices and arrived the morning of the meeting at the new Steinway Hall on Fourteenth Street, home to the New York Philharmonic. Inside, she took a seat on the stage where Charles Dickens had read on his last US tour. It was her first Eastern convention in over a decade. The seats were full, and only about a tenth of the audience were men.

After the prayer, Stanton, in a black silk moiré gown, her ringlets now snow-white, rose from a red velvet armchair to give the opening address and announced the proposal of "a Sixteenth Amendment to the Federal Constitution . . . The Right of Suffrage in the United States shall be based on citizenship, and shall be regulated by Congress; and all citizens of the United States, whether native or naturalized, shall enjoy this right equally without any distinction or discrimination whatever founded on sex."

She summarized the arguments for women's suffrage of the last twenty years. Bloomer had made many of them herself and agreed that "no man has yet made a fair, logical argument on the other side." This led to Stanton's central theme: the "aristocracy of sex" established by the Fifteenth Amendment. And now she displayed the prejudices that troubled her old friends. She spoke of "ignorant foreigners" and "the ignorant African just from his own land or the southern plantation, in whose eyes woman is simply the being of man's lust . . . If American women find it hard to bear the oppressions of their own Saxon Fathers, the best orders of manhood . . . think of Patrick and Sambo and Hans and Yung Tung . . . making laws for Lucretia Mott, Ernestine L. Rose, Susan B. Anthony or Anna E. Dickinson."

Her old friend Frederick Douglass sat nearby on the platform, his hair now streaked with gray.[449]

There were more speeches and the familiar sequence of reports and committee elections. Bloomer was reelected vice president for Iowa. Then Stephen Foster, Abby Kelley Foster's husband, rose and objected to Stanton's nomination for president because she "had publicly repudiated the principles of the society" with her promotion of educated suffrage, the alliance with George Francis Train, and *The Revolution*'s opposition to the Fifteenth Amendment. He also accused Anthony of mismanaging the AERA's funds. Mary Livermore objected that Train had left *The Revolution*, but Anthony stated that they did not "repudiate him." After some painful argument, the committee nominations passed by a large majority.

Douglass stood. "There is no name greater than that of Elizabeth Cady Stanton in the matter of Woman's Rights and Equal Rights," he said, "but my sentiments are tinged a little against THE REVOLUTION," and in Stanton's address, there was "a sentiment in reference to employment and certain names, such as 'Sambo,' . . . that I cannot coincide with . . . I must say that I do not see how any one can pretend that there is the same urgency in giving the ballot to women as to the negro. With us, the matter is a question of life and death." He was greatly applauded, and he reiterated his gratitude for Stanton's long friendship.

Anthony retorted that if "justice and suffrage" were not to be given to everyone, they should be given "to the most intelligent first." The audience now applauded her. She said that despite what he suffered as a Black man, Douglass would not trade sexes with Stanton. This was met by such loud laughter and applause that she could not go on. After the meeting settled down, Lucy Stone argued against educated suffrage and said that though she believed women's suffrage was more imperative, she was glad to see Black men get the vote.

That evening, Olive Logan, a fashionable actress and author and, now, popular suffrage lecturer of fifteen months, expressed her scorn for women who "unsexed" themselves. "I am not yet ready to see women wear trousers (great laughter and applause)—nor men wear petticoats (renewed applause)." The speeches went on until after ten that night.[450]

The next day, Douglass asked the AERA to pledge support for the Fifteenth Amendment. Stanton, Anthony, and Paulina Davis opposed this. Frances Ellen Watkins Harper, the only Black woman on the stage, rose and said that "the question of color was far more to her than the question of sex." Henry Blackwell moved to vote. Stanton moved to defer it and turned to the audience. "All in favor," she called, "say Aye!" A clear minority of voices said "aye."

"All opposed, say No!" There was "a roaring thunder of noes."

"The Ayes have it!" declared Stanton, and she deferred the vote on Douglass's resolution. The audience laughed and groaned.[451]

Bloomer was disturbed by the strife but took great pleasure in the speeches and new faces. She still felt that no one could match

Stanton, Anthony, or Stone as speakers. And she defended Anthony as the hardest worker in the cause. She did not agree with everything that Anthony said or did, "but I know her to be good and true of heart, and wholly devoted to the interests of all women." She also praised Mary Livermore as a "strong woman and pleasant speaker," who would "soon become to the West, what Mrs. Stanton and Miss Anthony are to the East."[452]

Two days after the convention, Stanton and Anthony formed the National Woman Suffrage Association, or NWSA. Stone and Blackwell would claim it was a secret meeting, intentionally held after they left town. Stanton and Anthony claimed it was spontaneous and that "Western women" had pushed for it. They made *The Revolution* their official organ and took a strong stance against the Fifteenth Amendment and in favor of a Sixteenth Amendment to enfranchise women.[453] Bloomer did not join them, nor did she criticize them.

On July 5, Bloomer spoke at the Woman's Suffrage Convention in Buffalo, along with Stanton, Anthony, and Livermore, before returning home. The railroad had finally given her access to "the excitements" of the women's movement again.

Council Bluffs now had a population a little over six thousand and began to feel like a town. Mansions were going up, as well as an opera house.[454] Post office cars would soon be put on the route from Chicago to make mail delivery from the East faster and more reliable.[455] The total solar eclipse on the afternoon of August 7 attracted parties of scientists and tourists from the East. The sky was clear, and the Bloomers drove up to the top of a high bluff to watch it through smoked glass. "It was magnificent," wrote Dexter.

At the end of August, a letter arrived for Bloomer from Lucy Stone with a printed circular advertising an "American Woman Suffrage Association" convention. On the blank side, Stone wrote that this would be a new organization "in addition to that of Mrs. Stanton. Nearly all the anti-slavery people feel repelled from them on account of their attack on the 15th Amendment ... People who cannot work with Susan, can work in the new organization which will make no war or quarrel." According to the circular, their plan was to empower state delegates, a decentralized approach in direct contrast with Anthony's.[456] Bloomer replied that yes, she would support them too.

She wrote to Iowa suffrage associations to ask about their activities and suggest a state convention to appoint delegates. One person she wrote to was Mrs. Annie Savery in Des Moines. Dexter had a business correspondence with Mr. Savery, a wealthy real estate developer. Mrs. Savery was a well-known philanthropist and had given a talk on women's suffrage in Des Moines, the first by any woman there. But she did not write back.

Dress reform was still a source of controversy, which flared up at the Ohio State Woman's Suffrage Society convention in Cincinnati that autumn. Dr. Mary Walker was an established woman's rights advocate who had been awarded the Medal of Honor for her service as an army surgeon in the Civil War, and whose wardrobe choices embarrassed many in the movement. Walker had worn trousers before Bloomer and criticized Stanton and Stone when they abandoned them. In 1866, she had been arrested twice in New York City for wearing "male costume" in public. The *Cincinnati Enquirer* called her "The Distasteful Bloomer" and described how she was hissed and hooted when she arrived at the convention. She wore a black broadcloth suit with loose trousers and frock coat, and a cloak "hanging rakishly from her left shoulder." At the midday recess, the *Enquirer* wrote, "Mrs. Dr. Walker put on her, or his, hat ... and started out to refresh the inner man." Boys and men jeered at her on the street.

Though Walker was starting a new lecture tour, the organizers did not want her to speak. But others did. On the second day, they shouted her name from the gallery. Mary Livermore stood, "looking very savage," and informed them that gentlemen did not "indulge in cat-calls at a woman's convention ... I must appeal to those who believe in personal freedom to help put down any demonstrations of disorder." Walker spoke twice that day, wearing green trousers, her frock coat, and her medal.[457]

Bloomer did not know Walker and felt conflicted as she read this report. She wrote to Livermore, "I am glad you spoke a good word for her ... *I* know that a woman may be just as good, just as true, just as much of a lady in a short skirt and pants, as in a trailing skirt."

She had reservations too. "It would be well, in the present state of public opinion, if Dr. Walker could conform to the fashionable style, or else make herself less conspicuous. Her costume ... is odious to the public, and calculated to bring reproach upon woman's cause in the minds of those who have not the good sense to distinguish between truth and raiment ... So would I counsel Dr. Walker, while defending her right to choose her own costume."[458]

Though she had hoped to attend the founding meeting of the AWSA in Cleveland, she told Mary Livermore that she would probably not be there.[459] Livermore packed as much emphasis as she could into a one-page reply. "Mrs. Bloomer, there never has been a time, since our woman movement was started, when your presence was so important as at this Convention ... Do come."[460]

Bloomer did not go. Cold weather, disruptions to the rail and steamer services, and her health were all likely reasons. But there were other delegates from Iowa, including Belle Mansfield.[461] At age twenty-four, Mansfield had a master's degree and was the first woman to pass the bar in the United States.[462] Bloomer read that the convention had been attended by about a thousand people, and that the celebrity minister Henry Ward Beecher agreed to be elected president in absentia. They did not discuss the Fifteenth Amendment. They formed a constitution that made both sexes of all races equal members and gave controlling power to the delegates, not a central power.[463]

Anthony attended and was invited to sit on the stage and to speak.[464] Stone announced a new newspaper. Mary Livermore's paper of one year, *The Agitator,* would move with her from Chicago to Boston and be renamed the *Woman's Journal.*[465] Bloomer subscribed.

On December 10, 1869, the Wyoming Territory passed Democratic Party legislation giving married women property rights—and the vote. There were few white women in the territory, and some thought it would attract more. Others wanted to embarrass President Grant's appointed Republican governor and assumed he would veto a women's suffrage bill. He did not, and Wyoming became a test case for women's suffrage.[466]

Around the same time, months after she had given up on a reply from Annie Savery, Bloomer got a friendly note from her confirming she would "do all in my power" for women's suffrage and encouraged Bloomer to write often.[467] Bloomer replied immediately and suggested that they hold a convention that winter. Savery suggested that they propose a women's suffrage amendment to the legislature, or it would be "two years before we can have another opportunity." She was an autodidact and a religious freethinker, and like Bloomer, she had no biological children. She had never involved herself with the women's rights movement before Bloomer wrote to her, but she was eager to start.

She invited Bloomer to visit and discuss strategy.

CHAPTER 16

Iowa Suffrage and the Free Love Scandal

Unfortunately for women's suffrage in Iowa, Bloomer's broken health deteriorated once again and made her unable to travel.[468] She was homebound when, in January 1870, an obvious opportunity arose that called for action. Democrats in the Iowa Legislature took up the now popular tactic of forcing debate on women's suffrage to embarrass the Republicans and stall ratification of the Fifteenth Amendment. They proposed a state suffrage amendment, and the Republicans called their bluff and created a committee to investigate it.[469]

Henry Blackwell wrote to Savery about forming a "Woman's Association," but she told him she would "not dare—without the advice and instruction of a competent leader."

"You certainly have the experience and ability," she wrote to Bloomer. If Bloomer's health was an obstacle, Savery was willing to be her student. But Bloomer was too sick to visit her.

Stone and Mary Livermore launched the *Woman's Journal* with a mission statement that echoed the familiar old words: "Devoted to the Interests of Woman." Bloomer told Stone about the germinating movement in Iowa and the proposed amendment.[470]

Savery offered to visit Bloomer and bring her back to Des Moines to meet with her legislator friends. Bloomer wrote to her and outlined all that would have to be done to organize the women of the state. It was not the work of a month. Blackwell and

Stone pressed Bloomer to make Iowa "auxiliary to the American Woman Suffrage Association of which you are a prominent officer" rather than part of Stanton and Anthony's organization. With so much to consider, Bloomer and Savery gradually decided that it made more sense to prepare for the next general session in two years.[471]

Women's suffrage supporters around Iowa began to write to Bloomer. A married couple introduced themselves by letter so that "we will be in communication and ready to work when canvassing begins. We know of no one else in this state, prominent in the cause, to whom we may write."[472] One woman in Decatur County wrote a letter that could have been from a woman twenty years earlier in New York. They had "heard but very little about the Woman Suffrage Movement. A few of us are trying to organize a woman's club, not under the name of Woman's Rights however. We want to … discuss various topics so that we may learn to express our opinions publicly, as men do."[473]

Bloomer finally made her first trip to Des Moines to stay with Savery in March 1870. She found her a true kindred spirit, enthusiastic and kind and sharp-witted; a small elegant woman with black hair, a high forehead, and large expressive eyes behind wire-rimmed spectacles.

On the afternoon of March 29, they sat with a crowd of other women in the House to watch the debate of a motion to allow them to vote and hold office in Iowa.[474] Bloomer's expectations were low. But to her astonishment, after strong speeches by old supporters and recent converts, it carried, 52–32. The crowd broke into applause and cheers.

The next day, everyone packed into the Iowa Senate. The woman who reported the House action was greeted by the senators with a standing ovation. They remained on their feet while she read it, applauded when she finished, suspended the rules, and took immediate action. "All attempts at debate were choked off and the measure was approved on a roll-call vote of 32–11. Once again the audience cheered."

Bloomer was floored. And then she was elated. All the effort invested by the abolitionist and women's movements had finally put forth this flower, like an apple tree that took a decade to mature. No current women's organization in Iowa had lifted a finger. It seemed possible that the next general assembly would approve the amendment a second time as required by law and submit it to state referendum for ratification.[475]

She and Savery struggled through the crowd to shake hands with some of the supporting legislators and thank them. The next day, Savery hosted a meeting in her parlors to discuss the plan for a state women's suffrage organization. The atmosphere was joyous, grateful, and earnest. But it was not clear who the leaders would be. Bloomer was a popular choice, but she could not promise more than some writing and occasional meetings and lectures near home.

Bloomer returned to Council Bluffs, welcomed her sister Elvira for a visit, and wrote to Stone for the *Woman's Journal.* "We have much to do to enlighten the people . . . No field is now more inviting— no other gives greater promise of success."[476] Stone placed her letter on the front page of the *Journal,* next to the report of the American Woman Suffrage Association convention in New York City and an ode to the Fifteenth Amendment by Julia Ward Howe.

Bloomer also responded to Stone's invitation to join forces with AWSA to say she did not want to take sides in the Eastern disputes. Stone wrote back several pages in response to "your good sensible letter." She had tried to approach Anthony and Stanton when she announced the AWSA but had been met with suspicion. She had told Stanton that with two associations, "each attracting those who naturally belong to it, we shall be far more likely to secure the hearty, active cooperation of all the friends of the cause than we otherwise could." And she told Bloomer about a merger forced through by Stanton, Anthony, and Theodore Tilton in New York City creating a new "Union Woman Suffrage Association" (UWSA) that absorbed the old AERA "by a vote of 16 against Mr. Blackwell and me . . . three persons voted who had never even met with us before." Stanton and Anthony's NWSA, with their mouthpiece, *The Revolution,* was also absorbed by the new UWSA. For Stone and the AWSA, it may have looked like a consolidation of forces before battle. She asked Bloomer to prevent the Iowa meeting "from organizing auxiliary to the 'Union' Society . . . If not auxiliary to the American let it be independent—or friendly to both."[477]

Amelia and Dexter traveled to Mount Pleasant for the first meeting of the State Woman Suffrage Society of Iowa, organized by Joseph Dugdale and Belle Mansfield. There they met Hannah Tracy Cutler of Ohio, a journalist, lecturer, and a friend of Frances Gage who was covering the meeting for the *Woman's Journal*, and they went to the meeting together.[478] When they arrived at Dugdale's house, they found the publisher of *The Revolution*, Edwin Studwell, already there. They all walked over to the hall, where a large audience was gathering and "placards announcing *The Revolution*" were "scattered like autumn leaves." The Union Woman Suffrage Association contingent was there in force.

One paper had called Bloomer "the leader of the woman suffrage party in our State" and said Susan B. Anthony would be there.[479] But Anthony did not attend. Belle Mansfield was elected president of the convention. Like Bloomer, she hoped to unify the two factions, and Bloomer was glad to see that she took her seat and conducted the meeting as if she had done it all her life. This was the younger blood she had hoped for.

A committee was appointed to form the state organization and constitution, and the chairman on resolutions added Anthony to it, thinking she might be present. At this initial sign of allegiance to the UWSA, Bloomer jumped up to object. Why, she asked Mansfield, should Anthony's name be thrust upon their state, or upon a committee? Iowa had enough workers and speakers to manage their own business.

Shock went through the room. Many assumed that this was a personal attack on Anthony. A Methodist elder censured her. Bloomer relented and was later appointed head of the resolutions committee. Throughout the meeting, Cutler took rapid notes for her *Woman's Journal* report, while Studwell watched the "scattered" efforts of his UWSA friends.[480] The Iowa attorney general, Henry O'Conner, was made president in absentia, with Belle Mansfield as secretary, Annie Savery corresponding secretary, and Amelia Bloomer first vice president.[481]

The next day, Bloomer took the train to Oskaloosa with Cutler to distribute handbills in the shimmering heat and hold a suffrage meeting that spilled into the next day. From there, they visited the Saverys. Bloomer addressed "a large Temperance gathering on the Capitol grounds," and in the evening, she and Savery spoke on women's suffrage at the Baptist church.

In response to its reporting, the *Woman's Journal* received "sundry indignant epistles from Iowa" to deny that they were aligned with the UWSA. "The one thing the convention did most decidedly was to *express its determination to remain aloof from Eastern organizations* . . . We are an independent association, and cannot be swept into anybody's net."[482]

In July, the Iowa Senate allowed mothers to inherit their children's property, and, as a direct result of Mansfield passing the bar, they removed the words "white" and "male" from the qualifications for admission.[483] Savery was inspired to study law.

That summer, Dexter expanded their house again, to eleven rooms with a parlor and a library and a broad sunny veranda.[484] A South American explorer who was collaborating with him on some writing gave them a cockatoo with a pink crest. Amelia already had a pet cardinal, and when she learned how long a cockatoo could live, and how destructive they could be, she hesitated. But she didn't want to offend the giver. They named the bird Dickey, and he became a feature of their house.

Eddie turned sixteen and moved out. As he grew, the Bloomers had "told him everything they knew about his parents and the Mormons." At twelve, "he could choose what kind of work he wanted to be educated for," including to become an attorney with Dexter. But he preferred garden work and printshops and wanted to reconnect with the Mormon community. In time, he made a home with them in Arizona, but he always stayed in touch with the Bloomers.[485]

Mary was back in Iowa with her family, in Exira, midway between Des Moines and Council Bluffs. Her husband was a lawyer, and they had two little girls: Rosa, age three, and Nellie, age one.[486] Perhaps she had not chosen as badly as the Bloomers thought. And they may have reconciled to some degree. In 1876, the Straights would name their new daughter Blanche Amelia, and nine years later, they named a son Harry Bloomer.

Bloomer's niece Jennie Frost finished high school, trained as a teacher, and returned to live with them in Council Bluffs, where she taught in the local schools and sang in choirs.[487]

The Bloomers also hosted friends, including Amelia's new friend Hannah Tracy Cutler. Cutler wrote to Stone, "Were I called on to say in what State I find the truest fitness for the reception of women into political relations, I should say Iowa . . . If Iowa shall first give suffrage to women, we will all vote to make her the Capitol State, and locate our national center at Council Bluffs."[488]

In late September, Bloomer and her friends, including Ruth Ann Dodge, organized a Council Bluffs Woman Suffrage Society. Despite her reluctance, they elected Bloomer their president.[489] At the end of November, she wrote to *The Revolution* that "the woman suffragists are all in working order in Iowa, and . . . we may expect to see the fur fly shortly."[490]

Back east, the spirit medium Victoria Woodhull and her sister Tennessee Claflin had been in the papers. The two had opened a brokerage firm and started a newspaper that promoted free love, women's rights, spiritualism, radical labor politics, and communism, and Woodhull announced her candidacy for president.[491] In January 1871, Woodhull became the first woman to speak to Congress. She argued that the Fourteenth and Fifteenth Amendments gave women the right to vote, an idea that would be called the "New Departure." Anthony thought she was a genius, and the Union Association threw all their resources behind this new idea. Stone and other leaders of the American Association thought that Woodhull's promotion of free love would repel the general public. They would be proven correct.

In early February, Susan B. Anthony, all in black, arrived at Bloomer's door. She was fifty-one now, strong and healthy except for her teeth, and more driven than ever. She had never been able to find financial backing for *The Revolution* after Train. Stanton's radicalism had driven off supporters and subscribers, and Anthony still owed $10,000 to creditors after selling it for a dollar to a wealthy UWSA secretary. She had been on the road for almost a month, earning money to pay this down. Bloomer welcomed her, put her up, and hosted her lecture to what Anthony called "a fine audience," though it was small.[492] No doubt they talked for hours by the warm parlor stove about the state of the movement. They had disagreed before, but they maintained their friendship, and Bloomer never lost her admiration for her and Stanton.

At the beginning of June, Stanton traveled out to join Anthony on a western tour and spoke twice in Des Moines. Anthony was impressed by the society there and pressed the New Departure. She hated the idea of working state by state. "Slow, tedious, humiliating process."[493] Bloomer had hopes for the New Departure, but Savery, now studying law, was unconvinced. Like Lucy Stone, she viewed it as, at best, an accidental loophole that would not allow women to gain suffrage for long, if at all.

After Stanton attended the Nebraska Constitutional Convention, she showed up at Bloomer's home for a friendly and political visit. Bloomer took her for drives through the valleys. Stanton thought that Bloomer should be the president of the Iowa Woman Suffrage Association, and she called Dexter "a large, fine-looking man, and considered by his neighbors one of their most able and reliable citizens . . . it is generally supposed that strong-minded women must have inferior husbands, when the facts, as far as I know, are just the other way."

She also told Bloomer some ugly Eastern gossip and swore her to secrecy. Bloomer told no one, but within months, the whole nation would know about it.

Bloomer held a reception for Stanton and luxuriated in the lively political conversation. Afterward, Stanton wrote that she would "not be surprised if the women in Iowa and Nebraska voted for the next President."[494] On the fourth of July, a notice in *The Revolution* nominated Bloomer and Savery as NWSA representatives for Iowa.[495]

That August, Stanton wrote to *The Revolution* from what she called "The Yo-Semite" with rapturous descriptions of the scenery, including a party of ladies "in sea-side hats and bloomers" riding horses down into the valley. Anthony was with her, also in bloomers for the occasion, and rode her horse astride without concern. Stanton struggled, and she recommended that any women who followed them imitate Anthony.[496]

Anti-suffragists were organizing, stirred up by Woodhull's scandalous opinions and the fear that the moral character of the nation was at risk. In the *Des Moines Register* that summer, one anonymous writer quoted passages that shocked her from the women's rights papers. "Twenty or thirty years ago, if a woman . . . conveyed such obscene meanings" or "stood up before the public and used such language as did Mrs. Stanton in Des Moines . . . they would have been shunned by all respectable citizens."[497] Savery's call for the Iowa suffrage convention in Des Moines that year emphasized their independence from the East and their devotion to traditional marriage in an attempt to head off the accusations of immorality.[498]

With their president absent, Vice President Bloomer called the large convention to order. Savery offered resolutions, starting with a request to organize aid for women victims of the Great Chicago Fire.

That afternoon, the convention dodged the specter of free love by refusing "any responsibility for the opinions or utterances" of anyone outside their organization. The discussion seemed to establish that all present stood for "good order and the morals of society" but did not wish to denounce "other organizations." This was what Bloomer wanted: a civil difference of opinion. She was elected president for the coming year.

Newcomer Nettie Sanford then offered the resolution that Bloomer and Savery had hoped to avoid. "That this association denounce the doctrine of free love, believing that marriage is sacred and binding . . . and that the Bible is the palladium of our liberties."

Savery said she thought it made no sense to denounce something that nobody thought they believed. Bloomer agreed and said they were not gathered to debate the matter. Debate happened anyway, but in the end, the *Woman's Journal* reported, "the emphatic opinion of the Convention was that . . . it did not endorse, and was not responsible for, the individual opinions of any one upon social or religious reform." They tabled Sanford's resolution and moved on.

Initially, Sanford did not seem to be a threat. She reported that the convention was "harmonious and pleasant" and described Bloomer as "a handsome woman of over fifty, and instead of wearing the stumpy suit which bears her name, was elegantly dressed in grosgrain silk with sweeping drapery."[499]

But at least one person was not done talking about the issue. An anonymous letter to the *Des Moines Register* said the "Radicals," which included Bloomer and Savery, wanted to "set aside all Stantonian and other side issues" including free love, trial marriage, easy divorce, education, and religion, to focus on the single issue of suffrage. She said the Iowa suffrage leaders, Savery in particular, were under the influence of Anthony, Stanton, and Woodhull, and "every free woman should do all in her power to oppose the enfranchisement of the sex." She believed in women's equality and that they should be well educated and equally employed and paid, but why should they make laws when they could not serve in the military?[500]

Savery replied in the *Register*, and Bloomer wrote a follow-up. Among other things, Bloomer denied that Woodhull had convinced her of the New Departure. "Able lawyers, Senators and Judges . . . have argued the case so clearly that it leaves no room for doubt." But Woodhull had publicized the New Departure well, and though Bloomer disagreed with her on other matters, "for this service done to woman's cause, I thank her most heartily." She regretted that such a talented woman had exposed herself to scandal, but "we cannot deny the right of any woman to labor in woman's cause, or withhold our own hands from the work" because they disagreed on other matters. "Nor is it any part of our work to go out of our way to denounce her . . . The Lord is her judge."[501]

Now Sanford claimed that "the best ladies in the convention" had favored her resolution but were "brow-beaten out of their nerve by the Savery and the Bloomer." She called them part of "the free love ring" and said they had the editor of the *Des Moines Register* in thrall, "a dish of oysters, a smile from painted lips, or an ogle of the eye from a bedizened beauty of three score years will secure his services."

That editor replied that no one had tried to influence his report except Sanford, "who asked us to suppress a portion of the proceedings, for reasons that she can explain better than we can take the trouble to do . . . as to our 'free love report' we may say, in our ignorance, we didn't know there was any of that kind of folks in the convention . . . and have heard of nobody but Mrs. Sanford that did."[502]

No reasonable argument could quiet the hysterical reactions to the tabling of Sandford's resolution. But Bloomer stood her ground.[503] At the executive committee meeting in January, they reasserted the morality of their movement and again refused to denounce any suffragist for their social or religious beliefs. Bloomer offered to speak to the legislature, but she did not return to Des Moines that session. Her health may have betrayed her again. Or perhaps she felt she had become a divisive figure.

The Polk County Suffrage Society in Des Moines panicked and formally condemned free love, declaring that they only believed in divorce for "good scriptural reasons," i.e., adultery.[504] And they ostracized Savery for her mild defense of Woodhull. The leaders also asked Stanton and Anthony to stay away while the legislature was in session. But Savery continued to talk to legislators and hosted a grand reception in her home for all the members and their families. Not one Des Moines paper mentioned it. The new little societies all over the state went silent in "the wake of the free-love storm." This was not the prepared ground for the general session of 1871 that she and Bloomer had planned two years earlier.

Women crowded the capitol for the debates on the suffrage amendment. The House approved it but then sent it back to committee rather than submitting it for ratification. Senator Benjamin Billings Richards told Savery and Lizzie Harbert that he would move to hear them speak but then tried to back out. They insisted and made him promise he would not speak against the amendment, but he took the floor and went on an emotional rant about the disgrace it would be to the state. As a result, his motion to hear them lost.

Savery attacked Richards in the papers for his betrayal. Jane Swisshelm wrote that the Polk County Suffrage Association was behind the refusal to hear Savery and Harbert and had convinced senators to vote against the amendment.

On the morning of March 29, 1871, the Senate chamber of Iowa was packed. At 10:00, the president of the Senate "facetiously announced" the discussion to strike "males" out of the state constitution. The men burst into laughter.

A German Republican spoke, in a heavy accent, and argued that women would make "ignorant and indifferent voters" and that they would have voted to end the Civil War before it was won.[505] The bill was defeated 24–22, with four absent or abstaining.

The national impression of these events was that the suffragists— Savery, Harbert, and Swisshelm in particular—had said too much and offended the legislators. Mary Livermore thought that the failure "damaged the entire cause everywhere, more even than the infernal Mrs. Woodhull."[506] Bloomer said nothing that spring.

In November 1872, Woodhull exposed the affair of the celebrity minister Henry Ward Beecher with the wife of his friend, the newspaper editor Theodore Tilton. Stanton was her source. Bloomer wrote to the *Nonpareil* that she believed Woodhull's allegations were true, because a year and half earlier, Bloomer had heard the same story from "one of the parties given as an authority." This was almost certainly Stanton, on their buggy rides in the valleys near Council Bluffs. Bloomer said she "never would have revealed her knowledge if it had not come so fully before the public." She hoped that "truth will be elicited and justice done" and that the blame would center on the adulterers rather than on Woodhull.[507]

And she finally wrote about the events of the previous year. "The attempt on the part of some of our friends to force the discussion of 'free love' and other outside issues, upon our convention last fall ... resulted disastrously to the cause for a time, and made us a mark for the opposition ... Disappointment and ill feeling were engendered, from the effects of which we have not fully recovered. Had not two or three Senators betrayed the trust reposed in them and refused to let us go with our claims to the people for their decision this fall, we should all have been up and doing, and have a more than usually interesting and exciting campaign."

Since Woodhull had been arrested for obscenity and her presidential campaign had come to nothing, Bloomer hoped the newer reformers had learned a lesson. "It is folly to turn aside from our great work to get up a doughty personal campaign against one lone woman." She could only hope that "our State Senate will reconsider its action of last winter, and vote to submit the question to the people two years hence."[508]

In March 1873, Bloomer went to Des Moines to preside over the annual state suffrage convention again. The Iowa general assembly had given women all their rights except suffrage, and Dexter would write that Amelia had a hand in that action. But this year, she undramatically stepped down. Lizzie Bunnell Read was elected president for the following year. The wealthy and conservative Martha Callanan was made vice president for Bloomer's district. And the convention formally repudiated any sympathy with free love.[509] After this, Bloomer's involvement would remain occasional, as her strength allowed.

That spring, Savery's house burned and was looted. They had no insurance or money to rebuild and moved into the Savery Hotel. Bloomer remained her sympathetic friend.[510] Neither of them attended the 1874 state suffrage convention, though Bloomer was elected to the executive committee in absentia, and Martha Callanan lost the presidency to Lizzie Harbert.[511]

The Woman's Crusades reinvigorated the temperance movement with the largest public demonstrations by women that century. Starting in 1873, in Xenia, Ohio, temperance women held "pray-ins," in which they prayed and sang at saloons for days and, in some cases, threw the alcohol into the street. This culminated in a Cleveland meeting in November 1874, where over a hundred women delegates from temperance societies in fifteen states and territories met to organize the Woman's National Christian Temperance Union (WCTU). It would become the largest and most powerful women's reform organization of the nineteenth century. They elected Annie Wittenmyer their president. Wittenmyer opposed women's suffrage, and women who were spooked by the immoral reputation of the suffragists were willing to join the WCTU.[512]

In May 1875, the Supreme Court upheld the decision in *Minor vs. Happersett* that ruled that the Fourteenth Amendment did not give women in the United States the right to vote. That was the end of the New Departure. Bloomer spent some time at the Cleveland Sanitarium that year.[513] She did not attend the Iowa suffrage meeting, though she was listed as a vice president.[514]

Over the next few years, Bloomer saw women's status continue to improve. The constitution of Iowa still barred women and Black men from major political offices, but in 1876, Annie Savery became one of the first three women admitted as attorneys in the state Supreme Court.[515]

Anthony and Stanton began a new project with the historian Matilda Joslyn Gage: a monumental history of the fight for women's suffrage. Anthony wrote to Bloomer for assistance, and Bloomer began to write to significant women for information. She also responded promptly to a request from the new Nebraska Historical Society for an account of her speech to their legislature, and she began to write her memoirs.

In the spring of 1877, Bloomer helped to organize a Council Bluffs women's temperance society. They recruited members and petitioned the city council for enforcement of the liquor law and amendment of the license law.[516] But as usual, their petitions were ignored.[517] Women's rights was making better progress. In May, to

Bloomer's surprise, Mrs. Jane Baldwin was appointed postmaster of Council Bluffs. Not everyone was happy, but no one questioned it.

Before dawn on August 25, Bloomer woke to a violent storm that hammered her roof and made the house and the trees creak alarmingly. In the morning, she and Dexter learned that a cyclone had struck the new iron railroad bridge over the Missouri, wrenching off two 250-foot spans that weighed thousands of tons and tossing them into the river. The Bloomers rode out to see the damage, which was so stunning that Frank Leslie's *Illustrated Newspaper* published a picture of it. The telegraph line to California was repaired, and traffic was running on temporary trestles within days, but the cost of the damage was immense.[518]

Summer 1879 marked Bloomer's first trip to Colorado, at sixty-one. Jennie had married and had her first child in February. Dexter and Amelia went out to meet the baby and see the sights.[519] They visited the resort town of Manitou Springs, where camp tents dotted the hills around hotels crowded with tourists and patients. They visited therapeutic bathhouses and rode out to see Cheyenne Cañon. One cool clear morning, they went for a day trip with a friendly couple from Memphis and a local guide to see the "remarkably beautiful" red rock formations, Glen Eyrie, and Queen's Cañon. From there, the party voted to continue to Monument Park, five miles away. Bloomer was amazed by the strange carved landscape. "Men have their theories, but the mystery is buried in the darkness of ages and none solve it satisfactorily. We leave them to their solitude and silence and, awe-stricken and subdued, turn our faces whence we came."[520]

CHAPTER 17
I Beg Leave to Correct

In the summer of 1879, Bloomer experienced an echo of the days when supposed friends sent her nasty criticisms from the papers. Several of her friends and family sent her an article by Mary Bull, the daughter of Ansel Bascom, on "WOMAN'S RIGHTS AND OTHER 'REFORMS' IN SENECA FALLS." Bloomer read it with interest and nostalgia, and then with growing irritation.

Bull confidently stated many errors and sniped at Bloomer as if she held a grudge against her. She was "certain" that everyone at the 1848 convention signed the Declaration. She described Bloomer as, "in all respects Mrs. Stanton's opposite, thin, almost meagre, in her proportions, short, with a small head and a dark complexion; not at all a handsome woman" with "no particular advantages of education, nor was she naturally an intellectual, nor a woman of talent," but someone involved with "such organizations as were to be found then in country towns, sewing societies and the like." She called *The Lily* "a small insignificant sheet," the conservative voice of the Woman's State Temperance Society. Stanton made it a women's rights paper. Bull insulted Stanton's appearance in the short dress and said Bloomer wore it to imitate Stanton. Bloomer went on tour to display herself in the dress, with neither "voice, manner, or anything particular to say." When Stanton happily abandoned the dress, "a slight coolness ensued between the two ladies," and Bloomer criticized her in *The Lily*.[521]

The words "small insignificant sheet" rang in Bloomer's head. She mailed a copy of Bull's article to Stanton and composed a letter to the *Seneca Falls Reveille*, which had reprinted it.

> As Mrs. Bull has given considerable space to me and my
> doings, I beg leave to correct some of her misstatements
> concerning my affairs . . . matters occurring when
> she was but a child of fourteen years, in which she
> had no part, and of which she knew nothing.
> Mrs. Bull says that it was the Bloomer dress and *The
> Lily* over all other reforms that gave to Seneca Falls its
> notoriety. Thanks for the admission . . . How strange that
> the "small insignificant sheet" conducted by an uneducated
> woman who had "nothing in particular to say" should
> have attained such a circulation, held its own through so
> many years, and been productive of such grand results.

Bloomer went on to correct Bull's article point by point: about her speaking tour, Mrs. Stanton's opinion of the short dress, and their relationship, and Stanton's status as a contributor to *The Lily*, nothing more.

> If any coolness ever existed between Mrs. Stanton and
> myself, it grew out of a difference of opinion in regard
> to changing the constitution of the Woman's State
> Temperance Society . . . On my part there was no such
> feeling . . . We always kept up an occasional correspondence
> and have ever been friends. It has been my pleasure . . .
> to entertain her for days at a time in my own home. In
> the main, I have endorsed her views ever since I knew
> them; yet there are points on which we differ . . .
> It is not pleasant to be written down by one who was
> but a child at the time of which she writes. Her charges
> and insinuations of betrayal of trust, disloyalty to principle,
> truckling to the wishes of others, being bought up by a little

attention, etc, do me great injustice . . . I think I am known to
have an individuality of my own, and something to say when
I speak, and my integrity has never before been questioned.

Stanton replied to Bloomer's personal letter. She was "quite
amused" by Mary Bull. "She seems to think that no one can have
a higher motive in doing anything than the use of notoriety. But
so long as we cannot make men and women to order, we must let
them say and write what they please." She had given up correcting
them. "It is of no use."[522]

The *Reveille* printed Bloomer's letter in full, but the editor
undermined it with a long comment, calling her sensitive and
biased. He called Bull's research "entirely reliable" and claimed that
"those familiar with the 'reform' movements inaugurated here seem
to regard it as quite truthful."[523]

Stanton had a point about correcting people. Bloomer did not
pursue it further.

In the autumn of 1880, the Bloomers went east to visit friends
and relations and to sightsee. Stanton invited them to visit her in
Tenafly, New Jersey, but before they could, a telegram came to tell
Bloomer that her sister Elvira was dangerously ill. They went straight
up to Waterloo, where Bloomer stayed with her sister until she died.
At sixty-two, Bloomer was now the only one of her siblings left.[524]

Not long after this, Anthony wrote to her from Tenafly. They
wanted her to write them a chapter of reminiscences and a thirty-
page Iowa chapter for their *History of Woman Suffrage* and asked for
details of New York women's history.[525] More friendly letters followed
with information requests and scraps of political news.[526] When
Bloomer told them her illnesses limited her activities, Anthony
wrote, "Sorry you are so out of health—you must pull through to
the day of woman's enfranchisement."[527]

A history of the Polk County Suffrage Society arrived from
Mary Work, and Bloomer found that her name and Savery's were
not included in the first two meetings of the state society. Work
apologized, asked Bloomer to write what she knew, and said, "You

pioneers have borne the burden of misrepresentation and ridicule but the tide has changed."[528]

Work was only about eight years younger than Bloomer, but the recent history of the movement, let alone before the war, was largely a blank to her. This reinforced the need for good histories and memoirs. The difficult relationships within the Iowa movement were another concern. If her Iowa chapter was not fair and complete, Bloomer would never hear the end of it.

The writing of the history tormented Bloomer for years. She corresponded with Anthony and Stanton, who confused her with their demands for more information in a limited space.[529] Anthony promised to use her chapter just as she wrote it, and when Bloomer got the revised proofs, she was horrified by Stanton's changes. She disliked being edited, and these edits were both ruthless and biased. Many contributors were similarly upset. Their often-uncredited coauthor Matilda Joslyn Gage called them "very lawless, and sometimes far from just."[530] Both apologized to Bloomer and assured her they meant well.[531]

In March 1881, an anti-temperance Democrat was elected mayor of Council Bluffs by thirty-six votes.[532] The Missouri River thawed and rose until it overran the banks in a flood worse than anything the white settlers had ever seen. All the bottom lands, where the Native people never built lasting structures for this very reason, were covered with four to five feet of water. Livestock drowned or starved.[533] Bloomer was grateful for the elevation of her house.

Anthony and Stanton forgot to return her Iowa chapter for corrections or mention that they had cut it to save for the next volume. The fragment of her reminiscences was also cut to make room for a profile of Ernestine Rose. She discovered these things when she received her published copy.

In bitterness, she scribbled a list of extracts from Anthony and Stanton's letters, all their praise and promises, and from this, she composed a bitter letter to Anthony.[534] She heard back almost immediately, but Anthony's letter seemed to have crossed hers in the mail. Anthony fished for compliments on the book and pressured Bloomer to sell copies, to review it for the Western papers, and to send them lists of typos.[535]

Bloomer wrote to Stanton about her grievances, and Stanton replied that she "knew nothing" of what Anthony had promised her and that they meant well.[536] Anthony finally replied from Rochester. She had been called away to the deathbed of a friend. Her distress at Bloomer's letter was apparent. "What can I say— but that I am very very sorry that we found it impossible to do what I had thought we could and should do." She explained her thought processes. "I can assure you Mrs. Bloomer—that in the whirl of getting out that book—working 12 and 14 hours nearly every day . . . for six months and more—I got to where I couldn't do everything that everybody wanted me to." She asked Bloomer to fix her Iowa chapter and send it to them for the next volume, but this time made no promises.[537]

And so Bloomer dove in again. She ended up managing the Nebraska chapter as well, with several contributors, and wrote an article for the *Western Woman's Journal*.[538] Mary Work helped her find more material, and Bloomer worked with her on a resolution for their next convention.[539] Maria Orwig, a Des Moines suffragist from Philadelphia, sent letters and asked Bloomer to be sure to return her letter from Annie Savery. "If you have not already said a 'good word' for Mrs. Savery *I would ask you to do so*—I think you know all about the opposition to her in our State Society." She had used the letter "many times to refute the accusation of free-lovism brought against her . . . she is my next door neighbor and I think she has been fearfully slandered by our Suffragists."[540]

On September 12, Bloomer went to the thirteenth annual meeting of the AWSA in Omaha. It was the largest and best meeting Bloomer had been able to attend in years, though she could not speak at it. Anthony spoke at one session, and Bloomer spoke on the early days of the movement at Anthony's NWSA meeting the following week. She told the crowd that the first time she gave a speech in public, she did it because Anthony asked her to.[541]

Despite the best efforts of the national and local societies, the Nebraska suffrage bill failed too. And again, at the last minute, Bloomer could not attend the annual state meeting and sent a letter to her friend Mary Coggeshall, a current secretary of the Polk County Society. "The defeat in Nebraska was, I know, a great disappointment . . . but to outsiders, success was hardly looked for." She blamed the failure on "the large foreign element, the entire liquor and gambling interest, the ignorant and prejudiced as well as the conservative," and said, "let us turn our attention to congress and a Sixteenth Amendment, which I think is more hopeful . . . It is very doubtful if the Fifteenth Amendment, enfranchising the negro, would have carried had it been submitted to the popular vote, and can we expect men to be more just to woman?"[542]

That November, Washington Territory became the third to enfranchise women. Coggeshall wrote to Bloomer, saying, "Dear friend, you will think me great in my demands upon you but to whom shall we go!" Would Bloomer help find writers to promote suffrage in the Iowa papers?[543] Bloomer received other invitations to speak and write and was at her desk in the bay window of their little library every day that her health permitted.[544]

Convenient, comfortable, idiosyncratic dress still lived. An article that year quoted women all over the country who still wore reform dresses. A woman in Vineland, New Jersey, had worn "the science dress" for over thirty years. A Michigan woman said she had not owned a long dress in twenty-five years. Women from New York to Iowa to California were quoted. And last, a "Home School" at Aurora, New Jersey, where women, men, and children "dress just alike, in a combination suit, with skirts."[545]

A women's suffrage bill would again go up before the Iowa state legislature in 1885. Mary Coggeshall and Martha Callanan wrote to Bloomer for support, advice, and reports.[546] Anthony sent her the call to the NWSA's seventeenth annual Washington, DC, convention, in January 1885. They also planned to meet in New Orleans, a first.[547] But Bloomer tried to shake them off. She resigned from the Iowa society and made no plans to attend either convention.

The Iowa women's suffrage bill passed the state Senate, but not the House.

In June 1885, Bloomer heard from Anthony again about the *History of Woman Suffrage*. Would she fix up her proof for them? It was hot in Council Bluffs, and Bloomer had guests from the East on the way. She told Mary Coggeshall that her chapter "had been so pruned down and altered, and sometimes I was misrepresented ... Mrs. Stanton making it read as she would like it to be and not as facts made it—that I was disgusted and disheartened, and never sent back the proof, not believing that it would ever be used after all these years." She had stopped keeping records of Iowa suffrage activities. The whole thing needed to be rewritten, but she had no heart for it. "It don't make much difference I suppose, but one don't like their writings so tampered with."[548]

Coggeshall praised Bloomer's "good nature" in revising the Iowa chapter. Bloomer said it was no such thing. "If I had the entire matter out of their hands I would not touch it. But they have the advantage." She asked if Coggeshall might be interested in taking it on, but Coggeshall declined.[549]

When Bloomer felt angry or resentful or hurt, she said so, but she still regarded Anthony and Stanton with affection and respect. In 1885, she was invited to contribute to a special issue of the *New Era* for Stanton's seventieth birthday, and she wrote an essay that also corrected the record on her own work. Of Stanton's partnership with Anthony she said, "Neither would have done what she has without the other. Mrs. Stanton had the intellectual and Susan the executive ability to carry forward the movement ... The writer is glad for the part she had in bringing two such strong characters together." Her birthday wish read, "May she live long to enjoy the fruits of her labors, and the consciousness that the world is better for her life and works."[550]

Anthony sent Bloomer the Iowa chapter proof for final corrections, and said she thought it read "splendidly now!! And I hope you'll think so too—and never again think or speak of your fearful ordeal . . . my feelings have never been hurt—only, because I felt I had hurt yours!!"[551]

Seneca Falls held a grand centennial celebration of its founding that July Fourth, which the Bloomers attended. The organizers made Amelia an honorary member of their press committee.[552]

In early February 1888, two parcels arrived for Bloomer, one from Representative A. J. Holmes of some documents that he thought might interest her, and one from the commissioner of agriculture of unusual flower seeds, sent by Holmes's request, to thank her. He had read her Iowa chapter in the *History of Woman Suffrage* and found that she had included his full remarks in support of awarding a medal to the heroine of an Iowa train wreck.[553] This might have been the most appreciation she had for her work on the *History of Woman Suffrage*.

Anthony forwarded a letter from a mutual friend remembering *The Lily*. Bloomer answered that she knew many hundreds of people across the country had first learned of the women's movement from it. "I gave my eight years to the work, but my seventy lectures, in addition to the care of the paper, overtaxed a constitution never strong, so that my later years have been passed in enforced inactivity."[554]

The fame of the trousers still harassed her, even now that she was white-haired and almost seventy. With the new dress reform promoted by Annie Jenness Miller and the popular embrace of baggy knickerbockers for women as active wear, Bloomer's name continued to be mentioned as the originator of these modern garments. Journalists visited her for interviews and wrote to her to ask about them and to get her thoughts on women's suffrage.[555] If they were respectful, she was polite and kind with them.

A particularly vulgar headline appeared in an April 1888 issue of the *Chicago Tribune*: "Amelia Bloomer's Boom: The Great Sensation Which She Made Forty Years Ago." The article was worse. The writer called the short skirt and trousers her own "peculiar ideas" and described them as purple and white silk with flamboyant trims.

He claimed her appearance "literally paralyzed" people in Boston, where Bloomer had never set foot. He referenced several articles from that time, including the one about the Bloomer bride in white satin, the young men in Syracuse who gave the dress to the Black woman, and the family of "Bloomers," which to her special outrage, he took literally as a description of Dexter.[556] But based on past experience, she decided to ignore it.[557]

That decision was not universally applied. Nettie Sanford Chapin, who had given Savery and Bloomer so much trouble over Woodhull, complained to the *Woman's Standard* about the Iowa chapter. Why had Bloomer left so much out? "Can women ever do justice to women?" This was why men distrusted women's suffrage: "this lack of fairness, this personal pique."[558] Bloomer could have said similar things about Sanford Chapin's attitude to herself. She replied that Stanton had warned her that "my turn would come after a while; that when my Iowa chapter appeared there would 'be a howl about my ears from Blanche, Tray, and Sweetheart.'" But Sanford Chapin was the first dog to howl, "and it is so faint, so uncalled for, so untrue, so easily refuted, that it does not hurt me." It was incomplete because it was one chapter on one state in a full history of women's suffrage. "That injustice was intended, or done to any, I deny, on my own behalf and that of the editors of the History."[559]

At the end of November, the *Chicago Tribune* printed a column with the words "FREE LOVE AND BLOOMERS" in the headline, and again she had to respond. It was on the Oneida Community, the religious society that engaged in nontraditional "complex marriage" from 1849 until 1879. The author said that Bloomer had learned of "the costume" there and "afterwards claimed it as her personal invention." He then gave a suggestive description of Noyes's sexual pairing of Oneida men and women.[560]

Bloomer sat down at her desk with its view of the garden and dipped her pen. She had never visited the Oneida Community or known anyone who had. "I never knew that the women there wore short skirts and trousers; and I never claimed that the short skirt as my 'personal invention.' It is said that 'nothing lies like history,' and, judging from your writers of history, I believe it." She told the true story again. For her and her friends, "the dress was but an incident." She had not worn it for thirty years. "I would that future writers would seek to learn the truth concerning me and my public career, or let my memory rest in peace."[561]

The family she created was a welcome respite. Jennie's children in Colorado, the closest the Bloomers had to grandchildren, were old enough to play with them when they visited. Bloomer would climb the short ladder into their attic and sit with them, looking over the family memorabilia brought from New York when Jennie's father died, telling the children stories, and giving them little lessons in observation. There were boxes of old letters, Betsy Frost's spinning wheel, a Revolutionary War cap and cartridge belt, and her sister Amanda's scrapbook.[562] In February 1890, the AWSA and the NWSA united as the National American Woman Suffrage Association (NAWSA), fulfilling Anthony's dream for national centralized control.[563] Bloomer was elected an honorary vice president along with many others not present. Some, like Bloomer, were absent due to old age and illness. Frederick Douglass was consul general in Haiti.[564]

That April would be Bloomer's fiftieth wedding anniversary. Friends and family sent congratulations and gifts. Letters arrived from people they had not heard from in years. Their tact varied. One suggested their infertility had freed them for "that generous care for the public welfare which has marked your long and honorable career." Anthony wrote that no married couple she knew, "where the wife belonged to the school of equal rights for women, have lived more happily, more truly one."

Bloomer's gown for the occasion was glossy black duchess satin, with an open front that displayed a contrasting vest and front panel of silver-gray damascene silk, patterned with calla lilies. She wore her diamond jewelry and a frill of antique lace at her throat. The house was filled with fragrant roses and lilies, green vines, and daffodils. "1840–1890" hung in gold numbers over the door to the library. In the front parlor, Bloomer sat under a reception canopy of vines and flowers to receive their guests, with a bouquet of pale yellow Maréchal Niel roses in her lap. Dexter stood beside her in a new black suit.

One reporter asked if she still had her wedding gown, and she laughed and told him she had "preserved none of her old-time costumes," with "a playful emphasis to the 'none.'"[565] A refreshment table in the dining room was staffed by two shifts of their friends to serve the parade of visitors, and in the evening, candles were lit among the flowers.[566] This event was reported nationwide, almost invariably with mention, and often an illustration, of the trousers.[567]

Bloomer was able to hire a full-time servant, usually a recently emigrated Danish or Swedish girl, which lightened her domestic workload in her last few years. The orchard and garden filled her kitchen with fresh produce in the summer. She still made preserves to use and give away and still made all her own breads and cakes and doughnuts, even for large parties and holidays.

Jennie and her family often came to visit them in the summers. One year, she decided to leave her eldest daughter, Maie, to keep them company for half the year, as she had. Maie would have been ten in 1890. Bloomer gave her Jennie's little upstairs bedroom and had her help with arranging papers, the cooking, and remaking clothing for the poor. Maie made friends in the neighborhood, and Dexter took her out for buggy and sleigh rides almost every day.[568]

Dickey, the pink-crested white cockatoo, was still alive and well. He perched next to Bloomer for supper and sat on the arm of her red velvet rocker in the evenings, while Dexter read aloud or they discussed politics and Maie did her homework. Maie and Dexter often had a game of checkers, and Amelia might tell stories of her childhood or show her a private case of letters from "persons of note from all over the world."

Maie decided that she wanted to be a doctor. Bloomer approved and let her pick two books on health from her collection. Maie picked one on food and one on the water cure. From the food book, she learned to cook with vegetables and breadcrumbs. The water cure did not go as well. After her bath, despite her pleading, Bloomer dashed a pail of cold water over her and then gave her a warm rubdown. Once was enough.[569]

Even now, she continued to support the causes she believed in as much as she could. When Frances Willard brought the WCTU around to women's suffrage, Bloomer became a member and officer of her local chapter. In 1890, she helped Mary Coggeshall promote another state suffrage amendment, and Coggeshall continued to press her to be an active member and attend meetings.[570] But Bloomer was increasingly homebound. She wrote to the annual Iowa meeting that "a large majority of the best people of the country are with us . . . sooner or later the ballot will be placed in the hands of women throughout the states."[571]

In April 1891, Annie Savery died in New York City and was buried in Des Moines.[572] That summer, after a day of lectures and music at the Council Bluffs Chautauqua, Bloomer suddenly lost her voice. It gradually returned but remained weak. She was seventy-three. Her mind was clear, but physically, she slowed until Dexter "was easily able now to keep up with her in their walks."[573]

Requests for copies of *The Lily* came often now, and Bloomer tried to locate more. Anthony visited her that spring and urged Bloomer to put her complete run in a library to preserve it.[574] Bloomer dismissed the suggestion but thought maybe she would will it to the public library or a friend. Anthony wrote later to suggest the new New York State Library in Albany, but Bloomer hesitated to let it go. It was her only proof of her eight years as editor and the facts of the early movement. She still referred to it all the time.

The Chicago World's Columbian Exhibition was planned to open in May, and an organizer asked her for *The Lily* for the Iowa display.[575] The New York committee also wanted it. Bloomer considered it and looked through the issues in their ribbon-tied black linen covers. She made pencil notes of the names of columnists next to their pseudonyms, especially Stanton's, and scratched out "a Committee of Ladies" in the masthead and wrote her name in its place.

At last, she talked herself into it.[576] She sent it via express and asked the committee to please acknowledge receipt. "It was like parting with a dear old friend and I do not expect to ever see it again."[577]

The Lily was safely exhibited in New York and Chicago and later sent to the state library in Albany. The *Woman's Journal* called it "the early woman's rights paper, published in the forties, by Mrs. Elizabeth Cady Stanton and Mrs. Amelia Bloomer."[578] Even friends kept getting the facts wrong.

Bloomer could not attend the Columbian Exhibition, but Dexter did, and he kept a detailed daily journal to share it with her.

The memory of the short dress and trousers of the 1850s did not age as well as *The Lily*, and consensus settled into the opinion that it had been "hideous."[579] But there were still some more positive comments, including one from the *Oskaloosa Herald*. "It was in 1851 that she began to wear the costume which is now known throughout the English-speaking world as the bloomer, and she has patiently waited forty-three years for the natty bicycle girl to demonstrate its utility and gracefulness."[580] The knee-length cycling breeches worn by women cyclists with blouses and jackets were a new variation on many old ideas of dress reform, but they were not the short dress and trousers.[581]

Her last journey was made to Colorado with Dexter, in late summer 1894, when she was seventy-six. She spent about two weeks at Colorado Springs and Manitou Springs, taking electric treatments at the sanatorium of her friend Mrs. Dr. Harriett Leonard. She could not tour much scenery this time. They spent a week with Jennie's family and returned home with Bloomer "somewhat improved in health and strength."[582]

She and Dexter spent Christmas at the home of their friend Nathan P. Dodge. She was happy, enjoyed the evening, and felt well enough to walk there and back. That was the last time she left her house. She sat in her library, reading, sewing, and talking to friends and neighbors, who visited her almost daily. On Friday, December 28, "several were with her during nearly the entire day; they remembered that she appeared remarkably bright and cheerful."

After supper that evening, at about six, she was reading with Dickey by her side and Dexter across from her, when she fell back in her chair and exclaimed: "I am sick; I am sicker than I ever was before in my life." Dexter dropped his book and came to her. He helped her to bed, but at one in the morning, she was struggling to breathe, and he called the doctor, who like most doctors all her life, could not do much for her. She was in agony, suffered intense nausea, and was unable to rest or sleep. Her dear cousin Hannah Kennedy arrived on Saturday morning to sit with them, and so did the doctor's wife, their minister, and two other friends. Bloomer had another attack that evening, and the doctor said she could not recover. But she was conscious and stoic. On Sunday morning, she worsened. But the pain faded, and she drifted into sleep. Dexter held her hand and felt her heartbeat slow, until at noon, "her pulse stopped beating, and she was gone forever."

CHAPTER 18

We All Have a Work to Do

Newspapers across the state, the nation, and the world reported Amelia Bloomer's death. The *Council Bluffs Nonpareil* said that "Mrs. Bloomer's circle of friends in Council Bluffs was large, and she was highly esteemed and loved by all who knew her. She was an excellent entertainer, and was a great favorite among the young people of the Episcopal Church of which she was a faithful member. She was very fond of society and took an active part in church and charitable work . . . The sudden announcement of her death came as a shock."[583]

The *Omaha World-Herald* ran an obituary on December 31 and another brief paragraph on New Year's Day. "Her youth was spent in wrestling for the rights and privileges of her sex. Many of those privileges are now accepted and enjoyed by women as a matter of course, with no thought of the effort exercised in securing them . . . She was a woman of exquisite refinement, of intensely affectionate nature, fond of the traditions of her eastern life and training, and alert to follow the progress of her country-women."[584]

Dexter and her other relatives and friends held her funeral on January 2, a cold sunny day.[585] As she had predicted, she was buried "on one of the high bluffs overlooking the mighty Missouri, and the beautiful plains of Nebraska beyond," in Fairview Cemetery. The tall white monument that Dexter ordered was inscribed, "A PIONEER IN WOMAN'S ENFRANCHISEMENT."

On January 5, the *Omaha World-Herald* printed excerpts from five more obituaries in major cities, beginning with a question in the *St. Louis Dispatch* as to whether Bloomer or Lucy Stone "was the first to wear bloomers. As both are now where bloomers are not worn, the subject may as well be dropped." The *Boston Herald* mentioned her "anxiety lest she should be remembered only because she once wore an odd costume. She appears to have come to a realization of the fact that when it comes to fighting against the tyranny of fashion, the enemy usually wins." The *Sioux City Tribune* said, "Thus ended a woman whose name has been one of the joke storm centers of the generation . . . It may surprise some to know that Mrs. Bloomer was a woman of every domestic virtue, gentle, kind, affectionate and universally beloved."[586] There were a few passing mentions in the international press, but most of the world had lost interest in her long ago.

On the thirteenth of January, 1895, Bloomer's rector, Reverend Babcock, delivered a memorial discourse at St. Paul's. Copies were printed and distributed to the mourners and mailed to friends and relatives who could not be there. He told of her hospitality and her commitment to her church. "Her kindness to me was ever constant and uniform, and her ingenuous frankness such as I always enjoyed. Plain and albeit of rugged candor in her speech, such is better for this world than the honey covering of deceit."

Dexter was left alone, except for Dickey the bird and Dolly the horse. Bloomer had advised him to move in with Jennie's family in Colorado if she died first, unless they could move to be with him. They could not, and Dexter did not want to leave his home and office. So they sent Maie again, now a young teenager, to keep house with him and Hulda, the current Danish maid.

Dickey grieved for Amelia, wandering the house, calling her with "a strange cry." Dexter still went out to his office most days, so he gave Dickey to another family where he thought he would have better care. But the cockatoo was so sad there that he took him back. Dickey would sit on his shoulder and caress his cheek.

In the library one day, Dexter opened Amelia's desk and began to sort through her papers. He felt he should write her biography, not just a memoir but a record of her work that made use of all the writings she had never made into a book herself. He wrote to friends to ask for publishing advice and settled on the radical press Arena, in Boston.

Dexter's book would have to be her most accurate and lasting memorial. He had experience writing and publishing historical essays and was soon deep in the work. He put her first in the narrative, with occasional fond memories of his own. One passage read, "it is here no more than strict justice to record that she was, in all her work of promoting temperance and woman's enfranchisement, aided and sustained by the cordial assistance and support of her husband. No note or word of discord ever arose between them on these subjects (and, indeed, very few on any other)."

On her character, he wrote, "Mrs. Bloomer was a great critic, and for that reason may not have been so popular with her associates as she otherwise might have been. Her criticisms, possibly, were sometimes too unsparing and too forcibly expressed . . . . No one ever attacked her, in print or otherwise, without receiving a sharp reply either from tongue or pen if it was in her power to answer. But no person ever had a kinder heart, or more earnestly desired the happiness of others, or more readily forgot or forgave their failings. Perhaps, she was deficient in the quality of humor and took life too seriously; this over-earnestness, however, if it existed at all, it is believed was brought out more fully by dwelling so much upon what she regarded as the wrongs of her sex . . . The same charge, that of taking things too seriously, has recently been made . . . against the women of the present day who are battling for what they conceive to be the sacred rights of women."

In the spring of 1896, *The Life and Writings of Amelia Bloomer* was published, in cloth hardcover for $1.25, and in paperback for fifty cents. There were a few reviews, including a long and sympathetic one in the *Woman's Journal*, and it was mentioned in lists of coming books. But Arena Publishing succumbed to its debts later that year, and no other press picked up Dexter's book until the feminist publishing wave of the 1970s.

Dexter still attended and spoke at suffrage meetings. In October 1898, he gave the welcoming address to the twenty-ninth annual convention of the Iowa Woman Suffrage Society, and Susan B. Anthony gave the opening address.[587] She told a reporter that a suffrage amendment would "undoubtably be passed" by the next state legislature.[588]

About five years after Amelia's death, at age eighty-four, Dexter was driving a sleigh in the snowy countryside, as he loved to do. Somehow, there was an accident, and he was thrown. He was badly bruised, but the doctor didn't think it was serious. About ten days later, he was sitting with Maie when he suddenly stopped breathing, and his head fell forward. When Maie and Hulda reached him, he was dead.[589]

With Dexter gone, Maie did her best for Bloomer's legacy, donating her letters and papers and personal effects to libraries and archives, and writing down some of her memories. Still, many of Bloomer's personal papers were lost or discarded or burned. There may yet be a box of letters from her in the closet of the descendants of some friend or collaborator or cousin.

A constitutional ban on alcohol finally passed in 1920, and by 1933, it was repealed. During Prohibition, rates of death from alcohol abuse, infant mortality, and domestic violence declined.

But since the end of Prohibition, changes in how we view our economic and political rights have shifted the historical memory of prohibitionists to a belief that they were motivated by their religion or culture, not by political and economic justice.[590] This has produced one more reason to view Bloomer as backwards in her advocacy for temperance.

But as of this writing, the CDC reports that 178,000 deaths a year are tied to alcohol abuse in the United States.[591]

Women did not win the vote until August 1920. Stanton had died in 1902, Anthony in 1906.

History can seem like one long game of telephone. If a writer invents a detail or reports hearsay, others will reprint the error endlessly and be taken for authoritative voices because they found it in an older source. Writers have claimed Bloomer lectured in London, or that Eddie and Mary were Civil War orphans. Half the pictures with her name on them are not her. A feminist children's book award from the American Library Association, the Amelia Bloomer Book List, was renamed in 2020 because the committee learned of Elizabeth Cady Stanton's private complaint to Anthony that Bloomer would not speak against the Fugitive Slave Act in *The Lily*.[592] Stanton's letter is easy to find online. *The Lily* is not.

While the bloomer outfit fell out of favor, the interest in dress reform did not. In a 1924 interview with designer Grace Ripley, she said the flapper was "the product of the dress reformers. No corsets, clothes hung from the shoulder, grace and freedom and comfort... Some day true modesty will be understood as a concept of personal dignity, having little or nothing to do with any arbitrary concealment of the body." She accurately described how Bloomer ran *The Lily* and adopted the new dress, "so light and free to walk in ... but to be comfortable was not enough and like most reformers she got laughed at for her pains."[593]

In the 1940s, when gender anxiety experienced another surge during the war, a musical called *Bloomer Girl*, set in 1861 with music by Harold Arlen, was a solid hit.

In 1956, a volunteer opened a trunk in the attic of the Seneca Falls Historical Society and rediscovered packages of letters to and from Bloomer, along with manuscripts of speeches, her autograph book, souvenirs of her golden wedding anniversary, and the daguerreotype of Bloomer in her short dress and trousers and pale beaver hat. No one knew how they had gotten there.[594]

In 1975, the Iowa legislature established the Iowa Woman's Hall of Fame. The first four women admitted to it were Carrie Chapman Catt, Ola B. Miller, Annie Wittenmyer, and Amelia Jenks Bloomer.[595]

In the late 1970s, Cheryl Schmidt, an English teacher in Council Bluffs, did a master's thesis on Bloomer and published an annotated bibliography in the *Annals of Iowa*. She visited the Bloomers' gravesite and found the tall, white granite marker badly neglected; it was filthy, tilted to one side, and crusted with decades of grime. She decorated it and enlisted the help of the county historical society. They restored the marker and added another with historical information about the Bloomers.

In 1984, Seneca Falls put up a historic marker for her, and in 1998, a trio of statues titled "When Anthony Met Stanton." Bloomer stands in the center. In 2012, the village of Homer, New York, installed a marker in front of her childhood home.

Ten years later, in May 2022, the Council Bluffs school board declared that Bloomer Elementary School would henceforth be named for both Amelia and Dexter, instead of Dexter alone. They placed a new historical marker to "Amelia Bloomer: President of the Iowa Suffrage Association 1871–73. Advocate for Temperance, Women's Rights, and Equal Pay for Women School Teachers in Council Bluffs."

In 1995, Bloomer was inducted into the National Women's Hall of Fame in Seneca Falls. Their statement claims that *The Lily* shifted focus to women's rights "under the guidance of Elizabeth Cady Stanton."[596]

Bloomer's name is still firmly attached to the general garment that was labeled as such by the press in 1851. She is often referenced in articles about women wearing trousers, or about fashion trends. Her name is occasionally attached to suffrage or women in journalism, but it almost never comes up when people talk about alcohol abuse.

The full scope of her work is worth remembering. She was a vital link in the early women's movement and helped to develop the foundational arguments. The discussions in *The Lily* are often still relevant now, sometimes with little change in language. And she was at the center of some of the first attempts by relatively ordinary women who had been trained for silence, weakness, and isolation to develop their abilities and risk their physical, emotional, and financial security to claim their equal rights as human beings and citizens.

This was not work they could leave to the authorities and the professionals. They had to take on tasks that seemed impossible at first and create what they did not have: a committee, a newspaper, an auxiliary society. A state organization, and then a national one. At different times in her life, Bloomer was both a visible leader and a less visible contributor, contributing what and when she could.

The mite pocket, a common women's fundraising ploy in the nineteenth century, is an image that sums up much of the work Bloomer did after the few years of her fame. A mite means a tiny thing and in this case references the Biblical story of the "widow's mite," the woman praised by Jesus because she put the only two pennies she had into the temple treasury while rich men made great displays of their donations, which they could well spare. Mite pockets were decorative bags hung on the wall to collect coins for a cause, to be donated at a "mite meeting" each month. When people wrote to Amelia Bloomer for autographs, she often responded with the same short sentiment: "In the grand providential movements of the age the individual is of little account. We all have a work to do, and it is a great joy to feel that we may aid with our mite in hastening the coming of the Truth and the Right."

Even if we are deeply committed to a cause, sometimes all we have to give is a mite. We may wish we had more time, or more money, or better health, or fewer responsibilities so that we could give what an Elizabeth Cady Stanton or Susan B. Anthony could give. But all contributions count. And when you become part of a community, you realize that we tag-team each other. If illness or poverty or grief sidelines one of us, others carry on, and our support for each other is part of the work too.

Bloomer understood the power of realizing that you can break away from isolation and the low expectations that others have for you and join with like-minded people to work for the change you want to see in this world. And that the inevitable conflicts, drudgery, and disappointments are an ordinary part of life and work, not a reason to break with those who share your ultimate goals, and never a reason to despair.

Isn't that a better story than a frilly pair of pants?

Acknowledgments

No book is created by one person.

The late Louise Noun and Cheryl Schmidt pointed the way with their research and bibliographies on Bloomer, which were part of the feminist publishing surge of the 1960s, '70s, and '80s that also produced a new paperback edition of Dexter's 1896 biography.

My research began with Bloomer's papers and objects at the Seneca Falls Historical Society. Nellie Ludemann was my friendly helpful contact there.

The Council Bluffs Public Library has the other large collection of Bloomer's papers and an excellent local history collection. My gratitude to librarian Daley Porter, who answered my emails and rummaged in their archive for me when I came by on my whirlwind research tour of Des Moines, Council Bluffs, and Omaha.

I am also grateful to Sophie Clough of the Cortland Historical Society, Anna Holland and Hang Nguyen of the Iowa University Libraries, Kelsey Berryhill of the State Historical Society of Iowa, and the New York State Library Manuscripts and Special Collections, the New York Public Library, and the New York Historical Society.

I have admired Belt Publishing for years and am delighted to be one of their authors now. Anne Trubek encouraged this idea when I first threw it together in her online book proposal class, said yes when I pitched it to her years later, and was patient when I found ten times the material I expected! Thank you to all the Belt staff who worked on this book, including cover artist David Wilson, and most of all my skillful and encouraging editor, Phoebe Mogharei, who helped me condense and focus and structure this book.

In July 2020, thanks to Amy Reading and Carla Kaplan, I was included in a remote Biographer's International Society roundtable on women's biography. They, Eve Kahn, Christine Cipriani, Allison Gilbert, Diane Prenatt, Elizabeth Harris, Harriet Reisen, Sallie Bingham, and Mary Ann Caws were a vital support when we and all the archives and libraries we needed were locked down in the worst of the pandemic. Thank you all for helping me to develop my ideas and my confidence. I'm amazed by all the good books we've produced!

My membership in Biographer's International has also given me access to priceless recommendations and talks, and early coaching by the expert and kind Anne Boyd Rioux.

Thank you to my sister Zoe Miller-Lee, my father and stepmother Mike and Marilyn Miller, and my dear old friends Anne Sawyer and Lisa Guevara, who encouraged me all along. And especially to my good friend Dana Wardlaw, who has been an interested and insightful sounding board for this project on our regular dog walks since the very beginning.

Simon Catterall has been my loving and constant support in every way for over twenty-five years. Sam and Rowan Catterall listened to me, fed me, and helped Simon keep our domestic sphere afloat while I ignored it all during the final crunch. All three have also given me excellent feedback over the last five years. Home is my safe harbor, and the women's movements have helped us to make it so.

Notes

Introduction

1. "Let This Woman Alone," *Chicago Daily Tribune*, December 8, 1889, 6.

Chapter 1

2. Amelia Bloomer, "Bloomers Weren't Invented Then," *Chicago Daily Tribune*, [1894].
3. H.P. Smith, *History of Cortland County, with Illustrations and Biographical Sketches of Some of Its Prominent Men and Pioneers* (D. Mason & Co., 1885), 49, https://lccn.loc.gov/08018098.
4. Smith, *History of Cortland County*, 213; CR4 Cortland Repository, Thursday, October 20, 1814.
5. CR4 Cortland Repository, Thursday, October 20, 1814.
6. "By Gone Days," *The Lily*, June 1849, 4.
7. Dexter Bloomer, *Life and Writings of Amelia Bloomer* (Schocken Books, 1975), 10–11; Maie Irvine Hoover, "The Home Life of Amelia Bloomer," typescript, Seneca Falls Historical Society (SFHS), Coll. 37, box 22; John H. Keatley, "Amelia Bloomer," *Annals of Iowa*, July 1874, 191.
8. "The Poor Indians," *Auburn Free Press*, June 2, 1830.
9. Bloomer, *Life and Writings of Amelia Bloomer*, 58–59.
10. Maie Irvine Hoover, "Mrs. Amelia Bloomer and My Early Recollections," 1, typescript in Amelia Bloomer Papers, SFHS.
11. Bloomer, *Life and Writings of Amelia Bloomer*, 12.
12. *History of Seneca Co., New York, with Illustrations Descriptive of Its Scenery, Palatial Residences, Public Building…and Important Manufactories* (J.B. Lippincott & Co., 1876), 107, New York Heritage Digital Collections, https://nyheritage.org.
13. Mrs. L.R. Sanford, "Early Industries," in *100ᵗʰ Anniversary of the Town of Junius* by the Seneca Falls Historical Society (1903), 43.

14. Bloomer, *Life and Writings of Amelia Bloomer*, 12.
15. Amelia Bloomer scrapbook, SFHS, Coll. 37, box 23.
16. "Woman's Influence," *The Lily*, September 1849, 8. She wrote this as fiction, but it is also obviously autobiographical and meshes with Dexter's memories. Her feelings about Dexter may have been different, but this is the best source available.
17. John H. Keatley, "Hon. D.C. Bloomer," *Annals of Iowa*, January 1874, 21–22.
18. Bloomer, *Life and Writings of Amelia Bloomer*, 13.
19. "Editorial Correspondence," *The Lily*, February 15, 1855, 5.
20. "After Fifty Busy Years," *Omaha World-Herald*, April 16 1890, 4.

Chapter 2

21. Isaac Fuller in 1840 Census, and North America, Family Histories, 1500–2000, via Ancestry.com.
22. "Woman's Influence."
23. Bloomer, *Life and Writings of Amelia Bloomer*, 14–15.
24. Edward Charles Eisenhart, *A Century of Seneca Falls History: Showing the Rise and Progress of a New York State Village* (Princeton, NJ: 1942).
25. Glenn C. Altschuler and Jan M. Saltzgaber, *Revivalism, Social Conscience, and Community in the Burned-Over District* (Cornell University Press, 1983), 58.
26. Bloomer, *Life and Writings of Amelia Bloomer*, 16–18.
27. Bloomer, *Life and Writings of Amelia Bloomer*, 17.
28. Larry E. Davis, "Unregulated Potions Still Cause Mercury Poisoning," *Western Journal of Medicine* 173, no. 1 (July 2000): 19.
29. Sok Chul Hong, "The Burden of Early Exposure to Malaria in the United States, 1850–1860: Malnutrition and Immune Disorders," *Journal of Economic History* 67, no. 4 (December 2007): 1001–35.
30. Elizabeth R. Varon, "Tippecanoe and the Ladies, Too: White Women and Party Politics in Antebellum Virginia," *Journal of American History* 82, no. 2 (September 1995): 494.
31. Ronald G. Shafer, "Women Openly Embraced a Presidential Campaign in 1840. Some Men Were Scandalized," *Washington Post*, August 5, 2020.
32. Bloomer, *Life and Writings of Amelia Bloomer*, 18.
33. *Seneca County Courier*, September 15, 1840, SFHS.
34. "Woman's Influence."
35. "Modern Flirtations," *The Lily*, July 1853.
36. "The Festival," *Seneca County Courier*, November 17, 1840.
37. *Seneca County Courier*, November 17, 1840, 3.
38. "Old Winter Has Come, Alack," *Seneca County Courier*, November 24, 1840.

39. "Wood! Wood!!" *Seneca County Courier*, January 26, 1841. A standard request, since rural subscribers often had everything but money. In 1821, the *Cayuga Republican* in Auburn asked for firewood in payment and "also, wanted Butter, Cheese, Lard, Wheat, Corn, Oats, Rye, Feathers, Flax, Wool, at fair prices, also a little Cash." In Frank Mott, *American Journalism: A History, 1690–1960*, 3rd ed. (Macmillan, [1962]), 203.

40. "Permanent Temperance Documents: Annual Report of the American Temperance Union, 1st–8th, 1837–44 6th Report Pp311/9," Gale, https://www.gale.com/primary-sources/nineteenth-century-collections-online; Amelia Bloomer, "Twenty Years Ago," March 1, 1862, typescript, Amelia Bloomer Papers, SFHS.

41. Altschuler and Saltzgaber, *Revivalism, Social Conscience, and Community*, 52.

42. *Seneca County Courier*, January 12, 1841, 1.

43. Ann Russo and Cheris Kramarae, eds., *The Radical Women's Press of the 1850s* (Routledge, 1991), 3.

44. Faye E. Dudden, "Women's Rights, Abolitionism, and Reform in Antebellum and Gilded Age America," *Oxford Research Encyclopedia of American History*, April 5, 2016, https://oxfordre.com.

45. *Seneca County Courier*, November 17, 1840.

46. *The Water Bucket*, microfilm, SFHS.

47. *Seneca Democrat*, January 1840, SFHS.

48. Frank Walker Stevens, *The Beginnings of the New York Central Railroad* (G.P. Putnam, 1926), 181–97, https://play.google.com/books; *Seneca Falls Democrat*, July 8, 1841.

49. Eisenhart, *Century of Seneca Falls History*.

50. Jeff Biggers, *The Trials of a Scold: The Incredible True Story of Writer Anne Royall* (Thomas Dunne Books, 2017).

51. Megan Marshall, *Margaret Fuller: A New American Life* (Houghton Mifflin Harcourt, 2013).

52. Sylvia D. Hoffert, *Jane Grey Swisshelm: An Unconventional Life, 1815–1884* (University of North Carolina Press, 2004).

53. *The Water Bucket* 1, no. 1 February 25, 1842, 1.

54. Ruth M. Alexander, "'We Are Engaged as a Band of Sisters': Class and Domesticity in the Washingtonian Temperance Movement, 1840–1850," *Journal of American History* 75, no. 3 (December 1988): 770.

55. "For the Water Bucket," *The Water Bucket* 1, no. 4 , April 1, 1842.

56. *The Water Bucket* 1, no. 5, April 8, 1842.

57. *The Water Bucket* 1, no. 8, April 29, 1842.

58. Ruth H. Bloch, "The American Revolution, Wife Beating, and the Emergent Value of Privacy," *Early American Studies* 5, no. 2 (Fall 2007): 223–51.

59. J. Quinlivan, "Where Should Research Now Be Focused in Domestic Violence and Alcohol?" *Journal of Substance Use* 6, no. 4 (July 2009): 248–50

Chapter 3

60. "Temperance Celebration! Of the Fourth of July," *The Water Bucket*, June 24, 1842, microfilm, SFHS.
61. "Oration" and "Grand Temperance Celebration of the Fourth of July in Seneca Falls," *The Water Bucket*, July 8, 1842, microfilm, SFHS.
62. Altschuler and Saltzgaber, *Revivalism, Social Conscience, and Community*, 276.
63. Altschuler and Saltzgaber, *Revivalism, Social Conscience, and Community*, 148.
64. Altschuler and Saltzgaber, *Revivalism, Social Conscience, and Community*.
65. Judith Wellman, *The Road to Seneca Falls* (University of Illinois Press, 2004), 127–28.
66. Bloomer, *Life and Writings of Amelia Bloomer*, 39.
67. Altschuler and Saltzgaber, *Revivalism, Social Conscience, and Community*, 45.
68. Altschuler and Saltzgaber, *Revivalism, Social Conscience, and Community*, 99.
69. Wellman, *Road to Seneca Falls*, 130.
70. Wellman, *Road to Seneca Falls*, 165–66.
71. Elizabeth Cady Stanton and Susan B. Anthony, *The Selected Papers of Elizabeth Cady Stanton and Susan B. Anthony*, vol. 1, *In the School of Anti-Slavery 1840 to 1866*, edited by Ann D. Gordon (Rutgers University Press, 1997), 25; ECS to Neall, November 26, 1841.
72. "Temperance," *Seneca County Courier*, March 12, 1847, microfilm, SFHS.
73. "Woman's Kingdom: Mrs. Bloomer Relates the Experience of the Editor of the First Woman's Journal," *Daily Inter Ocean*, March 12, 1881, 9.
74. Amelia Bloomer, "Letter from Mrs. Bloomer: Twenty Years Ago," typescript, March 1, 1862, Amelia Bloomer Papers, SFHS.
75. Bloomer, *Life and Writings of Amelia Bloomer*, 34–35; letter from Ida in *Auburn Temperance Star*, February 15, 1848, 52, Rutherford B. Hayes Presidential Library.
76. "Communications," *Temperance Star*, May 31, 1848, 166.
77. "Profession Vs. Practice," *Star of Temperance*, June 7, 1848.
78. Wellman, *Road to Seneca Falls*, 152–53.
79. *Seneca County Courier*, microfilm, SFHS.
80. Lori Ginzberg, *Elizabeth Cady Stanton: An American Life* (Hill and Wang, 2009), 57.
81. "Early Recollections of Mrs. Stanton," *The New Era*, 1885, In *Miscellany, 1840–1946 and Undated*, MS Papers of Elizabeth Cady Stanton, Library of Congress, Nineteenth Century Collections Online, https://www.loc.gov.
82. Elizabeth Cady Stanton, *Eighty Years and More (1815–1897)* (T. Fisher Unwin, 1898), 38, https://digital.library.upenn.edu/women/stanton/years/years.html.
83. Bloomer, *Life and Writings of Amelia Bloomer*, 34.

84. "Signers of the Declaration of Sentiments," National Park Service, https://www.nps.gov; 100 Signers Project, https://www.100signersproject.com/.
85. *The Lily* 1, no. 1, January 1, 1849.
86. "Communications," *The Star of Temperance*, October 11, 1848, 293.
87. "Mrs. Bloomer on Dress Reform," *The Sibyl*, September 15, 1856.
88. Bloomer, *Life and Writings of Amelia Bloomer*, 49.
89. Bloomer, *Life and Writings of Amelia Bloomer*, 41.
90. Harrison Chamberlain, "The Seneca Falls Press," 2, SFHS.
91. Hoover, "Mrs. Amelia Bloomer and My Early Recollections."
92. Kaima A. Frass, "Postpartum Hemorrhage Is Related to the Hemoglobin Levels at Labor: Observational Study," *Alexandria Journal of Medicine* (2015): 333–37.
93. Hoover, "Mrs. Amelia Bloomer and My Early Recollections," 3.
94. Louise R. Noun, *Strong-Minded Women* (Iowa State University Press, 1986), 20n5.
95. Susan E. Cayleff, *Wash and Be Healed* (Temple University Press, 1987), 42.
96. Bloomer, *Life and Writings of Amelia Bloomer*, 41.

Chapter 4

97. Bloomer, *Life and Writings of Amelia Bloomer*, 49. The best academic analysis of *The Lily* is Dr. Tracy Lucht's "Amelia Bloomer, *The Lily*, and Early Feminist Discourse in the US," *American Journalism* 38, no. 4 (2021): 391–415.
98. Bloomer, *Life and Writings of Amelia Bloomer*, 44.
99. *The Lily*, January 1, 1849.
100. Winifred Gallagher, *How the Post Office Created America* (Penguin Press, 2016), 88.
101. *The Lily*, January 1, 1849.
102. "An Admonition" and "An Incident," *Temperance Star*, January 10, 1849. See also "An Incident" and "We Met a Short Time Since," *The Lily*, January 1, 1849.
103. Bloomer, *Life and Writings of Amelia Bloomer*, 43.
104. Bloomer, *Life and Writings of Amelia Bloomer*, 49.
105. "The Slave Mother," *The Lily*, February 1, 1849.
106. *Massachusetts Cataract*, March 8, 1849.
107. "To Correspondents," *The Lily*, April 2, 1849.
108. "Owing to Circumstances," *The Lily*, April 2, 1849.
109. Bloomer, *Life and Writings of Amelia Bloomer*, 50.
110. Gallagher, *How the Post Office Created America*, 2.
111. "Post Office Arrangements," *Seneca County Courier*, January 1, 1851.
112. Gallagher, *How the Post Office Created America*, 87–88.

113. "A Word in Private with Mrs. Nichols," *The Lily*, May 1, 1850.

114. Bloomer, *Life and Writings of Amelia Bloomer*, 48.

115. Claire Prechtel-Kluskens, "The Nineteenth-Century Postmaster and His Duties," *NGS NewsMagazine*, 2007. See also "Owing to Many Complaints…of the Neglect of the Carrier to Deliver Their Papers," *The Lily*, January 1850, 6.

116. "De Forest," *The Lily*, May 1, 1849.

117. Paul, "The Lily: An Interpretation," 17, unpublished typescript at the SFHS.

118. "Mrs. Caroline M. Sweet," *The Lily* 1 no. 8, 5.

119. Frederick Blue, *No Taint of Compromise: Crusaders in Antislavery Politics* (Louisiana State University Press, 2006), 143.

120. "Plain Talk" and "Mrs Swisshelm Again," *The Lily*, June 1, 1849.

121. "'The Lily,' Comes This Week Again," *The Lily*, August 1849, 6.

122. Stanton, *Eighty Years and More*.

123. "Mrs. Bloomer" *The Lily*, August 1849, 7.

124. "Woman's Rights," *The Lily*, October 1, 1849, 5.

125. Ginzberg, *Elizabeth Cady Stanton*, 29.

126. "Sun Flower," *The Lily*, November 1849, 6.

127. Elizabeth Cady Stanton, Harriot S. Blatch and Theodore Stanton, *Elizabeth Cady Stanton as Revealed in Her Letters, Diary and Reminiscences* (Harper & Brothers, 1922), 23, accessed via HathiTrust, https://catalog.hathitrust.org/Record/001142964.

128. "Mrs. Bloomer," *The Lily*, December 1849, 7.

129. "Female Printers and Editors," *The Lily*, November 1849.

130. "Bad Habits," *The Lily*, November 1849, 2.

131. "Godey's Lady's Book," *The Lily*, November 1849, 6.

132. "Mrs. Kemble and Her New Costume," *The Lily*, December 1849, 6.

133. "Women's Dresses," *Water Cure Journal*, December 1, 1849, 186. Also, "kilt" here is clearly not a skirt. It seems that the word was used in nineteenth-century fashion to describe gathers or ruches more generally; this may have been a loose shirt or tunic gathered at the shoulders, with a simple collar.

Chapter 5

134. *The Lily*, January 1, 1850, misc items, 7.

135. "Woman's Kingdom Mrs. Bloomer Relates," *Daily Inter Ocean*, March 12, 1881, 9.

136. *The Lily*, January 1850, 2. Article from the *Rochester Evening News*.

137. "Miseries of Intemperance," *The Lily*, April 2, 1849.

138. "An Incident," *The Lily*, February 1850, 5.

139. "Have Women Any Souls?: From the Cincinnati Atlas," *The Liberator*, February 15, 1850, accessed via Proquest database American Periodicals.

140. "Woman's Rights," *The Lily*, April 1850, 6.

141. "A Word in Private with Mrs. Nichols," *The Lily*, May 1, 1850.

142. In the first volume of *The History of Woman Suffrage*, Stanton includes this note: "Gerrit Smith's home was ever a charming resort for lovers of liberty....Here one would meet the first families in the State, with Indians, Africans, slaveholders, religionists of all sects, and representatives of all shades of humanity, each class alike welcomed and honored...joining in all kinds of amusements and religious worship together (the Indians excepted, as they generally came for provisions, which, having secured, they departed). His house was one of the depots of the underground railroad. One day Mr. Smith summoned all the young girls then visiting there...ushered us into a large room, and there stood a beautiful quadroon girl to receive us. 'Harriet,' said Mr. Smith, 'I want you to make good Abolitionists of these girls by describing to them all you have suffered in slavery.' He then left the room, locking us in....One remark she made impressed me deeply. I told her of the laws for women such as we then lived under, and remarked on the parallel condition of slaves and women. 'Yes,' said she, 'but I am both. I am doubly damned in sex and color. Yea, in class too, for I am poor and ignorant; none of you can ever touch the depth of misery where I stand to-day.'" But this early impression never stopped Stanton from equating the lives of white middle-class women with genuine slavery.

143. Ana Stevenson, *The Woman as Slave in Nineteenth-Century American Social Movements* (Springer International Publishing, 2020), 14.

144. Documents available at "Underground Railroad, Abolitionism and African American Life in Seneca County," https://www.co.seneca.ny.us; Judith Wellman, "This Side of the Border: Fugitives from Slavery in Three Central New York Communities," *New York History* 79, no. 4 (October 1998): 359–92.

145. Stanton, Blatch and Stanton, *Elizabeth Cady Stanton*, 38–39.

146. "Slavery and Intemperance," *The Lily*, May 1, 1850.

147. Judith Wellman and Tanya Warren, "The Underground Railroad, Abolitionism, and African American Life in Seneca County, New York, 1820–1880," Historical New York Research Associates, 2005–06, http://www.co.seneca.ny.us.

148. "The Past and the Future," *The Lily*, January 1, 1851, 2.

Chapter 6

149. For a discussion of this history, see Charlott Jirousek and Sara Catterall, *Ottoman Dress and Design in the West: A Visual History of Cultural Exchange* (Indiana University Press, 2019).

150. Robert Halsband, ed., *The Complete Letters of Lady Mary Wortley Montagu,* vol. 1, *1708–1720* (Oxford University Press, 1965).

151. The respectable third Duchess of Richmond and Lennox, Mary Bruce, wife of one of the most radical British politicians of the eighteenth century, who supported American independence and universal suffrage, had her portrait done in accurate Turkish dress and printed for distribution.

152. Pascale Gorguet Ballesteros, "Women in Trousers: Henriette d'Angeville, a French Pioneer?" *Fashion Practice* 9, no. 2, (2017): 200–13.

153. Julia Pardoe, *The City of the Sultan, and Domestic Manners of the Turks,* vol. 1 (Henry Colburn, Publisher, Great Marleborough Street, 1837), 100, via Gutenberg, https://www.gutenberg.org/cache/epub/51879/pg51879-images.html.

154. Jill Fields, *An Intimate Affair* (University of California Press, 2007), 19.

155. Elizabeth Ewing, *Dress and Undress* (B.T. Batsford, 1978), 56–57.

156. Gayle Fischer, *Pantaloons and Power* (Kent State University Press, 2001), 36–37.

157. George Wallingford Noyes, *Free Love in Utopia: John Humphrey Noyes and the Origin of the Oneida Community* (University of Illinois Press, 2001), 147, 333.

158. Amelia Bloomer, "Our Rumsellers," *The Lily,* January 1, 1851, 6.

159. Bloomer, *Life and Writings of Amelia Bloomer,* 66.

160. Amelia Bloomer, "Female Attire," *The Lily,* February 1, 1851, 5.

161. Gretchen Sachse, "The Forest City Water Cure," *Ithaca Journal,* October 2, 1999, 2.

162. Norman Dann, *Ballots, Bloomers, and Marmalade* (Log Cabin Books, 2016), 67.

163. Amelia Bloomer, "Female Attire," *The Lily,* March 1, 1851.

164. Elizabeth Cady Stanton, "Sobriny Jane," *The Lily,* March 1, 1851, 7.

165. Bloomer, *Life and Writings of Amelia Bloomer,* 67.

166. "Woman's Sphere" from the *Pittsburgh Saturday Visitor* in *The Lily,* April 1850, 2–3.

167. Amelia Bloomer, "Now Don't We Feel Proud?" March 1, 1851, 6.

168. Elizabeth Cady Stanton, "Dreadful Uncomfortable," *The Lily,* April 1, 1851.

169. Amelia Bloomer, "Our Dress," *The Lily,* April 1, 1851, 6.

Chapter 7

170. *The Lily,* May 1851, 7.

171. "Ladies in Trousers," *The Home Journal: For the Cultivation of the Memorable, the Progressive, and the Beautiful,* May 3, 1851, 18, 273; American Periodicals, 1.

172. Bloomer, *Life and Writings of Amelia Bloomer*, 83.

173. "Ladies in Trousers," 18, 273.

174. "Progress of Turkish Fashion," *Alexandria Gazette*, May 14, 1851.

175. William Lloyd Garrison and Isaac Knapp, "Meetings in Central New York," *The Liberator*, May 30, 1851.

176. Bloomer, *Life and Writings of Amelia Bloomer*, 50.

177. Elizabeth Cady Stanton, Susan B. Anthony and Matilda Joslyn Gage, eds., *The History of Woman Suffrage*, vol. 1 (1889; Project Gutenberg, 2007), 457, https://www.gutenberg.org/cache/epub/28020/pg28020-images.html.

178. "Early Recollections of Mrs. Stanton," *The New Era*, 1885, Miscellany, 1840–1946 and Undated MS Papers of Elizabeth Cady Stanton, Library of Congress.

179. Sir William Ross (1794–1860), *Victoria, Princess Royal (1840–1901) in Turkish Costume*, 1850, Royal Collection Trust, RCIN 421115.

180. "The New Costume for Ladies: Favorable Notices of the Press," *New York Daily Tribune*, June 12, 1851, 6.

181. "Bloomerism," *Daily National Intelligencer* (Washington, DC), June 21, 1851.

182. "Bloomer Rig; Miss Anna Cruise," *Times-Picayune*, June 11, 1851, 1.

183. Fischer, *Pantaloons and Power*, 90–91.

184. "Heroine of the Bluffs," *Omaha Daily Herald*, February 19, 1888.

185. Bloomer, "Our Dress."

186. "The Progress of Bloomerism: From the New York Express," *National Intelligencer* 39, no. 11, June 26, 1851, 957.

187. "Bloomerism Alias Humbugism," *Missouri Courier*, July 24, 1851.

188. "Ladies in Pantaloons and Boots—The New Dress," *Macon Weekly Telegraph*, June 17, 1851, 2.

189. "Turkish Costume," *Harper's New Monthly Magazine* 3, no. 14, July 1851, 288.

190. "Correspondence," *The Lily*, June 1, 1851.

191. Amelia Bloomer, "Woman's Influence in the Temperance Cause," *The Lily*, November 1, 1851.

192. "Second Annual Announcement," *The Lily*, July 1, 1851.

193. "Bloomer Wedding," *Seneca County Courier*, July 1851, microfilm, SFHS.

194. Genin letter (mislabeled Genice), February 23 1852, Council Bluffs Public Library (CBPL).

195. "Amelia Bloomer," *Cayuga Chief*, August 26, 1851, 1.

196. "Bloomerism: A Latter-Day Fragment by Thomas Snarlyle," *Frederick Douglass' Paper*, December 18, 1851.

197. Amelia Bloomer, "The Boston Times," *The Lily*, July 1 1851.

198. Amelia Bloomer, "What Are We Coming To?" *The Lily*, June 1, 1851.

199. "Woman's Rights Convention," *The Lily*, July 1851, 1.

200. *The Lily*, February 1, 1853.
201. "The Past and the Future," *The Lily*, January 1, 1853.
202. C.F. Wells letter of December 5, 1851, CBPL.

Chapter 8

203. "The Athenaeum Building," *Daily Democrat*, June 28, 1849.
204. "The Woman's Temperance Convention," *Frederick Douglass' Paper*, April 22, 1852.
205. "My Dear Arthur," editorial in Amelia Bloomer Bio binder in CBPL, transcript from clipping in her missing scrapbook. Probably to T.S. Arthur in *Arthur's Home Paper*, reprinted in one of the NYS papers called *The Echo*. Dated March 11, 1852, but probably later due to touring with Anthony.
206. "Mrs. Bloomer's Reminiscences," *Woman's Journal*, September 25, 1880, 310; Susan B. Anthony to Amelia Bloomer, October 25, 1880, Amelia Bloomer Papers, SFHS.
207. "State Temperance Society," *Frederick Douglass' Paper*, June 24, 1852, signed J.T. In David Blight's biography, *Frederick Douglass: Prophet of Freedom* (Simon & Schuster, 2018), he states that in the summer and fall of 1852, "Douglass all but surrendered the editorship of his paper and allowed Julia Griffiths and his assistant, John Thomas, to take the reins," 268.
208. "A Heroic Woman," *The Lily*, July 1852.
209. Bloomer, *Life and Writings of Amelia Bloomer*; "A Noble Past," National Council of the International Organization of Good Templars, http://www.iogt.us.
210. "Asylum for the Sick," *The North Star*, September 5, 1850.
211. Bloomer, *Life and Writings of Amelia Bloomer*, 85.
212. "Geneva Courier vs. Us," *The Lily*, November 1852.
213. *The Proceedings of the Woman's Rights Convention, Held at Syracuse* (J.E. Masters, 1852), 103, HathiTrust, https://babel.hathitrust.org.
214. Walter P. Rogers, "The People's College Movement in New York State," *New York History* 26, no. 4 (October 1945), 415–46.
215. "Waterloo and Seneca Falls Post-Offices," *The Lily*, May 15, 1853.
216. Robert N. Hudspeth, *The Letters of Margaret Fuller*, vol. 2 (Cornell University Press, 2018), 86–87; Bloomer, *Life and Writings of Amelia Bloomer*, 132.
217. "A Seneca Pic-nic," *The Lily*, December 1852.

Chapter 9

218. "Our New Head," *The Lily*, January 1, 1853.
219. "Our New Head."

220. "Characters For Analysis," *Phrenological Journal* 16, no. 6 (December 1852): 1.
221. Phrenological reports.
222. "$10 Premium," *The Lily*, February 15, 1853, and various issues.
223. Bloomer, *Life and Writings of Amelia Bloomer*, 90.
224. "Mr. Marsh and the State Society," *The Lily*, January 1, 1853.
225. Frederick Douglass, "A Scene at Albany," *Frederick Douglass' Paper*, January 28, 1853.
226. Douglass, "Scene at Albany."
227. Bloomer, *Life and Writings of Amelia Bloomer*, 95.
228. "Editorial Correspondence," *The Lily*, February 15, 1853, microfilm, Cornell.
229. "Editorial Correspondence."
230. Bloomer, *Life and Writings of Amelia Bloomer*, 102–10.
231. "Editorial Correspondence."
232. Bloomer, *Life and Writings of Amelia Bloomer*, 111.
233. "Our Travels," *The Lily*, April 1, 1853.
234. "Heroine of the Bluffs," *Omaha Daily Herald*, February 19, 1888.
235. "Dress Reform," *Water Cure Journal* (October 1853): 16, 4; American Periodicals, 84.
236. "Slavery of Fashion." Reprint from the *New York Tribune* in the *Water Cure Journal* (October 1853): 16, 4.
237. "Our Young Girls. An Essay Read Before the Seneca Falls 'Conversational,'" *The Lily*, March 1, 1853.
238. "Burr on the Rappings," *Geneva Courier*, April 16, 1851, 2.
239. "Spiritual Rappings," *The Lily*, May 1851, 1.
240. "Temperance and Woman's Rights," *The Lily*, April 1, 1853. There is no additional information in the article as to which *Telegraph* this is.
241. "Waterloo and Seneca Falls Post-Offices," *The Lily*, May 15, 1853.
242. "Mrs. Bloomer's Lecture," *Seneca County Courier*, reprinted in *The Lily*, May 15, 1853.
243. *Document 5: The Whole World's Temperance Convention, Held at Metropolitan Hall in the City of New York . . . Sept. 1st and 2d, 1853* (Fowler and Wells, 1853), 1–8, included in *How Did the Rival Temperance Conventions of 1853 Help Forge an Enduring Alliance between Prohibition and Woman's Rights?*, documents selected and interpreted by John McClymer (Alexander Street Press, 2012).
244. Mary C. Vaughan, "World's Temperance Convention—Delegates Rejected," *The Lily*, May 15, 1853.
245. "The World's Temperance Convention—Syracuse Outrage Repeated in New York!!" *The Lily*, May 15, 1853.

Chapter 10

246. "The Annual Report," *The Lily*, June 15, 1853, 2.

247. "Women's State Temperance Society," *Frederick Douglass' Paper*, June 10, 1853, 1.

248. "Annual Meeting—Woman's N.Y. State Temperance Society," *The Lily*, June 15, 1853, 1–4; Bloomer, *Life and Writings of Amelia Bloomer*, 121–23.

249. Alling, P. L., "My Dear Mrs. Bloomer," transcribed newspaper clipping, page 165 of a binder titled The Amelia Bloomer Letters, transcriptions of an archival collection at the Council Bluffs Public Library (CBPL).

250. Frederick Douglass, "Woman's New York Temperance Society," *Frederick Douglass' Paper*, June 10, 1853.

251. Amelia Bloomer, "Annual Meeting" and "Ithaca," *The Lily*, June 15, 1853, 5–6.

252. "Mrs Bloomer's Lecture," *Penn Yan Whig*, reprinted in *The Lily*, July 1, 1853, 6.

253. "Editorial Correspondence," *The Lily*, August 1, 1853.

254. "Editorial Correspondence."

255. Bloomer, *Life and Writings of Amelia Bloomer*, 133.

256. Whole World's Temperance Convention, Lucy Stone and National American Woman Suffrage Association Collection, *The Whole World's Temperance Convention, Held at Metropolitan Hall in the City of New York, on Thursday and Friday, Sept. 1st and 2d* (Fowlers and Wells, 1853), https://www.loc.gov.

257. "The Last Vagary of the Greeley Clique," reprinted from *The (NY) Daily Herald*, September 8, 1853, in *The Liberator*, September 16, 1853, 148.

258. "Vegetarian Festival. Banquet at Metropolitan Hall," *New York Times*, September 5, 1853, 1.

259. "Woman's Rights Convention" *The Lily*, November 1, 1853, 1–2.

260. "Editorial Correspondence," *The Lily*, October 15, 1853.

261. "Editorial Correspondence," *The Lily*, February 15, 1855.

262. "Removal: The Lily in Ohio," *The Lily*, December 1, 1853.

263. *Seneca County Courier*, quoted in Bloomer, *Life and Writings of Amelia Bloomer*, 144.

Chapter 11

264. *The Lily*, January 1, 1855, 5.

265. *The Lily*, January 15, 1854; *The Lily*, September 1, 1854.

266. Bloomer, *Life and Writings of Amelia Bloomer*, 149.

267. Bloomer, *Life and Writings of Amelia Bloomer*, 151–54.

268. "From the Western Home Visitor. Golden Rules for Wives," *The Lily*, February 15, 1854.

269. Type cost in Katie Moodie, et al., B. Correspondence, 1834–1917: August–December 1854, Caroline Wells Healey Dall Papers: I. Loose Papers, 1811–1917, Reel 2, Box 2, Folder 10, Massachusetts Historical Society, Nineteenth Century Collections Online, https://www.masshist.org.

270. "All About The Lily," *The Lily*, January 2, 1854.

271. Bloomer, *Life and Writings of Amelia Bloomer*, 156.

272. Bloomer, *Life and Writings of Amelia Bloomer*, 172–73.

273. Bloomer, *Life and Writings of Amelia Bloomer*, 171. Also *Zanesville Courier*, January 18, 1854, 3. "We think she *would* like it as a home, notwithstanding, after she 'kind o' got the bang of' the coal smoke, soot and other necessary attendants upon a manufacturing emporium, and learned that all these apparent objections were but evidences of progress and prosperity. Her opinion of the intelligence and liberality of our citizens we heartily endorse."

274. Bloomer, *Life and Writings of Amelia Bloomer*, 174.

275. Bloomer, *Life and Writings of Amelia Bloomer*, 173.

276. "In Senate, Yesterday," *Portage Sentinel*, January 18, 1854, 2. See also *The Lily*, January 16, 1854.

277. "I.O. of G.T.," *The Lily*, July 1, 1854; Bloomer, *Life and Writings of Amelia Bloomer*, 186.

278. "Shawls and Overcoats," *The Empire City*, September 30, 1854.

279. "Male Bloomers," *The Lily*, February 1, 1854.

280. "The Female Compositors," *The Lily*, January 1854.

281. Moodie et al., B. Correspondence, 1834–1917: August–December 1854.

282. Bloomer, *Life and Writings of Amelia Bloomer*, 177. See also "About Our Printers," *The Lily*, May 1, 1854.

283. Bloomer, *Life and Writings of Amelia Bloomer*, 179. See also "About Our Printers"; "Women and Printers," *New York Daily Tribune*, April 22, 1854, 4.

284. Bloomer, *Life and Writings of Amelia Bloomer*, 169.

285. Bloomer, *Life and Writings of Amelia Bloomer*, 181.

286. Bloomer, *Life and Writings of Amelia Bloomer*, 182–83.

287. "Woman's Rights in Ohio," *The Lily*, June 1, 1854.

288. "A Strike," *The Lily*, August 1, 1854, 4.

289. "Address of Mrs. A. T. Swift, of Penfield," *The Lily*, June 15, 1854.

290. *The Lily*, June 15 and July 1, 1854.

291. "I.O. OF G.T.: Crystal Fount Lodge," *The Lily*, August 15, 1854.

292. Bloomer, *Life and Writings of Amelia Bloomer*, 187.

293. John H. Keatley, "Amelia Bloomer," *Annals of Iowa*, July 1874.

294. Moodie, et al., B. Correspondence, 1834–1917: August–December 1854, MS Dall Papers.

295. *The Lily*, January 1, 1855, 5.

296. "A Change, but Not a Farewell," *The Lily*, December 15, 1854.

Chapter 12

297. Robert P. Swierenga, "The Western Land Business," *The Business History Review* 41, no. 1 (Spring, 1967): 1–20.

298. Dexter C. Bloomer, "Article Regarding Early Churches in Council Bluffs, with a Detailed Account of the Early History of the Episcopal Church in Council Bluffs," typescript, vertical file held by CBPL, 1.

299. "Council Bluffs," *The Council Bluffs Chronotype*, July 4, reprinted from *The Lily*, October 1, 1855.

300. "My House My Home," Dexter C. Bloomer journals, DM M2 Z3 box 1, folder 1, 48, State Historical Society, Des Moines.

301. "Snow and the Railroad," *The Council Bluffs Chronotype*, reprint from *Chicago Daily Times*, January 29, 1855.

302. "Editorial Correspondence," *The Lily*, February 1, 1855.

303. "The Weather," *The Council Bluffs Chronotype*, March 21, 1855.

304. "Mr. D.C. Bloomer," *The Council Bluffs Chronotype*, March 7, 1855; "The Lecture Delivered by D.C. Bloomer," *The Council Bluffs Chronotype*, March 21, 1855.

305. "The Following Letter," from "Martha," *The Lily*, March 15, 1855.

306. "Editorial Correspondence," *The Lily*, April 15, 1855.

307. Chestnut Street mentioned in 'Letter from Mrs Gage,'" *The Lily*, March 15, 1855.

308. "Editorial Correspondence," *The Lily*, May 1, 1855, 4–5.

309. "Letter From Mrs Gage," *The Lily*, May 1, 1855, 5.

310. "Editorial Correspondence," *The Lily*, May 15, 1855, 5.

311. "Editorial Correspondence," *The Lily*, May 15, 1855, 5. See also Bloomer, *Life and Writings of Amelia Bloomer*, 199–202.

312. Title abstract photocopy in Amelia Bloomer Bio binder, CBPL.

313. "Personal," *The Council Bluffs Chronotype*, April 18, 1855.

314. "Editorial Correspondence," *The Lily*, June 15, 1855; Elk in Bloomer, *Life and Writings of Amelia Bloomer*, 228.

315. Bloomer, *Life and Writings of Amelia Bloomer*, 205–207.

316. Bloomer, *Life and Writings of Amelia Bloomer*, 222–26.

317. Bloomer, *Life and Writings of Amelia Bloomer*, 211.

318. Bloomer, *Life and Writings of Amelia Bloomer*, 205–207.

319. "Council Bluffs," *The Council Bluffs Chronotype*, July 4, reprinted from *The Lily*, October 1, 1855, 5.

320. Bloomer, *Life and Writings of Amelia Bloomer*, 205.

321. CBPL Grimes to Bloomer, June 14, 1855, and "DC Bloomer, Esq.," in *The Council Bluffs Chronotype*, July 11, 1855.

322. "Lucy Stone," *The Lily*, June 1, 1855.

323. "Rights of the Rumseller," *The Council Bluffs Chronotype*, June 6, 1855.
324. "Editorial Correspondence," *The Lily*, June 15, 1855.
325. "Editorial Correspondence," *The Lily*, August 1, 1855.
326. Bloomer, *Life and Writings of Amelia Bloomer*, 208.
327. "Editorial Correspondence," *The Lily*, August 15, 1855.
328. "Woman's Right of Suffrage," *The Lily*, July 15, 1855.
329. "Editorial Correspondence," *The Lily*, October 1, 1855.
330. "To Correspondents" *The Lily*, October 15, 1855.
331. Amelia Bloomer, "Where Shall Our Daughters Be Educated?" *The Council Bluffs Chronotype*, October 24, 1855.
332. Editorial Correspondence," *The Lily*, October 1, 1855.
333. "Editorial Correspondence," *The Lily*, August 1, 1855.
334. "Editorial Correspondence," *The Lily*, October 1, 1855.
335. "Editorial Correspondence," *The Lily*, November 1, 1855.
336. "Editorial Correspondence" *The Lily*, November 1, 1855.
337. "The City Authorities," *Council Bluffs Chronotype*, November 7, 1855.
338. "Editorial Correspondence," *The Lily*, November 1, 1855.
339. "Editorial Correspondence," *The Lily*, November 1, 1855.
340. "Editorial Correspondence," *The Lily*, December 1, 1855.
341. "On the First Page," *Council Bluffs Chronotype*, November 7, 1855.
342. "Literary Association," *Council Bluffs Chronotype*, January 9, 1856.
343. "Amelia Bloomer Letters," 42, CBPL; "Thanksgiving: A Lecture by Mrs. Bloomer," *Council Bluffs Chronotype*, November 21, 1855; "Women Voting in Nebraska—A Triumph, Almost," *The Lily*, March 1, 1856, 36.
344. "Mrs. Bloomer's Lecture," *Council Bluffs Chronotype*, November 28, 1855.
345. Bloomer, *Life and Writings of Amelia Bloomer*, 212.
346. "Women Voting in Nebraska."
347. "Mrs. Bloomer Is Coming," *The Nebraskian*, January 2, 1856.
348. "Cold Weather," *The Nebraskian*, January 9, 1856.
349. Bloomer, *Life and Writings of Amelia Bloomer*, 213.
350. "Women Voting in Nebraska—A Triumph, Almost," *The Lily*, February 1, 1856.
351. "Mrs Bloomer on Woman's Right of Franchise," *The Nebraskian*, January 9, 1856.
352. Bloomer, *Life and Writings of Amelia Bloomer*, 214; "Mrs Bloomer on Woman's Right of Franchise."
353. "Extract from the New York Tribune Council Bluffs Correspondence," *The Lily*, March 1, 1856.
354. Nebraska State Historical Society, *Transactions and Reports of the Nebraska State Historical Society*, 58–60; "Women's Rights in Nebraska," *Richmond Whig*, February 19, 1856, 2; Herman S. Davis, *Reminiscences of General William Larimer and of His Son William H. H. Larimer, Two of*

the Founders of Denver (1918), 38. See also "Women's Rights in Nebraska," *Richmond Whig*, February 19, 1856; and "Mr Editor," *Council Bluffs Chronotype*, February 13, 1856, clipping with pencil notations, Amelia Bloomer Biography binder at CBPL.

355. "Women Voting in Nebraska—A Triumph, Almost," *The Lily*, February 1, 1856.

356. "Present Extraordinary," *Ohio State Journal*, October 29, 1856.

357. "Petticoat Presentation," *Council Bluffs Chronotype*, November 5, 1856.

358. John H. Keatley, "Hon. D. C. Bloomer," *Annals of Iowa*, January 1874, 22–23.

359. Bloomer, *Life and Writings of Amelia Bloomer*, 211.

360. Bloomer, "Article by Dexter C. Bloomer Regarding Early Churches in Council Bluffs," CBPL.

361. Bloomer, *Life and Writings of Amelia Bloomer*, 212.

362. "The Seneca Indians," *The Lily*, Febuary 15, 1856.

Chapter 13

363. "My House My Home," Dexter C. Bloomer journals.

364. Bloomer, *Life and Writings of Amelia Bloomer*, 72–73.

365. "From the Republican: National Dress Reform Association," *The Lily*, August 1, 1856.

366. "A Criticism on a Criticism," *The Sibyl*, July 15, 1856, 4–5.

367. "Mrs. Bloomer on Dress Reform," *The Sibyl*, September 15, 1856.

368. David Roberts, *Devil's Gate: Brigham Young and the Great Mormon Handcart Tragedy* (Simon & Schuster, 2009), 154.

369. "Human Mortality in a Natural Disaster: The Willie Handcart Company," *Donald K. Grayson Journal of Anthropological Research* 52, no. 2 (Summer 1996): 185–205.

370. "My House My Home," Dexter C. Bloomer journals.

371. Keatley, "Hon. D. C. Bloomer."

372. "Local Items," *Geneva Courier*, August 26, 1857.

373. "Letter from Mrs. Bloomer. COUNCIL BLUFFS, Iowa, May 20, '58," *The Lily*, June 15, 1858, 92.

374. Houghton, Edwin B. to Amelia Bloomer, November 16, 1857, Collection of Jeannette Bailey Cheek, 1857–1904, Author: Cheek, Jeannette Bailey Owning Repository: SCH Call Number: A/C515 Vol/Box/Folder/Item(s): 1 folder, Schlesinger Library, Radcliffe Institute for Advanced Study, Harvard University.

375. "Biographical Sketch of Joseph Lewis," Family Search, https://ancestors.familysearch.org; "Dear Mrs Birdsall," *The Lily*, July 15, 1858.

376. Bloomer, *Life and Writings of Amelia Bloomer*, 301–2.

377. *Daily Nonpareil*, December 5, 1857, 3.

378. Bloomer, *Life and Writings of Amelia Bloomer*, 215–16.

379. "Omaha Library Association," *Omaha Nebraskian*, February 17, 1858.

380. Robert P. Swierenga, "Land Speculator 'Profits' Reconsidered: Central Iowa as a Test Case," *The Journal of Economic History* 26, no. 1 (March 1966): 1–28.

381. "Letter from Mrs. Bloomer. COUNCIL BLUFFS, Iowa, May 20, '58."

382. "Dear Mrs Birdsall," *The Lily*, July 15, 1858.

383. "The Visit of Abraham Lincoln to Council Bluffs," *Annals of Iowa* 4, no. 46 (July 1900): 460; Julia R. Leverett, "Moved to Bluffs with Her Husband," *World Herald*, April 25, 1939, Amelia Bloomer Bio Binder CBPL.

384. *Council Bluffs Nonpareil*, May 8, 1858.

385. "County Nominations," *Daily Nonpareil*, October 9, 1858, 2; "State Aid to Rail Roads," *Council Bluffs Bugle*, December 22, 1858, 3.

386. *Weekly Nonpareil*, November 6, 1858, 3; *Council Bluffs Weekly*, October 23, 1858, 1; "Benevolent Society," *Weekly Nonpareil*, March 13, 1858, 3; *Council Bluffs Nonpareil*, November 13, 1858, 2; "Prof. S. M. Hewlett," *Council Bluffs Nonpareil*, November 20, 1858, 2.

387. "Death of Col. Kinsman," *The Weekly Nonpareil*, June 6, 1863, 2.

388. Dexter C. Bloomer Journals, DM M2 Z3 box 1, 1860 diary, November 28 entry, Des Moines Historical Society.

389. "Kane Township," *Daily Nonpareil*, November 10, 1860, 3.

Chapter 14

390. "Letter from Mrs. Amelia Bloomer," *The Mayflower*, March 1, 1861.

391. "Mrs. Bloomer's Letter," *The Mayflower*, March 1, 1861.

392. "Multiple News Items." *Daily Nebraskian*, March 19, 1861.

393. "Dear Miss Bunnell," *The Mayflower*, May 1, 1861.

394. "Ladies on the War Path," *The Mayflower*, May 1, 1861.

395. "Fourth of July Celebration," *Daily Nonpareil*, June 22, 1861, 2.

396. "Hoops," *The Mayflower*, May 1, 1861.

397. "For the Women," *The Mayflower*, July 1, 1861, 102.

398. "Regulation Dress," *The Mayflower*, July 15, 1861, 108..

399. "Army Nurse Uniform," *The Mayflower*, September 15, 1861, 142.

400. Tiya Miles, *Night Flyer: Harriet Tubman and the Faith Dreams of a Free People* (Penguin Random House, 2024), 210; quoting Tubman's dictated letter to Franklin Sandborn from Jean McMahon Humez, *Harriet Tubman: The Life and the Life Stories* (University of Wisconsin Press, 2005), 283.

401. "Dear Miss Bunnell," *The Mayflower*, August 1, 1861.

402. Keatley, "Hon D.C. Bloomer."

403. "First Quarterly Report of the Soldiers Aid Society of Council Bluffs," *Council Bluffs Nonpareil*, September 28, 1861.

404. Tom Emmet, "Dodge Connection—William Kinsman: 'Tell the Boys I Died Happy,'" *Council Bluffs Nonpareil*, July 19, 2020.

405. "History of the Recovery and Final Interment of the Remains of Col. W. H. Kinsman," *Daily Nonpareil* [1902?], 92, accessed via HathiTrust, https://catalog.hathitrust.org/Record/100535036.

406. Bloomer, *Life and Writings of Amelia Bloomer*, 279–80.

407. Bloomer, "African Ladies" *The Mayflower*, August 1, 1861.

408. "First Quarterly Report of the Soldiers Aid Society"; "Mrs. Bloomer and the Hospitals," *The Mayflower*, October 15, 1861.

409. Printed in *Nonpareil*, November 9, 1861.

410. "An Omaha Heroine," *The Mayflower*, October 15, 1861.

411. "The Woman for the Times," *The Mayflower*, November 15, 1861.

412. "In Closing the First Volume," *The Mayflower* December 15, 1861; "L. Mott," *The Mayflower*, December 15, 1861.

413. "What the War Is Doing for Women," *The Mayflower*, December 15, 1861.

414. "The Blessings of the War," *The Mayflower*, July 15, 1862, 18.

415. "Correspondence," *Daily Nonpareil*, July 19, 1862, 2.

416. "Woman and the Press," and "In Another Part of This Paper," *The Mayflower*, August 1, 1862, 117–18.

417. "A Call for Help," *The Weekly Nonpareil*, March 14, 1863, 2.

418. Amelia Bloomer to Mrs. Wittenmyer, March 2, 1863, Des Moines Historical Society.

419. "Mrs. Frances D. Gage," *The Mayflower*, June 15, 1863.

420. "Resolutions on the Death of Colonel Kinsman," *Weekly Nonpareil*, August 1, 1863, 2.

421. "Editorial Remarks," *The Mayflower*, April 15, 1863, 58–59.

422. "To Patrons," *The Mayflower*, October 15, 1863, 154.

423. Bloomer to Wittenmyer, November 16, 1863, in Annie Wittenmyer Papers, Correspondence November 1863, Vol 3, 35. DM MS 25, Des Moines Historical Society. See also Lockwood and Dodge, 36, same file.

424. Lisa Guinn, "Annie Wittenmyer and Nineteenth-Century Women's Usefulness," *The Annals of Iowa* 74 (Fall 2015): 315–77.

425. "Report of the Committee on Donations" and "The Soldiers Aid Society," *Weekly Nonpareil*, January 21, 1865, 2.

Chapter 15

426. "The Prohibitory Liquor Law" and "Report of the Committee in Charge of Donations," *Weekly Nonpareil*, January 21, 1865.

427. "A Nation In Tears: Council Bluffs," *Chicago Tribune*, April 17, 1865.

428. "To the Women of the Republic," address from the Women's Loyal National League supporting the abolition of slavery, January 25, 1864, SEN 38A-H20 (Kansas folder), RG 46, Records of the US Senate, National Archives.

429. Bloomer, *Life and Writings of Amelia Bloomer*, 283–86.

430. Bloomer, *Life and Writings of Amelia Bloomer*, 287; Dexter Bloomer Diary, May 21, June 15, 1865; Louise Noun, "Amelia Bloomer, A Biography: Part II, The Suffragist of Council Bluffs," *The Annals of Iowa* 47, no. 7 (Winter 1985): 593.

431. Carne Manuel, "Elizabeth Keckley's 'Behind the Scenes'; or, the 'Colored Historian's' Resistance to the Technologies of Power in Postwar America," *African American Review* 44, nos. 1–2 (Spring/Summer 2011): 35.

432. Bloomer, *Life and Writings of Amelia Bloomer*.

433. Jane Grey Cannon Swisshelm, *Crusader and Feminist: Letters of Jane Grey Swisshelm, 1858–1865*, ed. Arthur J. Larsen (Minnesota Historical Society, 1934); "Dear Mrs. Swisshelm," June 11, 1865, transcribed newspaper clipping in *Amelia Bloomer Letters*, CBPL.

434. Dexter C. Bloomer, March 4 entry in 1866 diary, DM Ma 23, Dexter Bloomer Papers, Des Moines State Historical Society.

435. "History of the Recovery and Final Interment of the Remains of Col. W. H. Kinsman Etc."

436. Noun, "Amelia Bloomer, A Biography Part II," 582.

437. "The Lecture," *Council Bluffs Weekly Bugle*, January 24, 1867; Dexter C. Bloomer journal, February 17, 1867, Des Moines Historical Society.

438. Bloomer, *Life and Writings of Amelia Bloomer*, 243.

439. Lisa Tetrault, *The Myth of Seneca Falls* (University of North Carolina Press, 2014), 21.

440. "Close of the Volume," *The Revolution*, December 31, 1868.

441. "William Lloyd Garrison Crucifies Democrats, Train, and the Women of 'The Revolution,'" *The Revolution*, January 4, 1868.

442. "We Were Pleased to Learn," *The Revolution*, September 17, 1868.

443. "Female Reporters," *Chicago Tribune*, May 28, 1868, 2.

444. Schomburg Center for Research in Black Culture, Photographs and Prints Division, New York Public Library, "Our Ticket, Our Motto: This is a White Man's Country; Let White Men Rule," Campaign badge supporting Horatio Seymour and Francis Blair, Democratic candidates for President and Vice-President of the Unites States, 1868, https://digitalcollections.nypl.org.

445. 1869 Council Bluffs Directory, Library Special Collections, CBPL, 34.

446. "Woman's Rights," *Weekly Nonpareil*, February 27, 1869, 2.

447. "Woman's Convention," *Daily State Register*, April 2, 1869; "Anniversary of the Equal Rights Association," *The Revolution*, April 15, 1869, 1.

448. *The Revolution*, April 22, 1869.

449. "The Women in Council," *Cincinnati Enquirer*, May 15, 1869, 2.

450. "Annual Meeting of the American Equal Rights Association," *The Revolution*, May 20, 1869.

451. Tetrault, *Myth of Seneca Falls*, 29–30.

452. "Views of an Honored Veteran," *Agitator*, June 5, 1869, 3.

453. Tetrault, *Myth of Seneca Falls*, 31.

454. "Various Items," *Quincy Daily Herald*, July 25, 1869, 1.

455. "Postoffice Cars," *Evening Argus*, July 21, 1869, 4.

456. "Dear Mrs. Bloomer," *Amelia Bloomer Letters*, 56, CBPL.

457. Theresa Kaminski, *Dr. Mary Walker's Civil War: One Woman's Journey to the Medal of Honor and the Fight for Women's Rights* (Lyons Press, 2020), 200–201. "Petticoats in Politics: Second Day," *Cincinnati Enquirer*, September 17, 1869.

458. "Letter from Mrs. Amelia Bloomer," *The Agitator*, October 23, 1869, 3.

459. "The Undersigned," *North American and United States Gazette*, October 21, 1869; "The Cleveland Convention," *The Revolution*, October 28, 1869, 265; "Woman Suffrage Call," *National Anti-Slavery Standard*, October 23, 1869; "Woman Suffrage Call," *Tama County Republican*, November 11, 1869, 2. This last only mentions the six Iowa signers of the call, Bloomer among them.

460. "Dear Mrs. Bloomer," Amelia Bloomer Letters, 59, CBPL.

461. "Woman Suffrage Call," Amelia Bloomer Bio binder at CBPL.

462. Craig Collins, "Arabella Babb Mansfield: America's First Woman Lawyer," in *Raising the Bar: America Celebrates 150 Years of Women Lawyers 1869-2019* (Faircount Media Group, 2019), https://issuu.com.

463. "The Suffragans," *Cincinnati Daily Enquirer*, November 26, 1869.

464. "American Woman's Suffrage Convention," *The Revolution*, December 2, 1869.

465. "American Woman's Suffrage Convention," *New York Independent*, December 2, 1869.

466. Virginia Scharff, "Race, Gender, and Empire: The Strange Career of Women's Voting Rights in Wyoming," *Transatlantica* 1 (2022), http://journals.openedition.org/transatlantica/18470.

467. "My Dear Mrs. Bloomer," Amelia Bloomer Letters, 60, CBPL.

Chapter 16

468. "Mrs. Bloomer," *Daily Evening Bulletin*, January 11, 1870.

469. Louise R. Noun and Rachel E. Bohlmann, *Leader and Pariah: Annie Savery and the Campaign for Women's Rights in Iowa, 1868-1891* (1891; University of Iowa Libraries, 2002), 33.

470. Amelia Bloomer, "A Scrap of History," *The Woman's Journal*, February 19, 1870.

471. "Dear Mrs. Bloomer," from Savery, February 10, 1870, Amelia Bloomer Letters, CBPL; Annie Savery to Amelia Bloomer, March 1, 1870, Amelia Bloomer Letters, CBPL.

472. Ewing and Sara F. Summers to Amelia Bloomer, February 20, 1870, Amelia Bloomer Letters, 74–75, CBPL; Mrs. M. Brown Haven to Amelia Bloomer, March 12, 1870, Amelia Bloomer Letters, CBPL.

473. Mrs. A. Frazier to Amelia Bloomer, April 3, 1870, Amelia Bloomer Letters, CBPL.

474. Noun and Bohlmann, *Leader and Pariah*, 31.

475. Noun and Bohlmann, *Leader and Pariah*, 131–32.

476. "Letter from Iowa," *The Woman's Journal*, April 23, 1870, 1.

477. Lucy Stone to Amelia Bloomer, May 16, 1870, Amelia Bloomer Letters, CBPL.

478. Amelia Bloomer letter to Joseph Dugdale, May 7, 1870, Des Moines Historical Society, Joseph A Dugdale correspondence 1866–1873, D 879.

479. "IOWA: Annual Meeting of the Iowa Press Association—State Woman Suffrage," *Chicago Tribune*, June 9, 1870, 1.

480. "The Iowa Convention: A Correction," *New York Daily Standard*, reprinted in *The Revolution*, July 21, 1870.

481. Tracy Cutler, H.M., "The Iowa Woman Suffrage Convention," *The Woman's Journal*, June 25, 1870, 197.

482. "Notes and News," *The Woman's Journal*, July 9, 1870.

483. "The Iowa Senate," *The Revolution*, July 14, 1870.

484. "My House My Home," Dexter C. Bloomer journals.

485. Bloomer, *Life and Writings of Amelia Bloomer*.

486. 1870 census, Exira Township Audubon County, Iowa, June 9, 1870, page 4, lines 13–16.

487. Hoover, "Home Life of Amelia Bloomer," typescript, SFHS.

488. Tracy Cutler, H.M., "Letter from Iowa," *The Woman's Journal*, Septuary 24, 1870.

489. "A Woman's Suffrage Society," *The Revolution*, September 22, 1870, and October 6, 1870, 212; "Certain Ladies at Council Bluffs," *Chicago Tribune*, September 17, 1870; Thomas R. Emmett, *Daily Nonpareil*, July 12, 2021.

490. "Mrs. Bloomer Writes," *The Revolution*, December 8, 1870.

491. Tetrault, *Myth of Seneca Falls*, 57.

492. "Words of Praise," *Des Moines Register*, February 10, 1871, 2.

493. "Mrs. Stanton and Miss Anthony," *The Revolution*, June 1, 1871; Susan B. Anthony, "Our Mail Bag: Let Us 'Carry the War into Africa,'" *The Revolution*, June 29, 1871.

494. "Our Special Contributors: Overland Letters," *The Revolution*, June 29, 1871.

495. "Letter of the National Woman Suffrage and Educational Committee to New Nominees," *The Revolution*, July 13, 1871.

496. "Special Correspondence: The Yo-Semite," *The Revolution*, August 3, 1871.
497. "Suffrage, and How the Women of Iowa Will Vote in 1872," *Des Moines Register*, August 10, 1871, 2.
498. "The Suffrage Convention," *Des Moines Register*, October 18, 1871, 2; *The Revolution*, October 5, 1871.
499. Nettie Sanford, "Correspondence to the Times," *Marshall County Times*, October 26, 1871.
500. "For Woman Suffrage—No," *Des Moines Register*, October 26, 1871, 2.
501. "Mrs. Bloomer on the Convention Question," *Des Moines Register*, November 8, 1871, 2.
502. "A Candidate for Notoriety," *Des Moines Register*, November 2, 1871, 4.
503. Convention proceedings, *Woman's Journal*, December 9, 1871, 387.
504. Noun, *Strong-Minded Women*, 195.
505. Harbert, "Iowa Women Indignant," *Woman's Journal*, April 13, 1872.
506. Noun, *Strong-Minded Women*, 208–16.
507. "Victoria Woodhull and Henry Ward Beecher," *Chariton Patriot*, December 4, 1872, 2.
508. Bloomer, "Letter from Iowa," *Woman's Journal*, November 9, 1872, 355.
509. "Iowa Woman Suffragists," *Des Moines Register*, March 5, 1873, 4.
510. Noun and Bohlmann, *Leader and Pariah*, 61–63.
511. "Suffrage," *Des Moines Register*, September 8, 1874, 4; Lizzie Harbert to Amelia Bloomer, September 10, 1874, Amelia Bloomer Papers, CBPL.
512. Henry Browne Blackwell, "The Woman's National Christian Temperance Union," *The Woman's Journal*, December 5, 1874, 390; Carmen Heider, "Suffrage, Self-Determination, and the Women's Christian Temperance Union in Nebraska, 1879–1882," *Rhetoric and Public Affairs* 8, no. 1 (Spring 2005): 85–107.
513. Bloomer, *Life and Writings of Amelia Bloomer*, 242.
514. Mary A. Work to Amelia Bloomer, December 9, 1880, Amelia Bloomer Papers, SFHS.
515. "Progress in Iowa," *Woman's Journal*, July 29, 1876, 242–43.
516. Amelia Bloomer, "Womans Rights in Iowa," *Woman's Journal*, May 12, 1877, 147.
517. Bloomer, *Life and Writings of Amelia Bloomer*, 235.
518. "Accident to the Union Pacific Railroad Bridge, at Council Bluffs, Iowa," *Frank Leslie's Illustrated Newspaper*, September 22, 1877, 45.
519. Bloomer, *Life and Writings of Amelia Bloomer*, 290–91.
520. Bloomer, *Life and Writings of Amelia Bloomer*, 291–93; Clapp to Amelia Bloomer, August 30, 1879, Amelia Bloomer Letters, CBPL.

Chapter 17

521. Mary Bull in *Woman's Journal*, August 14, 1880.

522. Elizabeth Cady Stanton to Amelia Bloomer, July 25, 1880 (year by context), Amelia Bloomer Papers, SFHS.

523. Amelia Bloomer, "Bloomerism, The Lily, and Mrs. Stanton," and "The Communication of Mrs. Bloomer," *Seneca County Reveille*, July 30, 1880, microfilm, SFHS.

524. Bloomer, *Life and Writings of Amelia Bloomer*, 288–90; Elizabeth Chamberlain to Amelia Bloomer, October 31, 1880, Amelia Bloomer Letters, CBPL, 122–123.

525. Susan B. Anthony to Amelia Bloomer, October 25, 1880, Amelia Bloomer Papers, SFHS.

526. Susan B. Anthony to Amelia Bloomer, November 4, 1880, Amelia Bloomer Papers SFHS.

527. Susan B. Anthony to Amelia Bloomer, November 20, 1880, postcard in Amelia Bloomer Papers, SFHS.

528. Mary A. Work to Amelia Bloomer, December 14, 1880, postcard in Amelia Bloomer Papers, SFHS.

529. Dexter C. Bloomer journal, 1881, Des Moines Historical Society.

530. Tetrault, *Myth of Seneca Falls*, 126–27.

531. Elizabeth Cady Stanton to Amelia Bloomer, January 29, 1880, Amelia Bloomer Papers, SFHS.

532. Walter Raleigh Vaughan, *Vaughan's "Freedmen's Pension Bill.": Being an Appeal In Behalf of Men Released From Slavery. A Plea for American Freedmen And a Rational Proposition to Grant Pensions to Persons of Color Emancipated From Slavery*, (Self-published, 1891), 56, accessed via HathiTrust, https://babel.hathitrust.org/cgi/pt?id=emu.010002407274&seq=1.

533. "The Western Floods," *Frank Leslie's Illustrated Newspaper*, May 7, 1881, 171–72.

534. Amelia Bloomer, "Extracts from Letters of Miss Anthony and Mrs. Stanton," Amelia Bloomer Papers, SFHS.

535. Susan B. Anthony to Amelia Bloomer, June 28, 1881.

536. Elizabeth Cady Stanton to Amelia Bloomer, July 30, 1881, Amelia Bloomer Papers, SFHS.

537. Susan B. Anthony to Amelia Bloomer, August 4, 1881, Amelia Bloomer Papers, SFHS.

538. Erasmus Correll to Amelia Bloomer, January 7, 1882, Amelia Bloomer Letters, CBPL, 125.

539. Mary A. Work, to Amelia Bloomer, postcards, January 4 and 27, 1882, Amelia Bloomer Papers, SFHS.

540. Mary Orwig to Amelia Bloomer, February 7, 1882, Amelia Bloomer Papers, SFHS.

541. "Speeches at Omaha," *Woman's Journal*, October 14, 1882; "Gentle Womans' Jaw," *Omaha Daily Herald*, September 28, 1882.

542. "Suffering for Suffrage," *Omaha Daily Bee*, November 26, 1882, 6.

543. Mary J. Coggeshall to Amelia Bloomer, undated, Amelia Bloomer Letters, CBPL, 169.

544. Bloomer, *Life and Writings of Amelia Bloomer*, 230.

545. "Female Dress," *Daily Evening Bulletin*, December 16, 1884, 2.

546. Mary J. Coggeshall, to Amelia Bloomer, December 25, 188?, Amelia Bloomer Letters, CBPL, 162.

547. "The Seventeenth Annual Washington Convention," printed call, Amelia Bloomer papers, SFHS; Martha Callanan to Amelia Bloomer, Des Moines, February 27, 1885, Amelia Bloomer Letters, CBPL 136.

548. Amelia Bloomer to Mary Coggeshall, June 29, 1885, Amelia Bloomer Papers, SFHS.

549. Amelia Bloomer to Mary J. Coggeshall, August 3, 1885, Postcard, Amelia Bloomer Papers, SFHS.

550. "Early Recollections of Mrs. Stanton," *The New Era*, 1885, Miscellany, 1840–1946 and Undated, MS Papers of Elizabeth Cady Stanton, Library of Congress, Nineteenth Century Collections Online.

551. Susan B. Anthony, January 8, 1886, SFHS.

552. Arthur J. Baker to Amelia Bloomer, June 14, 1887, Amelia Bloomer Papers, SFHS; E.L. Welch, "Seneca Falls Centennial," in *Grip's Historical Souvenir of Seneca Falls, NY* (1904), 64.

553. A.J. Holmes to Amelia Bloomer, February 13, 1888, Amelia Bloomer Letters, CBPL, 141; Stanton, Anthony and Gage, *History of Woman Suffrage*, vol. 3, *1876–1885*, 633–35.

554. Amelia Bloomer to Susan B. Anthony, March 19, 1888, from Wisconsin Historical Society, Colby Papers, box 1, folder 7.

555. William J. Bok letters to Amelia Bloomer, October 15 and undated, 1888, Amelia Bloomer Letters, CBPL, 142–4; Bloomer, *Life and Writings of Amelia Bloomer*, 244.

556. "Amelia Bloomer's Boom," *Chicago Daily Tribune*, April 22, 1888, 25.

557. "Let This Woman Alone."

558. Nettie Sanford Chapin, "Can Women Be Just?" *The Woman's Standard*, July 1, 1888.

559. Amelia Bloomer, "Do Justice to Women," *The Woman's Standard*, August 1, 1888, 2.

560. "The Oneida Community.: Free Love and Bloomers," *Chicago Daily Tribune*, November 23, 1889, 9.

561. "Let This Woman Alone."

562. Hoover, "Mrs Amelia Bloomer and My Early Recollections."

563. Tetrault, *The Myth of Seneca Falls*, 161–63.

564. "Honorary Vice-Presidents," *The Woman's Journal*, March 1, 1890, 69.

565. Bloomer, *Life and Writings of Amelia Bloomer*.

566. "After Fifty Busy Years," *Omaha World-Herald*, April 16, 1890, 4.

567. "Bloomer Celebration," *Milwaukee Journal*, July 28, 1890, 4.

568. Hoover, "Home Life of Amelia Bloomer," typescript in Amelia Bloomer Papers, SFHS.

569. Hoover, "Mrs. Bloomer and My Early Recollections."

570. Mary J. Coggeshall to Amelia Bloomer, August 31, 1890, Amelia Bloomer Papers, SFHS.

571. Amelia Bloomer, "From Amelia Bloomer," *Woman's Standard*, January 1892, 2.

572. Louise Noun, "Annie Savery: Pioneer Feminist," *Des Moines Register*, August 4, 1996, 1.

573. Bloomer, *Life and Writings of Amelia Bloomer*, 319–20.

574. Elizabeth Boynton Harbert, Series II of the Mary Earhart Dillon Collection, 1870–1939; Amelia Bloomer to Lillian G. Browne, March 21, 1893, A-68, folder X, Schlesinger Library, Radcliffe Institute, Harvard University; "Our New York Letter," *Woman's Journal*, April 8, 1893, 109.

575. Henry Stivers to Amelia Bloomer, September 6, 1892, Amelia Bloomer Papers, SFHS.

576. Elizabeth Boynton Harbert, Series II of the Mary Earhart Dillon Collection, 1870–1939; Amelia Bloomer to Lillian G. Browne, March 21, 1893, A-68, folder X, Schlesinger Library, Radcliffe Institute, Harvard University.

577. Elizabeth Boynton Harbert, Series II of the Mary Earhart Dillon Collection, 1870–1939; Amelia Bloomer to Lillian G. Browne, March 24, 1893.

578. "Our New York Letter," *Woman's Journal*, April 8, 1893, 109.

579. "A Talk About Cheap Dress," *Omaha World-Herald*, April 8, 1894.

580. "At Last," *The Herald*, September 27, 1894.

581. Ballesteros, "Women in Trousers," 200–13.

582. Bloomer, *Life and Writings of Amelia Bloomer*, 322.

Chapter 18

583. Bloomer, *Life and Writings of Amelia Bloomer*; "Death of Mrs. Amelia Bloomer," *Council Bluffs Nonpareil*, reprinted in the *Daily Inter-Ocean*, January 5, 1895, 14.

584. "Amelia Bloomer Is Dead," *The World-Herald*, January 1, 1895, 5.

585. "Memorial Sermon on the Death of Mrs. Amelia Bloomer," SFHS, Coll. 37, box 22.

586. "Amelia Bloomer," *Evening World-Herald*, January 5, 1895, 4; Hoover, "Home Life of Amelia Bloomer," SFHS.

587. "Annual Suffrage Meetings," *The Woman's Tribune*, October 29, 1898, 1; "Editorial Notes," *The Woman's Standard*, June 1, 1898, 11, 4; Gerritsen Women's History Collection of Aletta H. Jacobs, 2.

588. "Editorial Notes: War Is a Reality," *The Woman's Standard*, November 1, 1898; Gerritsen Women's History Collection of Aletta H. Jacobs, 2.

589. "Bloomer Funeral," February 1900, *Nonpareil* clipping in Amelia Bloomer Biography binder at CBPL.

590. Mark Lawrence Schrad, *Smashing the Liquor Machine* (Oxford University Press, 2021): 538–40.

591. "Alcohol Use and Your Health, " CDC, May 15, 2024, https://www.cdc.gov.

592. "About Rise: A Feminist Book Project for Ages 0–18," *Rise: A Feminist Book Project*, https://risefeministbooks.wordpress.com/; "Petition of Amelia Bloomer Regarding Suffrage in the West: Background," National Archives Educator Resources, https://www.archives.gov.

593. "Do Flappers Like Dress Reform Won for Them After Long Fight?: They Do Not," *Boston Daily Globe*, December 1, 1924, 17.

594. "Long Unseen Letters, Manuscripts of Mrs. Bloomer Are Brought To Light," *Seneca Falls Reveille*, July 4, 1956, microfilm, SFHS.

595. "Iowa Profile," The Iowa Legislature, https://www.legis.iowa.gov.

596. "Amelia Bloomer," Women's Hall of Fame, https://www.womenofthehall.org.

Index

I

immigrants, 34, 128, 206, 223
Indiana, 134, 141, 143, 189, 198. *see also specific names of towns*
Iowa. *see also specific names of towns*
  AWSA in, 214
  disunionists in, 191
  dress and trousers, 139, 179
  education of women, 172
  liquor bans, 166, 171
  Maine Laws, 164, 166
  political centrality of, 218
  Republican Party, 213
  suffrage, 209, 213–15, 218, 219–220, 222–23, 224, 232, 233, 238
  temperance, 171, 173, 179, 199, 217
  Woodhull scandal, 220–22
Iowa Army Sanitary Commission, 196, 197, 198
Iowa Women's Hall of Fame, 245
Irish immigrants, 34, 128, 206
Irvine, Florence Marie "Maie," 237–38, 242, 244
Ithaca, New York, 43, 96, 122, 123

J

Jackson, James, 76, 124
James, Thomas, 52, 82–83, 99
Jenkins, Lydia Ann, 37, 42, 52, 55, 62
Jenks, Adaline. *see* Sutton, Adeline Jenks
Jenks, Amanda. *see* Frost, Amanda Jenks
Jenks, Ananias, 2–3, 5, 6, 186
Jenks, Augustus, 1, 5, 197
Jenks, Elvira. *see* Lowden, Elvira Jenks
Jenks, Judson, 3, 5
Jenks, Lucy Curtiss Webb, 3, 186
Johnson, Andrew, 201

K

Kansas, 165, 181–82, 203
Kansas-Nebraska Act, 165
Kelley, Abby. *see* Foster, Abby Kelley
Kemble, Fanny, 64
Kennedy, Hannah (cousin), 172, 240
Kinsman, William
  death of, 197
  enlistment, 193
  hired by Dexter, 186
Knickerbocker Hall, 107, 111
knickerbockers, 234
Kossuth, Lajos, 80

L

labor rights, 33, 77, 83, 132, 133, 135–37, 138–39
land agents, 163, 170
Larimer, William, 175, 176–77
Leonard, Harriett, 239
Lewis, Edward Philip. *see* Bloomer, Edward Dexter ("Eddie")
Lewis, Joseph, 180–81, 182
Lewis, Mary. *see* Bloomer, Mary
Lewis family, 180–81
Lily, The, 35, 124. *see also Mayflower, The*; *specific names of writers*; *specific topics*
  alternative medicine in, 39
  Bloomer's Council Bluffs writings in, 178, 181, 184
  Bloomer's memory of, 189
  circulation of, 45, 56–57, 63, 75, 101, 133
  community building and, 44, 101
  discontinuation of, 185, 189–190
  dress reform in, 42–43, 63–64, 65–66, 68–69, 72, 74–75, 79–83, 99–100, 180

W

Walker, Mary, *158*, 209–10
washing machine, 192
Washington Territory, 232
Water Bucket, The, 17, 20, 26
Water Cure Journal, The, 43, 48, 64, 79, 102
water cures
  Avon Springs, 12
  Clifton Springs, 48
  Glen Haven Water Cure, 75–76, 123–25, 149
  home demonstration, 237–38
  Manitou Springs, Colorado, 226, 239
Waterloo, New York, 6, 7, 8, 21, 37, 164, 229
Weber, Helene Marie, 75, 194
Wesleyan Methodist Church, 25, 27, 28, 52, 93, 98
Western Home Visitor, 127, 132, 140
Western Woman's Journal, 231–32
Wheaton, Charles, 93
Whig Party, 11–14, 30, 36, 38, 100, 128, 177
Whitney, Edward Tompkins, 89–90
Whole World's Temperance Convention (1853), 113, 125–26
Willard, Frances, 238
Willie, James, 181
Windham County Democrat, 51
wine, 8, 10, 15, 21, 35
Wittenmyer, Annie, 196, 197, 198, 225, 245
woman suffrage. *see* suffrage, women's
Woman Suffrage Association, 203
Woman's Crusades, 224–25
Woman's Journal, 195–96, 210, 215, 216–17, 221

Woman's National Christian Temperance Union (WCTU), 225
Woman's State Temperance Society (NY), 87–91, 97, 98, 103, 104–7, 115–121, 138
Woman's Temperance Convention (Rochester, 1852), 87–89
women, duties of, 15
women leaders, historic, 67
Women's Loyal National League (1865), 200
women's rights, 46–47, 50–51, 192, 193–94. *see also* child custody; *Lily, The*; property rights of women
women's rights movement. *see also History of Woman Suffrage; specific activities; specific conventions; specific individuals; specific publications*
  East-West divide, 185, 196, 208, 217, 220
  New York, 164
  roots of, 16
women's suffrage. *see* suffrage, women's
Woodhull, Victoria, 218, 220, 223–24
Work, Mary, 229–230, 231
World's Temperance Convention, (1853), 113, 125–26
Wyoming Territory, 210–11

Y

Yazoo Whig, 50–51
Yosemite Valley, 220

Z

Zanesville, Ohio, 133–34

About the Author

SARA CATTERALL is a writer with a drama degree from NYU and an MLIS from Syracuse University. She was born in Ankara and grew up in South Minneapolis. She has worked as a librarian at Cornell University, as a reviewer and interviewer for *Shelf Awareness*, and as a professional book indexer. Her work has been published in the NEH's *Humanities* magazine and *The Sun* magazine, and she coauthored *Ottoman Dress and Design in the West: A Visual History of Cultural Exchange*. She lives with her family near Ithaca, New York.